Leveraging Corporate Responsibility

The Stakeholder Route to Maximizing Business and Social Value

The corporate social and environmental responsibility movement, known more generally as corporate responsibility (CR), shows little sign of waning. Almost all large corporations now run some form of corporate responsibility program. Despite this widespread belief that CR can simultaneously improve societal welfare and corporate performance, most companies are largely in the dark when it comes to understanding how their stakeholders think and feel about these programs. This book argues that all companies must understand how and why stakeholders react to such information about companies and their actions. It examines the two most important stakeholder groups to companies – consumers and employees – to comprehend why, when, and how they react to CR. Armed with this insight, it shows how companies can maximize the value of their CR initiatives by fostering strong stakeholder relationships to develop, implement, and evaluate compelling social responsibility programs that generate value for both the company and its stakeholders.

CB BHATTACHARYA is Dean of International Relations and E.ON Chair in Corporate Responsibility at ESMT European School of Management and Technology in Berlin, Germany.

SANKAR SEN is Professor of Marketing at the Zicklin School of Business, Baruch College, a senior college of the City University of New York.

DANIEL KORSCHUN is Assistant Professor at Drexel University's LeBow College of Business, where he is also a fellow at the Center for Corporate Reputation Management.

Leveraging Corporate Responsibility

The Stakeholder Route to Maximizing Business and Social Value

CB BHATTACHARYA

SANKAR SEN

DANIEL KORSCHUN

CAMBRIDGE
UNIVERSITY PRESS

CAMBRIDGE UNIVERSITY PRESS

Cambridge, New York, Melbourne, Madrid, Cape Town, Singapore,
São Paulo, Delhi, Dubai, Tokyo, Mexico City

Cambridge University Press
c/o Cambridge University Press India Pvt. Ltd.
Cambridge House
4381/4, Ansari Road, Daryaganj
New Delhi 110002
India

www.cambridge.org
Information on this title: www.cambridge.org/9781107401525

© CB Bhattacharya, Sankar Sen and Daniel Korschun 2011

This publication is in copyright. Subject to statutory exception and to the provisions of relevant collective licensing agreements, no reproduction of any part may take place without the written permission of Cambridge University Press.

First published 2011
First South Asian edition 2012

This South Asian edition is based on CB Bhattacharya, Sankar Sen and Daniel Korschun / Leveraging Corporate Responsibility / 9781107401525 / 2011

Printed in India at India Binding House, Noida

A catalogue record for this publication is available from the British Library

Library of Congress Cataloging-in-Publication Data
Bhattacharya, CB
Leveraging corporate responsibility : the stakeholder route to maximizing business and social value / CB Bhattacharya, Sankar Sen, Daniel Korschun.
p. cm.
Includes index.
ISBN 978-1-107-00917-2 (hardback)
1. Social responsibility of business. 2. Business ethics. I. Sen, Sankar, 1936–
II. Korschun, Daniel. III. Title.
HD60.B485 2011
658.4'08 – dc23
2011023017

ISBN-13   978-1-107-65238-5 (paperback)

Cambridge University Press has no responsibility for the persistence or accuracy of URLs for external or third-party Internet websites referred to in this publication, and does not guarantee that any content on such websites is, or will remain, accurate or appropriate.

To our parents:

Sisir and Amita Bhattacharya
Jyotirindra Nath and Bhabani Sen
Michael and Doré Korschun

Contents

List of figures	page viii
List of tables	x
List of exhibits	xi
Acknowledgements	xii
1 The long and winding road to CR value	1
Part I Deconstructing CR value	**25**
2 Viewing stakeholders as individuals	27
3 How stakeholders respond to CR	42
Part II Inside the mind of the stakeholder	**67**
4 What stakeholders see and hear	69
5 The psychological engine that drives CR reactions	85
6 How context influences the process	119
Part III Putting insight into action	**151**
7 Co-creating CR strategy	153
8 Communicating CR strategy	186
9 Calibrating CR strategy	213
10 Putting the framework to work	244
11 Conclusion: The long and winding road revisited	294
Appendix Our research program	306
Index	313

Figures

2.1	The changing face of CR	page 30
2.2	Two routes by which CR generates value	31
2.3	An overview of our framework	35
3.1	Examples of the direct route to CR value	43
3.2	Nestlé framework for creating shared value	47
3.3	Individual-level outcomes in consumption and employment realms based on a donation to a child development center	52
3.4	Consumption realm outcomes from oral health program participants	53
4.1	Communicating CR activity	77
4.2	The Reverse Graffiti Project "Powered by Clorox"	80
5.1	The three levers that drive returns to CR	86
5.2	Conflicting messages, Conflicted feelings. Apple and BP appear on both the best and worst of the green companies listing	93
5.3	The effect of CR efficacy on intent to reciprocate	98
5.4	The effect of CR on two forms of Usefulness	104
5.5	The effect of CR awareness on Unity	112
6.1	The influence of closeness on reactions to CR	127
6.2	The influence of participation on reactions to CR	129
6.3	The influence of Product Quality on reactions to CR	141
6.4	The influence of core business on business value	142
6.5	The influence of CR Positioning on reactions to CR	145

9.1	Calibrating CR activity	214
9.2	Identification measure	226
9.3	CR evaluation dashboard	238
10.1	Understanding and employee response	248
10.2	Identification and purchase loyalty	254
10.3	The influence of customer similarity	255
10.4	A simultaneous test of the framework	257
10.5	Impact factors for each of the links in the framework	258
10.6	A dashboard of stakeholder reactions to CR activity	264
10.7	Understanding and resilience to negative information	272
10.8	A simultaneous test of the framework	273
10.9	Impact factors for the predicted paths	274
10.10	Yoplait's "Save Lids to Save Lives" Program: How It Works	276
10.11	The Dannon Institute: About Us	277
10.12	CR associations for Dannon versus Yoplait among customer segments	278
10.13	Perceived CR activity across six domains: Dannon versus Yoplait	280

Tables

4.1	Representative CR inputs	page 70
4.2	Illustrative examples of CR implementation	72
6.1	Examples of how context influences the process	134
9.1	Sample items for quantifying how stakeholders RESPOND to CR	218
9.2	Sample items for measuring parts of the stakeholder psychological engine	222
9.3	Sample items for quantifying how STAKEHOLDER CONTEXT influences the process	234
9.4	Scales for quantifying how COMPANY CONTEXT influences the process	236
10.1	Awareness of CR activity in numerous domains	263

Exhibits

1.1	Chevron statement on Myanmar	page 2
1.2	Report on oil majors propping up Myanmar regime	4
7.1	Examples of benefits to stakeholders as a result of an oral health initiative	182
7.2	Examples of CR initiative concepts	183
10.1	Retail customer facing employee questionnaire items	286
10.2	Yogurt consumer questionnaire items	291

Acknowledgements

This book would not be in your hands without the help, guidance, and encouragement of many collaborators, reviewers, and supporters. First, we would like to thank our superb co-authors on the numerous research projects that comprise the book's foundation. Shuili Du has been with us since the beginning of this research journey, and she has our gratitude and admiration in equal measure. The contributions of our other collaborators have also been valuable. Our research has also benefited immensely from the feedback we have received at innumerable conferences, seminars, and corporate presentations, and from the reviewers and editors of the journals it has appeared in. They helped ensure both the rigor and relevance of our work and to all these individuals, both academics and practitioners, we are grateful.

Several organizations have supported us during this endeavor. We are very thankful to our employers past and present: Baruch College/CUNY; Boston University; Drexel University; and the European School of Management and Technology. Sankar Sen is equally grateful to the Sasin Graduate Institute of Business Administration at Chulalongkorn University, which was his welcoming and supportive professional home for two of the writing years.

A very special thanks is due to the large number of companies that provided the empirical basis for this book, for allowing us to examine, through their gracious and generous access, our premise that corporate responsibility is, at its best, for and by the people. Thanks are also due to the Aspen Institute; the Human Resources Policy Institute at Boston University; the Marketing Science Institute, and the Research Foundation of the City University of New York for their research support over the years. And, of course, without the faith, guidance, and professionalism of the Cambridge University Press this project would never have come to fruition. For this, we owe Paula Parish, Philip Good, and the rest of their team a big debt of gratitude.

Turning to individuals we leaned on, quite heavily at times, to help bring our book to completion, we cannot thank enough Christel Nelius for her indefatigable efficiency and seamless organization in all matters administrative; she was truly our manager par excellence. Research and writing support was also provided by Surya Dodd and Swaha Devi, both of whom have contributed immeasurably to the accessibility of the material. Daryl Fox was most kind in helping us navigate the publishing waters, for which we are grateful.

Finally, our deepest gratitude goes to our families and friends, without whose enthusiasm and love there would be no book. Our children, Felix Nondon and Sofia Elizabeth, inspired us in more ways than they will ever know. And our partners, Elfriede Fürsich, Robert Albert, and Marta Rodriguez accompanied us on this journey with forbearance and humor. They, most of all, have made this book possible.

ONE

The long and winding road to CR value

Corporate Responsibility (CR) and you

On September 5, 2007, the Buddhist monks of Pakokku, Myanmar joined the citizen protests that erupted in that impoverished country in August of that year. The uprising was triggered by a long-simmering array of discontents ranging from high commodity prices to human rights abuses, including the long-term detention of pro-democracy leader Aung San Suu Kyi. The ruling military government in Myanmar, in power since 1962, took action to quell the protests. A few days after the monks joined the protests, troops fired on protesters in a crackdown that left at least ten people dead by the government's account (opposition groups put the fatalities at around 200). Independent reports suggest that several monks were beaten and killed.

Amid the international outcry over these events, the only company in the US to issue a public statement was Chevron (see Exhibit 1.1). Why? Because Chevron is the only American company doing business in Myanmar, in the face of a systematic, comprehensive and sustained US trade boycott of that nation. Chevron acquired a minority stake in Unocal (a US conglomerate) that operates the Yadana Valley Project, which produces 650 million cubic feet per day of natural gas for export to neighboring Thailand. A loophole in US sanctions has allowed Chevron to operate in Myanmar.

> ### Exhibit 1.1 Chevron statement on Myanmar
>
> San Ramon, California, October 2, 2007
>
> Chevron supports the calls for a peaceful resolution to the current situation in Myanmar in a way that respects the human rights of the people of Myanmar. Chevron's minority, non operated interest in the Yadana Project is a long term commitment that will help meet the critical energy needs of millions of people in the region. Our community development programs also help improve the lives of the people they touch and thereby communicate our values, including respect for human rights.
>
> #### Myanmar Community Development Program
>
> The Yadana Project partners have invested in a model socioeconomic program that positively improves people's lives in Myanmar.
>
> The Yadana project community development programs have delivered the following benefits:
>
> - 50,000 people along the Yadana pipeline now have free and improved healthcare
> - Ten doctors now work in villages when there were none and thirty-three health care workers have been trained
> - Local infant mortality is 1/6th the national rate
> - Malaria mortality rates down by a factor of 10
> - TB mortality rate halved since 2002
> - Student enrollment in schools has doubled
> - Forty-four schools have been built and 20 renovated in 23 villages
> - Financial support to 350 teachers, library program to 16 schools, scholarship program for 1,050 pupils and computers at 8 schools

- Improvements to local roads and the building of 24 bridges have resulted in both public and private transportation that was nearly nonexistent before the pipeline project
- 6,300 projects loans for small businesses have been granted resulting in numerous enterprises that help generate economic development for local communities

Source: Chevron website

Not surprisingly, then, both the US Congress and human rights organizations the world over have been trying to pressure Chevron into pulling out of Myanmar, not least because, according to independent human rights groups, gas sales from the Yadana Valley Project account for the single largest source of revenue for the military government, helping it stay in power and suppress human rights in that country (see Exhibit 1.2).

Chevron, on the other hand, argues that its presence in Myanmar is a positive influence, because of its health, economic development and education programs in the Yadana Valley. Chevron insists that locals living near Yadana are "better off by virtue of Chevron and its partners being there," and that "multiple third-party audits have confirmed"[1] this point.

This may be the first time you are learning about Chevron's involvement in Myanmar. Or you may have already followed this story in the newspapers and on TV. Perhaps you went to the Chevron website to learn more about the company's point of view. Or you learned about this issue from blogs and the websites of human rights organizations. Or you work for Chevron and have discussed the Yadana Valley Project with your colleagues.

Regardless, take a minute to think about what you have just read about Chevron. How do you feel about the company? Do you believe that Chevron is demonstrating corporate responsibility (CR) – that is, being socially responsible – by operating in Myanmar?

Exhibit 1.2 Report on oil majors propping up Myanmar regime

Oil majors propping up Myanmar regime: rights group

By Danny Kemp (AFP) – September 9, 2007

BANGKOK – Energy giants Total and Chevron are propping up Myanmar's junta with a gas project that has allowed the regime to stash nearly five billion dollars in Singaporean banks, a rights group said Thursday.

France's Total and US-based Chevron have also tried to whitewash alleged rights abuses by Myanmar troops guarding the pipeline, including forced labour and killings, two reports by US-based EarthRights International said.

The group urged the international community to exert pressure on the two companies, which have long managed to avoid Western sanctions against the generals who rule the impoverished Southeast Asian nation.

"Total and Chevron's Yadana gas project has generated 4.83 billion dollars for the Burmese regime," one of the reports said, adding that the figures for the period 2000–2008 were the first ever detailed account of the revenues.

"The military elite are hiding billions of dollars of the peoples' revenue in Singapore while the country needlessly suffers under the lowest social spending in Asia," said Matthew Smith, a principal author of the reports.

The junta had kept the revenues off the national budget and stashed almost all of the money offshore with Singapore's Overseas Chinese Banking Corporation (OCBC) and DBS Group (DBS), the watchdog said.

"The revenue from this pipeline is the regime's lifeline and a critical leverage point that the international community could use to support the people of Burma," added Smith, the group's coordinator for the country.

But Chevron said related development projects had helped local communities.

"We believe that Total's health, economic development and education programs, which we support, are critical and substantively make positive improvements to the lives of the people in the Yadana project communities," a Chevron statement said.

Total questioned the accuracy of the reports.

"An initial reading has already enabled us to identify inaccuracies... lack of precision or mistaken interpretations," Total vice-president Jean-Francois Lasalle told AFP.

He added the rights group "at no moment recognizes the benefits of our presence, notably in the areas of education and health".

Total and Chevron are two of the biggest Western companies in Myanmar and have recently come under fire for their dealing with the regime, following the extension in August of the house arrest of pro-democracy icon Aung San Suu Kyi.

Total has been able to continue working there because EU sanctions against the country currently only cover arms exports, wood, minerals, gems and metals.

US lawmakers in July 2008 dropped plans for sanctions that would have ended tax write-offs enjoyed by Chevron and would have pressured it to pull out from the Yadana project.

Total has been a major investor in the Yadana project since 1992, holding a 31.24 percent stake. Chevron has a 28 percent stake in the field, production from which represents 60 percent of Myanmar's gas exports to Thailand.

EarthRights said that as a result of the hidden revenues, Total and Chevron were a "primary reason" why international and domestic pressure on the Myanmar military regime had been ineffective for decades.

The group meanwhile said that impact assessments of the pipeline by US-based CDA Collaborative Learning Projects, a US non-profit organisation commissioned by Total, had covered up adverse effects and abuses, the group said.

Report co-author Naing Htoo said CDA "willfully participated in whitewashing Total and Chevron's impacts in Burma and their role in forced labour, killings, and other abuses."

> CDA visited villages in the pipeline area on five occasions but only with escorts from the oil company and interpreters from Total, while villagers were warned by security members not to give bad news, the report said.
>
> The Chevron statement said however that the firm believed the CDA's findings "provide a credible assessment of the Yadana Project's community engagement activities."

Like many people we have talked to, you might have an immediate, gut reaction to the story. It might be obvious to you that Chevron is not being socially responsible, because no matter what it does for the people of Myanmar, there is no getting around its support of a military dictatorship. On the other hand, you might feel that Chevron *is* being socially responsible because it is actually taking concrete actions to alleviate the myriad of social problems in the Yadana region, something other companies that would take the place of Chevron might not do.

How do *you* decide whether or not Chevron is being socially responsible? Do you base your opinion on a cost–benefit calculus, where the gains from Chevron's contributions to the community need to be weighed against the harm done by its support of the junta? Is your judgment colored by your beliefs about CR in general, the oil and gas industry, and the company itself? Will you reason differently if you are a Chevron employee? Will it matter whether you live in Bangkok or Boston? And perhaps most importantly, will what you have just learned and thought about change your likelihood of pulling into a Chevron gas station next time you need gas?

There are no easy answers to these questions. We have heard almost as many opinions and intentions pertaining to the ethical and socially responsible implications of Chevron's involvement in Myanmar as the number of people we have polled. And Chevron is but one example of a much larger phenomenon. There is as much media coverage on "corporate green washing" as there is on "corporate responsibility," and contributing to the complexity in the CR context, many companies are portrayed *both* as model citizens and corporate villains depending on the news story. As a result, people's perceptions can vary greatly, even about a single company.

So today, not only Chevron but, we'd argue, *all* companies must understand how and why stakeholders react to such information about companies and their actions. Why? For the very simple reason that today *our reactions – as consumers, employees, investors, or even just the public – to a company's socially responsible actions (or the lack thereof) can have an unprecedented impact on its fortunes*. And while some companies are taking the lead, many, if not most, companies are at sea when it comes to understanding how their stakeholders think, feel and react to the impact that their actions have on not just the bottom line but the welfare of the world at large.

This book seeks to fill this void in our understanding of stakeholder reactions to CR initiatives. We delve into the minds of the two most important stakeholder groups to companies – consumers and employees – to systematically comprehend why, when and how they react to CR. Armed with this insight, companies can maximize the value of their CR initiatives by fostering strong stakeholder relationships and thus energizing stakeholders to respond positively to such initiatives. Specifically, by identifying the psychological levers behind desired stakeholder behaviors (e.g., employee retention, customer loyalty), companies can develop, implement, and evaluate compelling social responsibility programs that generate value for both the company and its stakeholders, be they consumers, employees, or others.

Why stakeholders matter

Let's step back a bit from the Myanmar example to locate it in the broader context of today's global corporate landscape. Few notions today have so totally captured the corporate consciousness the world over as the twin ideas of corporate responsibility (CR) and sustainability. It is all but impossible to find a Fortune 500 company today that does not engage in CR activities.[2] In fact, most executives view CR as a key ingredient in their corporate strategy. In a recent Accenture/Global Compact study, 81 percent of CEOs, compared to just 50 percent in 2007, stated that CR issues are now fully embedded into the strategy and operations of their companies (whether this is founded in reality or not).[3] This enthusiasm for CR is reflected in publications such as *The New York Times, The Economist, Business Week*, and other major publications that have devoted entire sections to CR.[4] Terms like corporate (social) responsibility, sustainability, strategic philanthropy, and corporate citizenship are firmly embedded in today's managerial vernacular.

But what do these terms mean? Rather than waste precious real estate on debating similarities and differences between them, we simply choose CR as the focal term for this book and use it to denote the unified sense – which pervades all these terms – that *a company's long-term success, and sometimes even existence, is inextricably tied to its stewardship of not just its own well-being but also that of the natural and social environment in which it operates.*

This realization has led more and more forward-thinking companies to take a strategic approach to CR, devoting unprecedented efforts and resources to creating and maximizing what Porter and Kramer, in their *Harvard Business Review* article, have called "shared value" (i.e., value for the company and for society).[5] In other words, companies are flocking to the CR concept not only as a way to improve society, but also because of the promise it holds as a way to enhance corporate performance.

This desire to "do well by doing good" is motivating many of the world's largest corporations to collectively invest billions of dollars in a wide spectrum of social and environmental issues. Communications touting CR activity as a means to entice consumers to purchase products and services are proliferating. CR is alive and well in many companies' communications to employees. And a recent KPMG study found that 86 percent of the major shareholders and board members believe that CR is "in the best interest of our company."[6]

At the heart of this strategic approach to CR is *the central and ascendant role of the stakeholder*. Specifically, companies are increasingly construing CR in terms of the interests of a specific but large and diverse set of stakeholder segments (e.g., consumers, employees, investors, communities, government, environment, etc.). These efforts are shaped by the strong belief that endeavors in the CR domain can elicit company-favoring responses from these stakeholder groups. In fact, we could go as far as to argue that CR cannot succeed without stakeholder demand for it. In other words, *if stakeholders do not ultimately value CR, rewarding companies for their efforts in this domain, the CR movement itself cannot be sustainable.*

Two of these stakeholder segments stand out as particularly critical for CR management: customers and employees. This is borne out by a McKinsey survey of companies that have signed on to the UN Global Compact. When McKinsey asked the CEOs of these companies which stakeholders will have the greatest influence on the way in which companies manage societal expectations in the next five years, the CEOs pointed squarely to customers and employees as their greatest priorities.[7]

Customers are already a frequent target of CR communications, as CR messages can be a potent ingredient of marketing messages. Since customers provide the lifeblood – revenues – for any commercial endeavor, they are likely to remain central to CR management into the foreseeable future. But now, employees are quickly becoming a key consideration for CR managers as well. Employees are critical from a dual perspective, because companies need to motivate employees and strengthen their relationship with the company, while employees also represent an excellent channel through which companies can make customers aware of their CR activities. With these considerations in mind, our primary focus in this book is on customers and employees. At the same time, however, we expect the fundamental psychological process behind stakeholder reactions to CR activity to be similar across the other stakeholder groups.

So, who is this ever-important stakeholder? The answer is: *all of us*. We are the consumer, the employee, the investor and the regulator, and we all lie at the heart of a successfully sustainable company. But do we really care about the CR activities of the companies we encounter?

But do we (the stakeholders) really care?

Even as recently as a decade ago, many of us knew and cared little about the actions of companies beyond buying from them, working for them and investing in them. Today that is no longer the case. A confluence of forces, headed by the information revolution, the environmental crisis, the widening gap between the haves and have-nots, declining faith in the public sector, and the coincidental ascendancy of the transnational corporation and global brands, has started a public movement which, while smaller in some corners of the globe than others, is unstoppable. Call these consumers the LOHAS ("Lifestyle of Health and Sustainability") segment or the Awakening Consumer;[8] whichever moniker we use, more and more people are not satisfied with just affordable products that satisfy their needs. Instead, they now want these products to come from socially responsible/sustainable producers. Thus, the actions of Chevron in Myanmar matter as much – if not more – to these consumers as the price of its gas.

This trend is reflected in marketplace polls that point to large and growing swaths of consumers who want to buy products and services that not only *are* good but also *do* good. In the most recent survey conducted by Cone Communications (2008), 79 percent of consumers said that they are likely to switch from one brand to another (price and quality being about equal) if the other brand is associated with a good cause.[9] Similar trends have been observed, of course, in the employment and investment domains. This is likely to give companies like Chevron pause, particularly if its empowerment of the people of the Yadana Valley is overshadowed, in its stakeholders' minds, by the company's financial complicity with the junta.

Or is it? Consider the sentiments expressed by one of the consumers we interviewed, which are not uncommon in our experience.

> It's great to be socially conscious, but I have a life too, and I have a house, and I have to paint it, and I have to keep my bathroom clean...so I don't really care if Q-Tips gave a million dollars to Alzheimer's...I just need Q-Tips. So it's all well and good, but you're a mother with three kids and a full-time job, what do you care? You're like: milk, orange juice, all right, pick the kids up, or whatever...

In other words, the results obtained by omnibus surveys done by Cone Communications and others are susceptible to social desirability biases, where respondents give the answer they believe interviewers want to hear. So the reality, as the above quote exemplifies, is far more complex. Not surprisingly, evidence for a positive link between CR investments and aggregate measures of financial performance has proven to be quite elusive; the numerous studies that have tried to examine this connection have produced at best weak and inconclusive results.

Companies need to understand stakeholder reactions

What does this all mean, then, for the likes of Chevron? Do you, as a current or prospective stakeholder, think it is being socially responsible by operating in Myanmar? The answer, we saw earlier, is that "it depends." Do stakeholders care whether or not Chevron is being socially responsible? Our discussion above seems to point to the somewhat puzzling answer: "Possibly."

So should Chevron then really care about and spend a lot of time and energy figuring out what its stakeholders think and feel about its

Myanmar operations? We believe the answer to this question is an emphatic "Yes" – not *in spite of* but *because of* the equivocal answers to the former two questions. In fact, the central assertion of this book is that it is precisely the complexity, uncertainty, and variety in stakeholder responses to CR that makes it essential for companies to understand the basis of such reactions. Companies need to move from thinking about *whether* their stakeholders care about CR to *who* cares, and *when* and *why*. Yet, such reactions are still not well understood by many companies. We need to look no further than the opening Chevron example to understand why this might be the case.

How is this book different?

Numerous books have already been written about how companies need to and can be strategic about their CR. Some of these have talked about how essential it is to engage and respond to stakeholders. Yet little is said that provides a concrete, systematic, comprehensive, and actionable sense of how stakeholders react (i.e., perceive, think, feel and behave) in the CR domain, to which companies can, therefore, respond. This sort of understanding is essential to stakeholder engagement; embarking on such a task without a guiding framework anchored in the psychology of stakeholder reactions today is akin to embarking on a journey without a compass (or a GPS).

Our book advances extant thinking and action in the CR domain by focusing squarely and wholly on the stakeholder. Based on our own decade-long research program, as well as the research of others, we enter the minds of these stakeholders to paint the big picture of whether, when, how, and why they might react positively to a company's CR efforts. The impetus and validation for this effort comes from our finding that when done right (i.e., based on a meaningful understanding of stakeholder reactions to CR), CR can foster strong, positive and enduring relationships with the company's stakeholders.

In the pages that follow, we will show that the key to creating what we call "CR value" lies in understanding stakeholders' personal interpretation and evaluation of CR activities. By getting into the minds of stakeholders, companies can more effectively foster the kind of relationships that contribute both to corporate performance and to social and environmental well-being.

In short, we identify the psychological levers that drive stakeholder behaviors. We also identify the conditions under which these psychological levers produce the desired behaviors (e.g., customer loyalty or employee commitment). With this understanding, companies can develop and implement compelling CR programs that invoke the psychological processes underlying stakeholder reactions. When these levers work harmoniously, they produce the greatest value for both the company and society, maximizing the triple bottom line: People, Planet, Profit.

About our research

As you may have noticed, our approach is firmly grounded in marketing thought. While some other treatments of CR concentrate on the operational changes that companies need to make in order to see rewards from CR (e.g., energy efficiency initiatives in factories), we rely on decades of research on *how companies build and sustain relationships* with those they seek to serve. As such, we focus on how people respond when they learn about a company's CR activity, given their desires, preferences, beliefs, emotions and idiosyncrasies. This approach enables us to show how CR can help companies build and sustain relationships not only with consumers, but with other stakeholders as well.

In other words, the fundamental premise of this book is that CR will create the greatest value for the company, when it, like successful products and services, actually fulfills, in an authentic and meaningful way, some of the most basic needs of its stakeholders. In that, this book is not about CR as yet another cynical instrument of corporate profit. Instead, the central belief guiding our thinking is that *for firms to gain value from their CR efforts, those efforts must improve the lives of their stakeholders in significant ways.*

Our book also diverges from others in our approach to understanding stakeholder psychology in the domain of CR. Current wisdom on the topic comes overwhelmingly from case studies of stakeholder engagement (or the lack thereof) by specific companies. While such a best/worst practice approach does much to edify us in an industry- and company-specific way, it highlights, at best, the dots in the CR puzzle that still need to be appropriately connected before a given company can use this knowledge for its own purposes, particularly if it is not in the same industry as the one showcased.

Our book responds to this need for a systematic yet actionable understanding of stakeholder reactions to CR by providing insights based on substantial empirical research, both our own and that of fellow scholars. This research not only has the desired conceptual approach we found to be missing in prior writings on this topic, but it is also conducted on a wide array of real companies, industries, CR issues, and consumption and employment contexts. Specifically, we researched multiple stakeholders who talked about or were affiliated with a variety of companies, including the likes of Dannon, General Electric, General Mills, Procter and Gamble, Walmart and many others.[10] In short, the research that forms the basis of this book is not only extensive, but also both rigorous and relevant. Moreover, the insights we provide are grounded in a broad set of research methods including exploratory, descriptive, and causal. Descriptions of many of these studies can be found in the Appendix of this book.

Here are examples of some of our methods. We have carried out *exploratory research* in the form of in-depth interviews and focus groups with hundreds of corporate stakeholders. For example, in one study done in partnership with a multinational corporation, we conducted focus groups with employees at multiple locations – including headquarters, international offices, and manufacturing plants. Our *descriptive studies* include field surveys that have been conducted in a variety of contexts. These surveys have used a number of techniques, ranging from paper and pencil studies to web-based surveys with online panels of consumers or employees. One study, for example, examined the reactions to CR activity among over 900 frontline employees in the retail and hospitality industries. Another study examined the responses of more than 1,000 yogurt consumers to CR initiatives.

We have also run *experiments in order to establish causal relationships* in our framework. One laboratory experiment, for example, examined how consumers respond to both positive and negative information about a company's social responsibility activity. Similarly, in a before-and-after field experiment we studied the responses of stakeholders in the consumer, employment and investor realms to an announcement of a $1 million charitable contribution to a child development center.[11]

The research with primary data has been enhanced with additional studies analyzing secondary data. For example, a couple of studies done by one of the present authors (Bhattacharya) with researcher Xueming Luo examined the effect of CR activity on stock market value and firm risk; these projects involved analyzing data from multiple third-party sources (e.g., *Fortune*'s ranking of "America's Most Admired Companies," the American Customer Satisfaction Index, COMPUSTAT, CRSP and others).[12]

How companies can benefit from this book

In 2009, the 43,000 residents of Barendrecht, the Netherlands, voted against granting Shell, the oil company, a permit to build the first of a new generation of CO_2 storage facilities in two depleted natural-gas fields more than a mile under the suburb, twelve miles from Rotterdam. Carbon capture and storage involves extracting CO_2 from power generation and industry, compressing it and injecting it into depleted oil and gas fields or saline aquifers. The technology would allow prolonged use of coal for electricity generation while reducing greenhouse gas pollution, a major step in the battle against greenhouse gas emissions. Emissions from a gasification hydrogen plant at Shell's Pernis refinery, about twelve miles away, would be sent by pipe to the site, preventing the greenhouse gas from reaching the air and harming the environment.

The project sufficiently addresses safety concerns and adequately demonstrates compliance with Dutch safety standards, according to the MER commission, an independent panel of experts appointed by the national and provincial governments to assess projects for their potential environmental impact. However, town residents and officials have cited safety concerns and the project's experimental nature as the reasons for their opposition. The people of this small Dutch town are not against pumping tons of carbon dioxide into the ground to fight global warming. They just wish it wasn't right beneath their houses. "Who wants to live in Barendrecht if one of these CO_2 things is built?" asked retiree Marianne van Heugten.

Real estate agent Frits Markus says worries about the project could affect the average $420,000 house price. People "will be scared that CO_2 will be stored under where they live; they will feel their houses will lose value, and [that they] will have trouble selling them. Shell's plans to pipe the gas to Barendrecht would turn the town into a waste landfill," claims local campaign group "CO2 isNee." It's being labeled a dump, of sorts, that seems to anger locals the most. "The value of houses, that's the real worry here," said resident Herman Bakker.

Barendrecht's town council is now concerned that the Dutch government could overrule its vote by citing the national interest. Councilman Zuurbier warned against that. "Here in Barendrecht there will never be any support for this," he said. "You need a general public support for the success of this new ambition. If you start this new policy with a conflict with Barendrecht... that is a very nasty start for your general public acceptance."

"The whole debate became quite emotional," Jeroen van der Veer (CEO, Shell) said in an interview in Lausitz, Germany. "There's still a long way to go." Matthias Ruete, the European Commission Director-General for energy and transport, has stressed that the Dutch would "pay a price" in terms of higher costs for new energy technology if the project doesn't go ahead.[13]

Shell's recent experience with the residents of Barendrecht underscores how even the best laid CR plans can unravel in the face of stakeholder opposition. Like Shell, many companies tend to assume that CR has a self-convincing quality; that the very fact that it is a virtuous act is enough to convince stakeholders of its worth. In doing so, companies underestimate the diversity, complexity and unpredictability of stakeholder reactions. If Shell had understood and anticipated how this important group of stakeholders might react to this issue, it would not only have saved a lot of time and resources, but also, more importantly, been successful at achieving its environmental CR goals.

That is precisely the point of this book. In it, we go beyond merely describing stakeholder psychology in the CR domain: We also articulate the implications of our findings for the optimal formulation, implementation, communication and evaluation of CR programs. Thus, the ultimate aim of this book is to help managers avoid being "Shell-shocked" as in the above example, by harnessing their understanding of their stakeholders to guide their CR strategies. Specifically, after reading this book, managers should be able to design, implement, and evaluate CR programs more effectively.

In sum, our research shows that if companies are to maximize the benefits of CR activity they must get into the minds of the very stakeholders who will contribute to enhanced performance (e.g., consumers who purchase products, employees who work hard). Managers, such as those working for Shell, need to design, implement, and evaluate CR programs with these reactions in mind. And they need to focus their communications accordingly as well.

What this book says (and doesn't say)

As we mentioned earlier, readers should not construe our marketing-based approach as a call to "manage" or "manipulate" stakeholders, deceiving them into behaviors that benefit the company alone. In contrast, our approach suggests the opposite: that companies need to align their behavior – especially in the CR realm – with the needs of stakeholders. We anticipate that engaging in deceptive CR practices will actually backfire because it will harm the stakeholder–company relationship once stakeholders figure out the company's true motives. And in today's hyper-connected world, managers can rest assured that stakeholders will know when a company is using CR activity as window dressing.

So this book is written for managers and scholars who are interested in what might be called "Positive CR," conducting CR in ways that generate real, tangible value for the company and its stakeholders, as well as society at large. Our focus is not on how companies should avoid unethical behavior. Rather, our principal goals are to enlighten managers in terms of when and how CR "works," and to articulate clearly the implications of important insights from our approach so that managers can make better CR-related decisions.

The overarching take-aways of this book include:

- Engagement in CR *can* produce long-term value, for both stakeholders and for companies, making it a source of durable competitive advantage.

- However, mere engagement in CR is not enough to create such shared value.
- Strong and enduring stakeholder relationships occur only when people are aware of a company's CR, gain a meaningful understanding of it, find the CR initiatives to be personally useful or relevant, and perceive a sense of unity with the company. These psychological levers are essential to value creation through stakeholder reactions.
- The optimal functioning of these psychological levers hinges, in turn, on an array of factors that operate at both the stakeholder and company level, such as the company's value chain and competitive context, as well as stakeholder demographics, culture, and role.
- Insight into these psychological levers allows companies to understand and respond to their stakeholders through their CR strategy and management, ensuring a desired set of reactions from them. Significant steps in this process involve articulating the relative importance of specific stakeholder groups, engaging them in the co-creation of CR in terms of both articulation and implementation, communicating appropriately with them, and assessing the reactions meaningfully.
- Assessing the total value created by CR requires a broader perspective than most managers are used to (for instance, not just measuring the value to business but also the value to society and the environment). Creating value for society and/or the environment is, in fact, a pre-requisite for creating business value.

These insights will become clearer as we lay out our approach in the chapters to come. Many chapters will provide empirical evidence that supports each insight. Other chapters will discuss the implications of these insights in terms of managerial decision-making. Overall, it is our hope that readers will obtain greater clarity on the subject while gaining an appreciation for the many complexities involved in CR management.

Who should read this book

This book is intended for three key audiences: managers; students; and scholars. First, it is meant for managers – particularly those with CR interests or responsibilities (in departments ranging from Human Resources, Marketing and Strategy to Sustainability) – who want to base their CR decision-making on empirically based insights.

Second, this book is designed for students taking graduate courses on CR and CR management. The book uses a combination of case studies and research-based frameworks to make its key insights both theoretically rigorous and accessible. In that, it could either be the primary or supplemental text, depending on the focus of the course.

Finally, this book is intended to be a scholarly reference for those engaged in CR research. While the roots of our approach are in marketing, the framework should prove useful for scholars in a variety of disciplines (e.g., organizational behavior, strategy, human resources); in fact, much of the research on which this book is based has appeared in non-marketing journals (e.g., *MIT-Sloan Management Review*, *California Management Review*, *Journal of Business Ethics*) and is frequently cited by scholars from other business disciplines.

What lies ahead

The book is laid out as follows:

Part I (Chapters 2–3) deconstructs the concept of CR value and makes the case for our approach of focusing on understanding stakeholder psychology to help companies create such value. We introduce our stakeholder psychology framework (Chapter 2) and highlight the stakeholder-driven, pro-company and pro-social outcomes a company can hope to reap through its CR (Chapter 3).

Part II (Chapters 4–6) is the conceptual heart of the book. It contains the details of our stakeholder psychology framework. More specifically, Chapter 4 focuses on the CR/stakeholder interface, wherein we discuss what stakeholders learn about CR and the ways in which they do so (i.e., the communication channels from which they typically acquire such information). Chapter 5 goes into the mind and heart of the stakeholder, revealing how stakeholders interpret CR information. Finally, Chapter 6 examines the contextual factors that influence the interpretations and responses of stakeholders.

Part III (Chapters 7–11) of the book unpacks the implications of the framework for managers. In Chapter 7, we focus on how companies can co-create CR programs with their stakeholders. Chapter 8 is concerned with how to communicate effectively with stakeholders about CR. Chapter 9 provides guidance on the challenging task of evaluating the effectiveness of CR activity. Chapter 10 describes two tests of the framework in realistic contexts, and provides illustrations of how the framework might be used by managers. We conclude in Chapter 11 by recapping the main themes and, looking to the future, outlining some issues that we believe will become increasingly important in years to come.

Endnotes

1 B. Ross, "Congress Moves to End Chevron's Myanmar Operations," *ABC News*, October 25, 2007; C. Schmollinger and D. Sethuraman, "Chevron Digs in its Heels over Myanmar," *International Herald Tribune*, October 30, 2007.
2 P. Kotler and N. Lee, *Corporate Social Responsibility: Doing the Most Good for Your Company and Your Cause* (Hoboken, NJ: Wiley & Sons, Inc., 2004).
3 P. Lacy, T. Cooper, R. Hayward, and L. Neuberger, A New Era of Sustainability – UN Global Compact-Accenture CEO Study 2010.
4 "The Business of Green," *The New York Times*, March 26, 2008; "Just Good Business," *The Economist*, January 17, 2008; "The Debate over Doing Good," *Business Week*, August 15, 2005.
5 M.E. Porter and M.R. Kramer, "The Link Between Competitive Advantage and Corporate Social Responsibility," *Harvard Business Review*, December (2006), 78–93.
6 KPMG, "The Directors & Boards Survey: Corporate Social Responsibility," in *Directors & Boards: Boardroom Briefing* (2006), available at, http://www.directorsandboards.com/DBEBRIEFING/December2006/Winter06BB.pdf, accessed March 18, 2011.

7 "McKinsey survey of 391 UN Global Compact participant CEOs" (2007), available at http://www.mckinsey.it/storage/first/uploadfile/attach/139881/file/cest07.pdf, accessed March 18, 2011.
8 The term was coined by GreenTeam, an ad agency in New York City.
9 www.coneinc.com/stuff/contentmgr/files/0/8ac1ce2f758c08eb226580a-3b67d5617/files/cone25thcause.pdf, accessed March 18, 2011.
10 Due to the confidentiality agreements we had with some of these companies, we are unable to refer to them by name while describing our research in subsequent chapters.
11 CB Bhattacharya, S. Sen, and D. Korschun, "Using Corporate Social Responsibility to Win the War for Talent," *MIT Sloan Management Review*, 49(2) (2008), 37–44; S. Sen, CB Bhattacharya, and D. Korschun (2006), "The Role of Corporate Social Responsibility in Strengthening Multiple Stakeholder Relationships: A Field Experiment," *Journal of the Academy of Marketing Science*, 34(2) (2006), 158–66; S. Sen and CB Bhattacharya, "Does Doing Good Always Lead to Doing Better? Consumer Reactions to Corporate Social Responsibility," *Journal of Marketing Research*, 38(2) (2001), 225–43.
12 X. Luo and CB Bhattacharya, "Corporate Social Responsibility, Customer Satisfaction, and Market Value," *Journal of Marketing*, 70(4) (2006), 1–18.
13 F. Pals, "Shell's Barendrecht CO2 Project has 'Long Way to Go,' CEO Says," *Bloomberg*, May 7, 2009; F. Pals, "Barendrechters Stand Up to Shell's Plan to Bury CO2 (Update 1)," *Bloomberg*, April 20, 2009.

Further reading

John Elkington, *Cannibals with Forks: Triple Bottom Line of 21st Century Business* (Gabriola Island: Capstone Publishing, 1999).

> In this pioneering book, Elkington unfolds the notion of the triple bottom line (people, planet and profit) and identifies seven dimensions for a sustainable future.

Bradley K. Googins, Philip H. Mirvis, and Steven A. Rochlin, *Beyond Good Company* (Basingstoke: Palgrave Macmillan, 2007).

> This book shows that the business world is changing and how global companies such as Shell, Unilever and GE have integrated CR with their core business strategies.

Jeffrey Hollender and Bill Breen, *The Responsibility Revolution: How the Next Generation of Businesses Will Win* (San Francisco, CA: Jossey-Bass, 2010).

> The CEO of Seventh Generation, a socially and environmentally responsible household company shows how companies can be part of the solution instead of the problem. He presents ideas and strategies for managers to realize that goal.

Lynn Sharp Paine, *Value Shift: Why Companies Must Merge Social and Financial Imperatives to Achieve Superior Performance* (New York: McGraw Hill, 2003).

> This book describes why successful companies will have to fulfill the social and financial expectations of their stakeholders by signaling a new business ethic and higher standards of corporate behavior.

Paul Hawken, Amory Lovins, and L. Hunter Lovins, *Natural Capitalism* (Oxford: Backbay, 1999).

> The authors of this book focus on the "planet" dimension of the triple bottom line and reveal that companies will create economic value by being environmentally responsible.

Joel Makower, *Strategies for the Green Economy* (New York: McGraw Hill, 2009).

> Makower focuses also on the "planet" dimension of the triple bottom line and offers a roadmap for companies to align environmental and business goals.

PART I

Deconstructing CR value

The corporate social and environmental responsibility movement, known more generally as corporate responsibility (CR), shows little sign of waning. All Fortune 500 companies now run some form of corporate responsibility (CR) program and the desire to "do well by doing good" motivates the world's largest corporations collectively to direct billions of dollars towards a wide spectrum of social and environmental issues, whether through donations, volunteer programs, or other means.

Numerous surveys show that senior managers, major shareholders and board members agree that CR is "in the best interest" of their company. Yet despite the widespread belief that CR can simultaneously improve societal welfare and corporate performance, it is rare that CR reaches its full potential as portrayed in the mainstream press. Simply put, even for a company with the best intentions, merely "doing good" is *not enough* to create business and social value.

In this first part, we make the case for understanding when, why and how CR value is created. We argue that to practice strategic CR management, managers need to see stakeholders as individuals who can create value for the company through their individual behaviors. Specifically, in Chapter 2, we deconstruct the value created by CR into its underlying components and provide an overview of the underlying psychology that drives stakeholder reactions. In Chapter 3, we outline what many of these behaviors are and show that much of the value from CR stems from stakeholders rewarding the company, and acting responsibly themselves.

PART I

Deconstructing CR value

TWO

Viewing stakeholders as individuals

The "Market for Virtue"

The roots of CR have a long and rich history. The idea that businesses can be managed in ways that benefit society dates back to at least the early eighteenth century. In those days "CR" initiatives, in the form of policies and programs helpful to workers, were implemented by industrialists. These were the days of CR's pioneers, idealists who single-handedly pursued a vision of using business to "give back" to society.

For example, Robert Owen was a Welsh-born textile entrepreneur, who in 1799 bought a cotton mill in New Lanark, Scotland so that he could conduct what he called "an experiment" in business practice.[1] Upon purchasing the mill, he instituted a series of socially responsible policies aimed at improving the lives of his workers. He created a fund for those who became sick. He abolished child labor in the factory town. He set up a bank and store to provide services and products at reasonable rates. Owen even started the "Institution for the Formation of Character," which functioned as a school for both children and adults.

In 1831, George Cadbury, the son of the philanthropist and chocolate maker John Cadbury, created a model village – for the benefit of his workers – that conformed to his Quaker ideals. Sir Titus Salt founded the manufacturing town of Saltaire in 1853 as an alternative for workers who lived under wretched conditions and intense pollution in nearby Bradford, England. When asked why he took on the ambitious project, Salt answered: "Outside of my business I am nothing – in it, I have considerable influence."[2]

Undoubtedly, the employees of Owen, Cadbury, and Salt appreciated the fruits of these efforts. But the employees were not the initiators of these innovations.

The face of CR looks very different today. In the twenty-first century, the impetus for many companies to engage in CR is driven by *demand from their stakeholders*. The model of CR as the brainchild of a single executive no longer holds sway. A substantial segment of the population now prides itself on rewarding "good" companies and punishing "bad" ones. Thus, today's companies are responding as much to market forces as they are to the societal issues themselves. This is what researcher David Vogel calls "the Market for Virtue," in his eponymous influential book.

> A substantial segment of the population now actively rewards "good" companies and punishes "bad" ones.

Never have these market pressures to engage in CR been more acute. In fact, *many people now believe that businesses are better equipped to solve the world's problems than the public sector*.[3] The reasoning goes that governments are resource-strapped, slow to change, and often ineffective in many endeavors; on the other hand, companies have considerable resources, are nimble enough to take on problems as they arise, and bring a performance-based attitude that makes them freer to solve issues quickly and efficiently. As a result, *companies are increasingly expected to be on the frontlines of the world's political, economic, and social transformations*.

Certainly, the wide diffusion and prominence of CR is still in part a response to the daunting social and environmental challenges we face as a society. Income disparity in both developing and highly industrialized economies is of unprecedented concern. Global climate change is widely accepted as real, and there is great unease that its potential consequences are imminent and devastating. Human rights continue to be routinely and flagrantly violated in many parts of the world. And with the power and numerous privileges that corporations are afforded by law, many citizens also believe the time has come for these companies to act differently.

Concerns about social justice, equity, and the environment have long been with us. But what we see today is a widely held belief *that companies can and should intervene* in addressing these societal issues.

Companies speak about CR

Former Toyota President, Katsuaki Watanabe, observes: "One of the greatest changes in the business environment in recent years is the heightened expectations towards corporate responsibility."[4] We see these expectations across the full range of stakeholders. Pringle and Thompson, the authors of *Brand Spirit*, are intensely aware that many consumers are pushing companies to engage in CR: "Consumers are going beyond the practical issues of functional product performance or rational product benefits... What they are asking for – and are drawn to now – are demonstrations of good."[5]

Meanwhile, Jim Copeland, the former CEO of Deloitte, finds a similar impetus from employees: "The best professionals in the world want to work in organizations in which they can thrive. And, they want to work for companies that exhibit good corporate citizenship."[6]

Investors are adding their voice as well; Judy Henderson, of the Global Reporting Initiative, notices a strong trend: "Discerning investors now recognize that *a company managed according to interests broader than those of only shareholders is more likely to profit over the long term*."[7]

Not surprisingly, many forward-thinking companies are gravitating towards more strategic approaches to meet CR demand. Figure 2.1 shows that this shift is occurring along three dimensions.

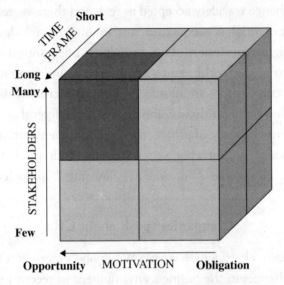

Figure 2.1 The changing face of CR

First, while CR was once considered an obligation, and often afterthought, companies are now treating it more as *an opportunity to create value for their business*. Some companies acknowledge this shift explicitly by using the phrase "Corporate Social Opportunity" in place of CR.

Second, while CR was traditionally thought to revolve around a few stakeholder groups, such as non-profits and possibly consumers, of late companies have realized that CR is important to *multiple* stakeholders such as *employees, investors, regulators*, and the *communities* in which they operate.

Finally, while companies used to see CR as a short-term, one-shot tactic (e.g., increased sales from cause-marketing initiatives), it is now seen as *an intrinsic part of the company's long-term, strategic thrust*. Companies that are most strategic about their CR tend to operate in the dark gray area of the cube; they see it as a long-term opportunity to relate to many stakeholder segments.

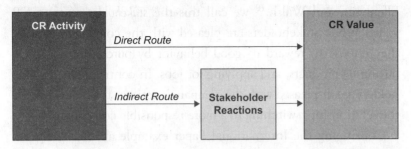

Figure 2.2 Two routes by which CR generates value

The stakeholder route to CR value

With this substantial shift in worldview, many companies are recognizing an important distinction in terms of how CR generates value. Specifically, there are *two routes* through which CR can create value for the company, the *direct* route and the *stakeholder* (or indirect) route (illustrated in Figure 2.2).[8] Each route is important, and the two routes should be seen as complementary. This simple, yet critical, distinction can shed light on why CR value can seem so idiosyncratic; that is, it generates value for some companies but not others.

The first route to CR value is more direct and obvious, and reported routinely in CR reports released annually by companies. Through this route, the CR activity – in and of itself – leads to cost savings or increased revenues. For example, from 2004 to 2006 International Paper reduced its overall energy usage by 0.7 percent and its fossil fuel consumption by 12.2 percent (even as revenues grew by about 6 percent). The company is also the largest producer of reforestation stock, which is likely to contribute directly to future revenues.[9] In this example of the direct route, the financial performance benefits of engaging in environmentally friendly programs are obvious, clearly assessable and a direct outcome of the company's actions.

In contrast, the second and more indirect route to CR value is through the reactions of stakeholders. In line with Margolis,

Elfenbein, and Walsh,[10] we call this the *stakeholder route* to CR value. When stakeholders are pleased with the company's actions, they choose to reward its good behavior by purchasing its stock, buying its products, and applying for jobs. In contrast, when stakeholders are displeased with the company's actions, they may dissolve the relationship, switching to a more responsible company.

Continuing the International Paper example above, it is possible that many stakeholders will react favorably to the company's actions in the environmental arena. For instance, certain *customers* may happily receive news of the company's reduced energy usage and reduction of fossil fuel consumption; some may even make an extra effort to buy the company's products and spread positive word-of-mouth on behalf of the company. The same is true for many of International Paper's employees. Many of them will feel proud to work for a company that is environmentally responsible.

These benefits may not be immediately apparent in financial statements, yet over time could well result in increased customer loyalty and advocacy, as well as an increase in employee morale, leading to greater employee retention and higher productivity.

Clearly, the stakeholder route is more indirect in that the value depends on the subjective reactions of the stakeholders. As a result, the value from this route, while potentially substantial and long lasting, is idiosyncratic and contingent on a host of contextual factors that influence stakeholder responses. Managing the stakeholder route is therefore very challenging, requiring a clear image of what stakeholders want so that CR can be properly designed, implemented, and evaluated.

The missing link: An individual stakeholder view

CR impacts a wide variety of stakeholder segments and each of these segments responds in diverse ways based on their personal preferences and tastes. Taking advantage of the stakeholder route to CR value requires managers to develop a much deeper understanding of how stakeholders think and behave. In essence, managers need to examine *stakeholder psychology* and develop an appreciation for how CR fits into the lives of stakeholders. Absent this sort of understanding, it is unlikely that we will be able to predict with any certainty whether CR will or will not create real value.

No two stakeholders are exactly alike. In the consumption realm, some people demand CR from companies, others are cooler about the idea. Some will pay a premium for socially responsible products, while others will purchase from responsible companies only when products are similar in quality and price to those of the competition. The same heterogeneity is found in the investment realm, where a growing number of shareholders actively seek good corporate citizens as a matter of principle, while others support responsible business practices only when it is seen to contribute to the profitability of the company.

Given this heterogeneity, managers need to know how *individual stakeholders* perceive CR initiatives. Managers need to get into the mind of the stakeholder, understanding how CR activity is interpreted. And managers need to relate the thoughts and feelings of stakeholders to behavioral responses to CR that contribute to the company's success.

> Managers need to examine stakeholder psychology and develop an appreciation for how CR fits into the lives of stakeholders.

We take this individual-level perspective in almost all of our research. For example, in our technology company study and in the childhood development center study we find that CR increases consumers' intent to purchase products because it signals to consumers that the company shares their values.[11] In our frontline employee study, we find that, if managed correctly, CR can contribute to employees' desire to fulfill customer needs.

We will revisit the details of these and other studies in upcoming chapters. What's important to note now is that the individual-level perspective is often much more revealing than the view from the aggregate level. Once a clear picture is formed at the individual level, managers can begin to aggregate up from the ground level in order to predict the overall market response to CR initiatives.

In pursuing such an understanding of stakeholder reactions, we build on and integrate affiliated disciplines – including psychology, consumer behavior, and marketing – to develop a framework that provides insight into how CR activity fulfills stakeholder needs. This understanding allows the company to optimize the impact of CR on itself, its stakeholders, the environment, and society at large.

The road to CR value: A framework

We have synthesized insights from our research and those of other researchers into a comprehensive framework. The framework is designed to trace stakeholder reactions to CR, from the moment they see or hear about it, to the time they purchase a product or apply for a job. This road to CR value can be long, and sometimes complex, but managers who understand these steps will be better prepared to respond to stakeholder pressures, and more likely to reap rewards from their CR efforts.

> Strong and enduring stakeholder relationships are critical to a company's success.

Our framework (Figure 2.3) has *four overarching components*, which are explained in more detail in the chapters that follow.

1. The first component is CR inputs (i.e., what stakeholders see and hear). Stakeholders make judgments about companies' CR

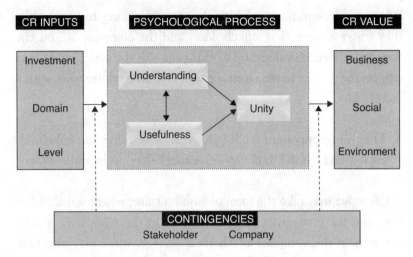

Figure 2.3 An overview of our framework

activity, and they make them based on a few key dimensions: the issue that CR addresses, how programs are implemented, and the extent to which the company allocates resources to programs.
2. The second component in the framework concerns the psychological process (i.e., how stakeholders interpret CR activity). This component is concerned with all the thoughts and feelings that stakeholders have about the CR activity and the company. As stakeholders learn about CR activity, developing what we call *Understanding*, they judge the appropriateness of the CR activity, try to uncover what motivated the company to engage in CR, and evaluate whether CR programs are improving societal welfare.

In addition to the impact on others, stakeholders – human beings after all – like to benefit themselves from CR. This may be something concrete, or it may be something as simple as "making them feel good." Whether they receive these benefits, something we call *Usefulness*, is a major factor in stakeholders' reactions to CR.

Understanding and *Usefulness* work in concert to forge a sense that there is *Unity* (or not) between the stakeholder and the company.

When Understanding and Usefulness are working harmoniously, they foster a sense that stakeholders and the company are on the same team, sharing values and working towards the same goals. *Unity* reflects the goal of having a strong and enduring relationship with a stakeholder.

3. The third component is CR value (i.e., how individual stakeholders respond to CR). It comprises actual behaviors by stakeholders.

CR value may take the form of *business value*, where stakeholders purchase the company's products, invest in the company, or otherwise help the company reach its goals. CR value may also take the form of *societal value*, a too-often overlooked outcome of CR, involving increases in donations, volunteering, or other important pro-social activities from the stakeholder.

4. The fourth and final component of the framework are the contingencies (i.e., how context influences the overall process). Each situation is unique, so managerial decision-making must be adapted to account for this reality. We have conducted our research in many industries and with many types of stakeholders. As a result, we have identified many of the critical contextual factors that may influence how stakeholders' interpretations and ultimate responses unfold.

These factors are often related to *individual differences in stakeholders, such as how much they care about an issue or how embedded they are in the organization*. Alert managers can leverage these factors, tailoring CR activity to generate the most favorable business and societal returns from CR investment.

The other set of factors that influence the road to CR value are based on differences across companies and industries. These may also be leveraged by managers for maximal advantage.

What the framework means for managers

Our framework is stakeholder-centric, recognizing that stakeholders have considerable control in responding to CR activity. However, the framework is really designed to help managers use this knowledge to make better decisions about their CR engagement.

> CR programs are most likely to be self-sustaining when they provide a "win-win-win" (company, stakeholder, cause).

Our intention is for managers to tailor CR activities so that stakeholders feel that the company is satisfying their needs and wants. Satisfying stakeholders is a responsibility of managers. We believe that the company is who its stakeholders are,[12] that without strong and enduring stakeholder relationships a company is bound to fail, collapsing under its own weight. But aside from this normative motivation, managers also need to be pragmatic in how they run CR programs. Our approach is designed to provide managers with the win-win-win (company, stakeholder, cause) that is necessary for CR programs to be self-sustaining. Unless CR programs are compelling to stakeholders, they are unlikely to survive in the long term, and maybe not even in the short term.

An illustrative example

We explain each of the framework's components in subsequent chapters. But to illustrate our overall approach, consider a real world example from our research: a corporate responsibility initiative of a global consumer products company designed to address the "silent epidemic" of oral disease. To achieve its goal of "combating America's oral health epidemic by helping 50 million children and their families by 2010," the company partnered with the Boys and Girls Club of America and local dental schools across the country to provide education, tools, and access to dental care services for children in economically disadvantaged neighborhoods across the US.

By partnering with a well known non-profit, the company was able to generate high awareness among the non-profit's members. The program provided both kids and their parents with many valued benefits. For example, *by inviting celebrities to speak to the children about dental hygiene, kids were highly motivated to participate,* resulting in healthier teeth – and happier parents. When parents saw the positive results of the program on their children's lives, it fostered a belief that the company was genuinely concerned about kids' oral health. One parent we spoke with said: "This company helps a lot and they think a lot about kids especially; they want to help the lower income people."

Parents with kids in the program now view the toothpaste brand as gentle and caring. *The relationship that has developed between these parents and the company has resulted in a number of positive outcomes.* For example, many parents have become loyal consumers not only of the toothpaste brand, but also of products marketed by the company in other categories (e.g., shampoos). They connect purchasing the company's products to their own well-being. As one parent noted: "By consuming their products we are contributing to the program's success."

Also, parents are more aware of their kids' oral health, which has led them to supervise their children to attain improved brushing habits. These outcomes are notably stronger depending on the characteristics of the parent; those who have immigrated most recently to the country – and are therefore still acculturating – react more positively to the program. (We will explain why this occurs in Chapter 6.) In sum, this example gives a sense of the underlying process behind many stakeholders' reactions to CR.

Summary

In this chapter we review some history and early examples of social responsibility before zooming in on the present state of affairs. In so doing, we underscore what is different about the challenges for today's CR manager, including the current "market for virtue" and the importance of generating value via the stakeholder route, a less direct but major key to a successful business venture in the twenty-first century.

We set forth our basic framework, each component of which will be discussed in greater detail in the chapters that follow. These include understanding what stakeholders see, how they interpret what they know about CR initiatives, how they respond to such CR activities, and how context influences the process.

Throughout this book, our approach is stakeholder-centric; yet our intent is to provide managers with the insights they need to tailor CR activities so that stakeholders feel that the company is satisfying their needs and wants. Ultimately, the goal is a win-win-win – for the company, the stakeholder, and the social or environmental cause.

The value of the framework to managers can be summarized more specifically thus: By defining how stakeholders interpret and respond to CR activity, the framework helps managers configure both their CR efforts and their communication of it to ensure that their CR is focused on issues that are most important to their stakeholders. It allows managers to design and implement CSR programs that make clear to stakeholders how these fit into the company's mission and benefit the stakeholders. As well, the framework guides managers so that they can effectively and comprehensively assess their CR campaigns' success and calculate return on CR investment. Finally, by understanding how context influences the entire process, the framework helps managers adapt their CR activities to their unique situation.

Endnotes

1 B. Kiviat, "A Brief History of Creative Capitalism," *Time*, August 11, 2008.
2 Rev. R. Balgarnie, *Sir Titus Salt, Baronet: His Life and Its Lessons*, London: Hodder & Stoughton 1878, Repr. 1970; J. Styles, *Titus Salt and Saltaire: Industry and Virtue* (Shipley, England: Salts Estates Ltd., 1994).
3 S. Hart, *Capitalism at the Crossroads: The Unlimited Business Opportunities in Solving the World's Most Difficult Problems* (Philadelphia, Pennsylvania: Wharton School Publishing, 2005).
4 P. Engardio, "Beyond the Green Corporation," *Business Week*, January 29, 2007; Toyota 2007 Sustainability Report, available at www.toyota-global.com/sustainability/sustainability_report/pdf_file_download/07/, accessed March 28, 2011.
5 H. Pringle and M. Thompson, *Brand Spirit: How Cause Related Marketing Builds Brands* (Hoboken, NJ: Wiley, 2001).
6 World Economic Forum, "Responding to the Leadership Challenge: Findings of a CEO Survey on Global Corporate Citizenship" (Geneva, Switzerland, 2003).
7 J. Hollender and S. Fenichell, *What Matters Most: How a Small Group of Pioneers Is Teaching Social Responsibility to Big Business, and Why Big Business Is Listening* (New York: Basic Books, 2003), 163.
8 J.D. Margolis, H.A. Elfenbein, and J.P. Walsh, "Does It Pay to Be Good?" 2007, available at http://www.unglobalcompact.org/newsandevents/articles_and_papers/margolis_november_07.pdf, accessed March 16, 2011.
9 International Paper Sustainability Report, 2006, available at www.ipaper.com, accessed July 2, 2008.
10 Margolis, Elfenbein, and Walsh, "Does It Pay to Be Good?"
11 For example, S. Sen and CB Bhattacharya, "Does Doing Good Always Lead to Doing Better? Consumer Reactions to Corporate Social Responsibility," *Journal of Marketing Research*, 38(2) (2001), 225–43; S. Sen, CB Bhattacharya, and D. Korschun, "The Role of Corporate Social Responsibility in Strengthening Multiple Stakeholder Relationships: A Field Experiment," *Journal of the Academy of Marketing Science*, 34(2) (2006), 158–66.
12 J.E. Post, L.E. Preston, and S. Sachs, *Redefining the Corporation: Stakeholder Management and Organizational Wealth* (Stanford University Press, 2002).

Further reading

R. Edward Freeman, *Strategic Management: A Stakeholder Approach* (Cambridge University Press, 2010).

This book is a re-issue of Freeman's path-breaking work in the field of stakeholder theory and management on the occasion of the twenty-fifth anniversary of publication.

R. Edward Freeman, *Stakeholder Theory: The State of the Art* (Cambridge University Press, 2010).

This book examines the manifold research in the field of stakeholder theory and assesses its relevance for business.

Jörg Andriof, Sandra Waddock, Bryan Husted, and Sandra Sutherland Rahman, *Unfolding Stakeholder Thinking* (Sheffield, Greenleaf, 2002).

The authors argue that stakeholder thinking has evolved into the study of interactive and responsive relationships that establish the very context of doing modern business, and create the basis for transparency and accountability.

THREE

How stakeholders respond to CR

For CR to have a legitimate place at the corporate table, it cannot be an end in itself. CR needs to produce tangible value not only for the environment and society, but also for the company. Otherwise, CR is simply not sustainable.

The global business community knows this. As a result, many companies, as a matter of course, try to measure the value created by their CR activities. That's why new emerging standards, like those set forth by the UN's Global Reporting Initiative, have made it easier for companies to evaluate their CR activity.

If annual CR reports are any indication, companies are making progress in tying CR actions to a variety of both social and business outcomes. Managers are setting ambitious CR-related goals, and, in many cases, achieving them. For example, 3M plans to reduce emissions by 50 percent over the next fifteen years with expected savings to the company of $200 million.[1] More examples of the direct route to CR value are shown in Figure 3.1.

While such progress is certainly laudable and is a clear step in the right direction, it is overwhelmingly focused on the *direct route* to CR value discussed in Chapter 2 (e.g., cost savings; reduction of carbon footprint, etc.). But ignoring the indirect route (i.e., through *stakeholder reactions*) to CR value provides only a *partial accounting* of the full value that CR generates. In other words, while direct route assessment should be seen as an important *starting point* for

Company	Year	Innovation	Revenue
Siemens	2009	Energy-saving and other green technologies constitute more than a quarter of total sales	€23 billion
GE	By 2010	Green portfolio "Ecomagination"	$17 billion
			Savings
Catalyst Paper Corporation	2002–2005	Reduced CO2 emissions by 46% (equivalent of 690,000 barrels of oil)	$13 million
Hewlett-Packard	Annually	Consolidated 85 data centers to six worldwide. This reduces energy usage by up to 450 million kWh	$25 million
BASF	Annually	By-products and waste from one plant can be used as raw materials for other plants	€500 million at Ludwigshafen plants

Figure 3.1 Examples of the direct route to CR value

companies that wish to be strategic about their CR management, companies also need to articulate, understand, and assess the CR value created through stakeholder responses to CR.

Executives are cognizant – at least in a general sense – that stakeholder reactions to CR activity can have important consequences for the company and society. In 2003, for example, the World Economic Forum conducted a global survey in which it asked executives to cite the three most important motivations behind their CR activity. Almost 80 percent cited reputation among constituents (i.e., the stakeholder route). A full 60 percent cited employee motivation, another indirect route. In contrast, less than 20 percent claimed operational efficiency (i.e., the direct route) as one of their top motivations.[2]

> Managers who ignore the indirect route are likely to miss much of the value generated by CR.

These findings are corroborated by a recent McKinsey survey (2009) of Chief Financial Officers (CFOs) investment professionals, and corporate responsibility professionals. (See below.)

> A 2009 McKinsey survey asked CFOs as well as investment and CR professionals to name how CR engagement benefits the company. Almost 80% claimed that CR helps a company's financial performance primarily through building and maintaining a good reputation and/or brand equity; and about 55% claimed that CR helps attract, motivate and retain talented employees. In contrast, only about 35% of these executives claimed that CR benefits the company mainly through the direct route of improved "operational efficiency, and/or decreasing costs."

Consider, too, the many benefits of CR as cited by Business for Social Responsibility (BSR), each of which is based on stakeholders' indirect reactions to CR:

> When done well, CSR builds business value in diverse ways: by enhancing brand image, establishing a more cooperative relationship with government regulatory agencies, and garnering the interest of investors who are interested in issues related to sustainability. It also helps: attract and retain talented, motivated employees; enhance the company's position in new markets; position the company as a good partner for peers, government, and NGOs; and improve risk recognition and avoidance. The list goes on and on.[3]

The missing element

Although many managers know that the stakeholder route to CR value is important, many continue to struggle to understand the ways in which it can truly inform their decision-making. Admittedly, making sense of the many potential stakeholder reactions can be daunting. Most companies have a wide array of stakeholders to satisfy, each with their own interests and needs. Moreover, there are precious few models to help practitioners or scholars make sense of the complexity. In their book, researchers Marc Epstein and Sally Widener point out this dilemma by stating: "While research suggests that organizations need to evaluate diverse stakeholder interests, be aware of social and economic impacts, and integrate this into decision-making, there is little guidance on the underlying process."[4]

In sum, then, companies want to know whether their CR investment is paying off. At the same time, however, it is not easy to delineate the links between CR actions and how or whether the value of such actions is created through stakeholder reactions. Given the need for greater clarity around the nature of stakeholder-driven CR value, this chapter delves into its components, providing a measurable and actionable sense of the "pro-company outcomes" inherent in stakeholder responses to CR.

Two types of CR value

Business value

WPP Group CEO, Sir Martin Sorrell, sees CR as: "a major area of potential revenue generation and profitability."[5] Moreover, he believes that CR is beneficial to companies because, "consumers, governments and non-government organizations will favor those companies that take a more constructive approach to issues such as the environment, food availability, obesity and water shortages."[6] Thus, as we argue at every stage of this book, CR value often stems directly from the behaviors of stakeholders in any number of stakeholder realms (e.g., consumption, employment, investment). This occurs because CR *activity can forge strong and enduring relationships with stakeholders, leading many to reward the company for its responsible behavior.* We call this set of behaviors *business value*. But CR can also create another type of value.

Societal value

Just as there is an indirect route linking CR activity to *corporate returns*, so, too, there is one linking CR to *societal returns*. This *societal value* stems from the social and environmental impacts of the company's CR activity *as wrought by stakeholder actions*.

For instance, when stakeholders become aware of or get personally involved with CR initiatives, it heightens their desire to "do good." This desire may express itself in the form of voluntary actions (e.g., donating money, volunteering) on the part of the stakeholder, which can benefit the cause beyond the formal boundaries of the CR initiative. Moreover, engagement in CR initiatives also prompts stakeholders to undertake behavioral changes in the social arena (e.g., lowering their carbon footprint, eating healthier foods).

A real world example: "Shared value"

Companies that practice strategic CR management actively track both business and societal value. Nestlé, for instance, is such a company, having made great strides in assessing both business and societal outcomes on a regular basis (see Figure 3.2). The company calls this approach "creating shared value."

In a manner similar to that of our approach in this book, Nestlé breaks shared value into two components: value to the company (and its shareholders), and societal value. With regard to value to the company, Nestlé has begun the process of understanding how CR improves its fiscal and strategic position.

Specifically, setting aside the *direct contributors* to business outcomes – such as lowering manufacturing costs – Nestlé cites

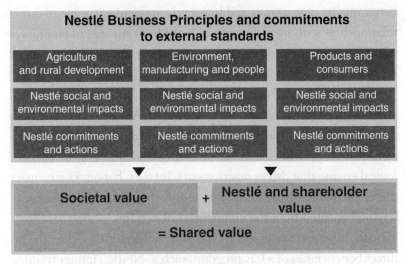

Figure 3.2 Nestlé framework for creating shared value

several *stakeholder-related drivers*. These include providing new R&D and expertise to suppliers and building brands through responsible marketing. This company has also organized and convened formal meetings to reach out to high priority stakeholders who can help the company achieve its performance objectives. Above is a breakdown of their approach.

Nestlé assessed the societal value of CR initiatives by looking at several outcomes. These include:

- widening access to nutritional products for consumers,
- reducing consumption of natural resources in manufacturing,
- creating jobs in local communities where Nestlé has a presence, and
- generating local investment and economic growth.

Specific measures of this value include the number of farmers trained through Nestlé programs, the number of products renovated for nutrition or health considerations, and the degree of reduction of both waste and carbon emissions. *Value for the company* takes the form of better quality of materials and lower procurement costs due to direct relationships with local farmers, reduced lost time due to employees injured on the job, and greater market share due to the enhanced reputation that CR provides.[7]

Nestlé's approach highlights the essential link between societal and company value – that is, *shared value*. And beyond that, it is apparent that such shared value is created through stakeholder reactions to CR. As will become clear in the delineation of the psychological engine that drives reactions to CR (see Chapter 5), a primary driver of pro-company behaviors is the stakeholder perception of having benefited from the company's CR actions.

Such benefits may come to the stakeholders either directly (as direct beneficiaries of a CR program, such as Nestlé's farmer training programs) or indirectly, through an increase in their psychological well-being. In some instances well-being may even be enhanced through their own greater pro-social and pro-environmental behaviors (e.g., buying from a company that cares about the environment).

The *value to society* of a company's CR is a *direct determinant* of the added value that stakeholders then go on to create for the company. They create that value through specific behaviors, once they feel engaged. Therefore, while the main thrust of this chapter is on CR company value, it is essential to acknowledge the underlying link between company value and societal value.

> The most impactful CR activity is often that which provides compelling benefits to the stakeholder.

Because of the central position of the stakeholder in this equation, it is important for managers to understand the behaviors of individual stakeholders. The discussion therefore moves next to the different individual-level components of CR company value, providing evidence for each from our own research studies and those of other scholars. As shown in our framework (see Chapter 2), *such value is created through a set of pro-company behaviors exhibited by individual stakeholders.*

CR business value

Conventional wisdom suggests that the biggest return to CR spending stems from an *increased intent to purchase products* from or *seek employment* with or *invest* in a firm that is deemed socially responsible. For example, a poll by Cone Communications in 2007 found that when price and quality are equal, 87 percent of American consumers are likely to switch from one product to another that is associated with a good cause; this number has gone up from 66 percent in 1993. Similarly, 77 percent considered a company's commitment to social causes when considering employment (up from 48 percent in 2001) and 66 percent considered such commitment while making investment decisions (up from 40 percent in 2001).

In fact, when stakeholders reward a company for its CR initiatives, they do so in multiple ways that are reflective of a strong relationship in which purchase, employment, and investment are but the starting points. Deep relationships can result in valuable behaviors across a variety of stakeholder realms. These are described below in more detail, with particular emphasis on the consumption and employment domains, which are critical to strategic CR management.

The consumption realm

While many managers – especially marketing managers – view CR as an opportunity to grow short-term sales, our research suggests that the real value of CR transcends any single transaction. Instead, CR *value stems from the deep, meaningful and enduring relationships that CR can encourage stakeholders to develop with the company.* Consider the following focus group quotes:

> If I saw something I didn't like, I would still give them [Good Earth Company] another chance.

> Talk about Patagonia – people would just leave the magazines at my door, leave an article about the company – it's really supposed to be great.

> I will only buy Stonyfield and I'll only buy Tom's of Maine toothpaste no matter how cheap the other stuff is.

> Even though their product is not unique, I am very loyal to them. If their prices went up relative to similar products, I would still buy it, even if I had to cut down on the total amount.

Managers who work to cultivate high quality relationships based on identification and trust (see Chapter 5) are likely to find this sort of broad-based support from stakeholders in the consumption realm. Among the measurable aspects of consumption are purchase, loyalty, willingness to pay, and positive word-of-mouth behaviors.

> CR value stems from the deep, meaningful and enduring stakeholder relationships that CR can produce.

Purchase: Much research, including ours, points to consumers' increased likelihood of purchasing the products and services of a socially responsible company. Across numerous studies we conducted, consumers consistently express a desire to reward companies that engage in CR activity. For example, we conducted an experimental study, measuring the purchase intent of respondents as a function of their perceptions of the company's CR record. Holding other factors constant, we found that respondents had significantly higher intent to purchase from a company with a positive CR record than from one with a poor record.

In another study of stakeholder responses to CR, a large corporate donation to a child development center by a large consumer goods company heightened stakeholders' intentions to purchase its brands (See panel a of Figure 3.3).

Interestingly, the findings from our study of the oral health program demonstrated that such increased purchase behavior by program participants can, under certain conditions, end up taking share from an entrenched market leader. Before being exposed to the program, the parents were very loyal to the market leader brand. Once the parents saw the positive effects of the initiative on their children's oral health, they sought to support the initiative by purchasing the company's toothpaste. The parents in our focus groups described the dramatic effect of CR in these words:

> My kids are benefiting, the community is benefiting, why would I not buy it?
>
> As parents we all have to support the company that is sponsoring the program so that it can have more money [to continue this program].
>
> Sometimes we buy a product and ... that's the end of it. But when you see something like what [the brand] is doing, you realize that they are trying to help the community, especially the Latinos and the African Americans, because we are the poorest, and they are trying to help us. [The initiative] is expensive but they are giving it to us for free.
>
> By consuming their products we are contributing to the program's success.

To confirm that these intentions were actually acted upon, we surveyed more than 350 people that fit the ethnic and socio-economic profile of beneficiaries of the initiative. We compared responses of three groups: the *participants* in the initiative, a second group comprised of *non-participants who were aware* of the initiative, and a third group representing the *general population* (who were unaware of the initiative). When we asked how often they buy the brand when shopping for their children, the results from the parents were

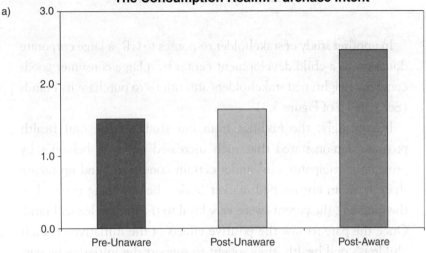

Figure 3.3 Individual-level outcomes in consumption and employment realms based on a donation to a child development center

Note: (a) Purchase intent scores were constructed by multiplying the response to the purchase intent item (1–5 scale, 5 indicating high intent to purchase) and a second item that tested whether or not the respondent knew that the brand belonged to the corporation that made the donation (1 if they knew the brand was manufactured by the company and 0 if they did not). For example, a respondent who indicated a high intent to purchase the brand but did not know the company that manufactured the brand (4*0) was given a score of 0 while a respondent who had the same purchase intent but knew that the company manufactured the brand was scored as 4 (4*1). Employment and Investment intent are based on a simple 1–5 scale (higher values represent greater intent). (b) Pre-unaware equals participants polled before the donation, post-unaware equals unaware consumers after the donation, and post-aware equals participants who are aware of the donation.

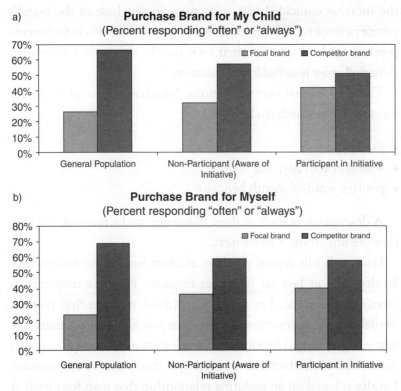

Figure 3.4 Consumption realm outcomes from oral health program participants

eye-opening. Only 20 percent of the general population said that they purchase the brand "often" or "always," compared to 66 percent for the main competitor brand. In contrast, 32 percent of parents who were merely aware of the program purchased it often or always – already a large bump up from those unaware of the program. Purchase by participants in the initiative was even higher (42 percent).

> CR value is manifested in a range of consumption behaviors such as purchase, loyalty, and positive word-of-mouth.

Figure 3.4a suggests that some of the increase in purchase likely came at the expense of the sales of the competitor's toothpaste;

the increase coincided with a decrease in purchase of the brand's primary competitor. Figure 3.4b shows very similar effects for parents purchasing the brand for their own use. In short, *the CR program converted entire households into customers.*

Three additional outcomes in the "purchasing" realm that were measured in research studies were:

- loyalty,
- willingness to pay, and
- positive word-of-mouth behavior.

A description of each of these outcomes, and a rationale for why they are important, follows next.

Loyalty. While repeat purchase is often used as an indicator of loyalty, it is at best an imperfect measure. Purchase frequency is often more influenced by promotions (think frequent-flyer points), availability, and convenience than a true psychological commitment towards the brand. Therefore, we view loyalty as consumers' commitment to a brand, which runs much deeper than mere repeat purchase. Loyalty is based on an enduring relationship that manifests itself as repeat purchase and a resistance to purchasing from other companies. As one respondent told us about the Body Shop in a separate study:

> What brings me back to their stores is the feeling that every purchase from them is in a way a contribution to the improvement of life in places where their product comes from and, at the same time, a way to take care of myself.[8]

Our research has revealed many such examples of loyalty that stem from a company or a brand's CR initiatives. For example, in our study of more than 1,000 yogurt consumers, we found that frequent buyers of Stonyfield Farm (hereafter "Stonyfield") professed stronger loyalty to their brand compared to frequent buyers of Dannon and Yoplait. Furthermore, these differences could be traced directly to consumers' beliefs that Stonyfield is more socially responsible. Overall, our body of research shows that CR can help not only immediate sales, but also the intent of consumers to purchase into the foreseeable future.

Willingness to pay. When CR enhances the relationship between stakeholders and the company, it often leads to a heightened willingness to pay for products and services. Across a range of product categories, CR makes products and services more desirable to stakeholders because it is socially desirable and because purchase *enables stakeholders to affirm their personal values through purchase of the company's offerings.*

An interesting experiment conducted by researchers Trudel and Cotte asked consumers how much they would be willing to pay for T-shirts and coffee. Some consumers were told that the goods were ethically produced (the "ethical group"), while others were told that production was unethical (the "unethical group"). A third group, given no information other than the basics about the product, served as a control.

For coffee purchases, the control group was willing to pay, on average, $8.31. In contrast, the mean price of coffee for the ethical group was significantly higher, $9.71. The unethical group, on the other hand, was willing to pay only $5.89, significantly less than both the control group and the ethical group. The same results were found for T-shirts, where the price consumers were willing to pay reached $21.21 for ethically produced 100 percent organic cotton shirts, but only $17.33 when told that production of the shirts harms the environment (the control group was willing to pay $20.04). Notice that in each case, consumers were willing to pay premiums for good behavior (+17 percent for coffee and +6 percent for T-shirts compared to the control group), but enacted even steeper discounts when the company was perceived to be engaged in irresponsible practices (−29 percent for coffee and −14 percent for T-shirts compared to the control group).[9]

In sum, many stakeholders are cognizant of this added value created by CR and are willing to pay for it. However, social irresponsibility can destroy value as well, a fact that is reflected in lower willingness to pay for unethically produced commodity products such as coffee and T-shirts.

Word-of-mouth. When people enter into strong relationships with companies, they often go beyond simply purchasing products and services at a premium. Sometimes, they attempt to sway others, spreading news of the company's good works, and recommending the company's products and services to friends and family. *Consumers often tell us that they talk-up the company in an effort to provide additional rewards to the company for its CR activity.*

Word-of-mouth is also a way of supporting the programs in a more roundabout way, because it generates additional sales that the consumers expect will be used to bolster the impact of the programs in question. For instance, in our study of yogurt consumers, respondents had significantly higher intentions to engage in relationship strengthening behaviors, such as positive word-of-mouth, for Stonyfield, the brand positioned on CR, than they were for its competitors.[10] The reason is that Stonyfield's close association with CR activities engenders strong relationships with stakeholders. Stakeholders then wish to contribute to the brand's success; they do this not only by purchasing the product themselves, but also by recruiting others.

The employment realm

The outcomes that various research studies have measured in the employment realm include:

- recruitment,
- work performance,
- turnover.

Recruitment. Analogous to the consumption context, an important way in which companies can benefit from their CR activity is by *attracting talented workers.* As mentioned in the previous chapter, prospective employees look for companies that match their values because they expect that working at such a company will provide an environment where they can express themselves fully.

The study of a large donation to a childhood development center bears this out (see panel b of Figure 3.3 above). In addition to the increase in purchase intent reported above, we found that stakeholders who were aware of the gift had significantly greater intent to apply for jobs than either of the control groups.

Corroboration of this finding comes from other studies, such as one conducted by researchers Greening and Turban.[11] They examined the choices that prospective employees make as they search for jobs. Respondents in their study preferred socially responsible companies over less responsible peer companies not only when deciding where to apply for jobs, but also in their likelihood of accepting offers.

> Prospective employees seek companies that match their values because they expect that working at such a company will provide an environment where they can express themselves fully.

In still another study, which surveyed 800 MBA students in North America and Europe, researchers found that 94 percent are willing to accept a lower salary in order to work at a socially responsible company. On average, these students were willing to take a 14 percent drop in pay to work for a company that is environmentally friendly and caring about employees and other stakeholders.[12]

Work performance. It has been written that "a paycheck can keep a person on the job physically, but it alone will not keep a person on the job emotionally."[13] The best companies not only look to reward employees through traditional rewards such as salary and benefits, but also by *producing a culture of engagement,* where employees become fully immersed in their job tasks. This sort of engagement often leads to exceptional individual and group performance because engaged workers show up for work consistently, are attentive on the job, and work hard to be as productive as possible.

For example, Google has a very progressive approach to CR in the employee realm.

> Google's progressive approach to CR, aimed at engaging its employees, is exemplified by its "20 percent rule." Engineers are encouraged to "think outside the box" by being allowed to devote one day per week (20 percent of their work time) to projects and ideas that are beyond their job descriptions.
> Not only are these stakeholders pleased with this culture of engagement, but some of these projects have also evolved into highly successful products.

A basic and significant finding across many studies is this: When *employers* engage in compelling CR activities, CR very often fosters heightened engagement on the part of *employees* as well. This engagement is often derived from the fact that CR is highly effective in strengthening employee–employer bonds. Once these bonds are formed and employees feel a sense of Unity with the company, they will work hard to achieve its goals, because the goals are also their own.

For instance, this factory worker at a Fortune 500 company responded to a question about how CR affected his work by saying: "The responsibility of what you're doing out there, what you're making, and the pride in the product. Everything goes up, quality, your focus on not only what you are doing, but the machines you're working with. If you see something, right away you fix it."

In some cases, CR can cultivate a desire to help other stakeholders. For example, in another of our research studies, the effect of CR on frontline employees' behavior towards customers was quite telling.

Employees who felt that customers shared their interest in the company's CR were motivated to "treat each customer as the only customer" by listening carefully to their needs and doing whatever is necessary to provide them with exceptional service. In contrast, employees who did not have a mutual interest in CR with customers felt little Unity with the company and its customers and were less likely to report customer-benefiting behaviors. In other words, under the right circumstances, CR can enhance the degree to which a company's workforce is customer-centric. Further discussion of this concept appears in Chapter 6.

Turnover. A final outcome of CR that we have identified in the employment realm is related to retention. Employees are more wedded to companies that share their values. These sorts of companies make going to work pleasurable for employees and give them pride in their association with the company. As one respondent reported: "One of the things that keeps me here is some of the positive things that we do in the community and being able to be part of that as a result."

Our findings are corroborated by companies like Green Mountain Coffee Roasters, twice ranked by the journal *Business Ethics* as the world's best corporate citizen. Green Mountain actively encourages its employees to create new and innovative volunteer initiatives, reasoning that "these programs contribute to job satisfaction and lower turnover."[14]

Such CR value is particularly useful to companies during difficult times, when one of the first things to be affected is employee morale. In the words of Bobbi Silten, the Chief Foundation Officer of GAP: "We have been going through some challenging times at the GAP. When you ask employees 'why are you staying?' one of the reasons... is the values of this company. And some of those... come from the [CR] work we do."

We also find that employees who perceive a sense of Unity with their respective employers – thanks to CR – also exhibit a variety of citizenship behaviors such as positive word-of-mouth and employee recruitment.

CR societal value

CR activity intends – by definition – to improve societal welfare (the terms societal and social are used interchangeably throughout the book). But sometimes the impact on societal or environmental issues comes not from the company itself, but rather, from stakeholders who become interested in helping the cause. Societal value created by CR can therefore be measured at least in part by how effective it is at engendering stakeholder behaviors that benefit society. We now discuss two specific ways in which CR can change stakeholder behaviors in ways that benefit society: *cause advocacy* and *behavior changes*.

Cause advocacy

When stakeholders develop a strong and enduring relationship with a company, they often personally take on the company's commitment to the causes addressed by the CR activity. For example, employees who find a company's volunteer efforts to be compelling will often volunteer themselves. One respondent we spoke with, an employee at a consumer goods company, described it this way: "It encourages you to go out as a person and volunteer, or do a Habitat for Humanity, and be involved in the community as well."

The sense of Unity fostered by a company's CR activity reminds stakeholders of the need to behave responsibly and to contribute to societal welfare. It raises people's awareness of the issue and demonstrates that progress can be made. Furthermore, CR illustrates the values of the company in unmistakable terms.

Stakeholders who subscribe to the company's engagement in CR will likely support similar issues through volunteering, generating word-of-mouth, or donating money. In a field experiment of beneficiaries' responses to CR, we found that beneficiaries who were aware of a company's involvement with children indicated stronger support for children's issues compared to those who were not aware of the company's involvement. In other words, *CR efforts by a company can act as a catalyst, igniting a small movement of indirect and additional efforts by stakeholders.* Over time and across many stakeholders, these efforts can lead to a substantial impact on the intended cause.

A fine example of CR stimulating additional giving by stakeholders is a creative study conducted by researchers Lichtenstein and colleagues.[15] They surveyed 1,000 customers at four national food chains in four cities to document individual-level outcomes of CR. Survey respondents were given a $3 voucher as an incentive to participate in the study. The catch? The voucher could be redeemed for either: (1) $3 off the respondent's next purchase at the restaurant, or (2) a $3 donation to a local non-profit with which the company had partnered. Consistent with our framework, rates of using the voucher for a donation – as opposed to using it as a discount coupon – increased significantly as Unity increased.

In other words, as stakeholders deepened their relationships with the restaurant as a result of its CR activity, they were more likely to go out of their way to support the cause as well, even if it meant missing out on an opportunity to save money on a future restaurant purchase. Overall, study findings demonstrate that people give disproportionately to a charity that is sponsored by a company with which they identify. They do this as part of a desire to express the values they share with the company.

Behavior changes

One of the goals of CR engagement is to encourage stakeholders to think about the consequences of their actions on the environment, their communities, society at large, and of course, themselves. For example, consumers indicated in interviews we conducted that buying organic food products from socially responsible companies (e.g., Stonyfield, Newman's Own) influences them to increase the overall proportion of organic foods in their diet.[16] Similarly, participants in the oral health program reported brushing and flossing their teeth more regularly. Not surprisingly, they also reported that the improved dental health lowered the number of missed school days for their children.

An interesting anecdote profiled in *The New York Times* shows that Walmart's recent commitment to CR has encouraged employees to change their behavior at work and how they approach their jobs. Specifically, Walmart's recent accent on CR has empowered employees to initiate innovative and responsible business practices that also provide benefits to the company's customers.[17] During the summer of 2007, some employees refused to sell Styrofoam coolers that were thought to be harmful to the environment. Alert managers responded by offering coolers made from more eco-friendly materials. Thus, Walmart's CR activity is encouraging employees to look for opportunities to behave responsibly themselves.

Summary

CR can benefit the company through both direct and indirect routes. The direct method includes such things as savings and increased revenue from a company's actions. But this book focuses on the less understood *indirect stakeholder route* through which CR can create both company value (i.e., corporate performance) and societal value (i.e., social and environmental welfare) through stakeholder reactions to the company's CR. Stakeholders' perception that they are benefiting from CR initiatives, either directly or indirectly, acts as a significant driver of their reactions to CR and influences the stakeholder–company relationship.

While CR drives *individual* behaviors across many stakeholder realms, the outcomes, in turn, can create clear benefits at the *aggregate* level. Companies that are able to "scale-up" CR value such as loyalty and advocacy across the stakeholder base are likely to see substantial improvements in both business performance and societal welfare.

The concept of "shared value" – that is, value for both the company and society – is, then, key to success and is based in large part on stakeholder reactions. Business value is manifested in a variety of stakeholder realms such as consumption and employment. For instance, CR value tends to enhance consumers' intention to continue purchasing the company's products, to be loyal to the brand, and to engage in positive word-of-mouth behavior. CR also tends to attract high quality job candidates. Societal value includes not only the obvious social or environmental impacts, but also behavior changes that can stem from a stakeholder's increased sense of Unity with the company. Stakeholders play a pivotal role in the success of CR initiatives because when they find a program engaging they may alter their own behavior to improve their life and the lives of others.

Endnotes

1 BSR 2008 Spring Forum: Corporate Social Responsibility, available at www.asiabusinesscouncil.org/docs/BSR.pdf p.10, accessed April 9, 2009.
2 World Economic Forum, "Responding to the Leadership Challenge: Findings of a CEO Survey on Global Corporate Citizenship," (Geneva, Switzerland, 2003).
3 BSR, "Value Driven Leadership: Responsible Companies Committed to Tackling Global Societal Woes Have Discovered that They Gain Strategic Advantage, Advertising Supplement," *New York Times: Business For Social Responsibility* 2007, available at www.timeinc.net/fortune/services/sections/fortune/pdf/111307CorpSocialRespon.pdf, accessed March 21, 2011.
4 M.J. Epstein and S.K. Widener, Performance Measurement: Measuring Stakeholder Reactions for Facilitating Corporate Social Responsibility Decision-Making, Working Paper (2008).
5 A. McMains, "The Top Ten Trends of 2007," *Adweek* 48 (2007).
6 www.marketingweek.co.uk/cgi-bin/item.cgi?id=60281, accessed July 1, 2008.
7 Nestlé, The Nestlé Creating Shared Value Report, 2007, available at www.nestle.com/Common/NestleDocuments/Documents/Reports/

CSV%20reports/Global%20report%202007/Global_report_2007_English.pdf, accessed March 18, 2011.
8 CB Bhattacharya and S. Sen, "Doing Better at Doing Good: When, Why, and How Consumers Respond to Corporate Social Initiatives," *California Management Review*, 47(1) (2004), 9–24.
9 R. Trudel and J. Cotte, "Does Being Ethical Pay? Companies Spend Huge Amounts of Money to Be 'Socially Responsible.' Do Consumers Reward Them for It? And How Much?," *Wall Street Journal*, May 12, 2008. Also R. Trudel and J. Cotte, "Does It Pay To Be Good?" *Sloan Management Review*, 50(2) (Winter 2009).
10 S. Du, CB Bhattacharya, and S. Sen, "Reaping Relational Rewards from Corporate Social Responsibility: The Role of Competitive Positioning," *International Journal of Research in Marketing*, 24(3) (2007), 224–41.
11 D. Turban and D. Greening, "Corporate Social Performance and Organizational Attractiveness to Prospective Employees," *Academy of Management Journal*, 40(3) (1997), 658–72.
12 www.workforce.com/section/06/article/23/93/45_printer.html, accessed April 8, 2009.
13 B.L. Berry and A. Parasuraman, "Marketing Services: Competing Through Quality," *New York Free Press* (1991).
14 Green Mountain Coffee Roasters, "Brewing a Better World," 2007, available at www.gmcr.com/PDF/gmcr_csr_2007_final.pdf, accessed March 21, 2011.
15 D.R. Lichtenstein, M.E. Drumwright, and B.M. Braig, "The Effect of Corporate Social Responsibility on Customer Donations to Corporate-Supported Nonprofits," *Journal of Marketing*, 68(4) (2004), 16–32.
16 CB Bhattacharya and S. Sen (2004), "Doing Better at Doing Good."
17 T.L. Friedman, "Lead, Follow or Move Aside," *The New York Times*, September 26, 2007.

Further reading

Martin Christopher, *Relationship Marketing: Creating Stakeholder Value* (Oxford: Butterworth-Heinemann, 2002).

This book comprehensively demonstrates how to formulate and implement a successful stakeholder relation strategy.

Alex Harris, *Reputation At Risk: Reputation Report* (Sydney: Masterstroke Group, 2009).

Harris's handbook for managers addresses the difficulty for companies to attract and retain employees, customers and investors. It identifies reputation as key to improving stakeholder relations and offers guidelines for managers.

John Peloza and Lisa Papania, "The Missing Link between Corporate Social Responsibility and Financial Performance: Stakeholder Salience and Identification," *Corporate Reputation Review*, 11 (2008), 169–81.

The authors identify the ability of stakeholders to reward or punish a company based on its CR performance as a link between CR and business value.

Maria del Mar García de los Salmones, Angel Herrero Crespo, and Ignacio Rodríguez del Bosque, "Influence of Corporate Social Responsibility on Loyalty and Valuation of Services," *Journal of Business Ethics*, 61(4) (2005), 369–85.

This article relates customers' perception of CR performance with service quality and loyalty.

PART II

Inside the mind of the stakeholder

In the previous section, we explained that when it comes to managing CR, *stakeholder reactions matter*. That is why a critical pathway linking CR activity to improvements in business and societal performance (i.e., CR value) lies in what we call the stakeholder route. As a result, CR value is often best understood by examining the behaviors of individual stakeholders. For example, consumers may become loyal patrons, and employees may make the extra effort to perform well on the job.

Of course, such positive or desired responses to CR activity are not guaranteed. Responses are driven by a psychological process in which stakeholders interpret the CR activities of the company. Companies with an understanding of this psychological process are the ones best prepared to engage in the types of CR activity that stakeholders find most compelling. And these activities ultimately lead to the sort of CR value that managers seek.

In this Part we reveal how stakeholders perceive CR activity and how they think and feel about it. In Chapter 4, we show how stakeholders become exposed to CR information, highlighting the fact that the sources from which stakeholders draw CR information are varied and often lack the ability to provide a comprehensive picture of a company's CR activity. In Chapter 5, we explain how stakeholders interpret CR activity. More specifically, we show that the interpretive process is driven by three "psychological levers": Understanding, Usefulness, and Unity. Finally, in Chapter 6, we identify conditions under which stakeholder reactions to CR can be expected to be strongest or weakest.

PART II

Inside the mind of the stakeholder

FOUR

What stakeholders see and hear

Interested readers already know that there are innumerable ways in which companies enact their commitment to serve society. This chapter focuses on how stakeholders learn about CR and what characteristics of CR stakeholders are looking for when they evaluate socially responsible activity. Such information is vital to know, because what managers care about may be very different from what stakeholders care about. Moreover, what companies *think they are saying* may be quite different from what stakeholders are *seeing and hearing*.

There are two aspects of communications that CR managers need to be aware of in order to have the impact they need for success:

- First, they must understand *what CR characteristics stakeholders look for* as they evaluate CR activity. This is important because it enables managers to make these characteristics prominent in communications.
- Second, managers must understand that *stakeholders acquire information from a variety of communication channels*. Getting a handle on the costs and benefits of these channels is the first step to designing integrated communications campaigns for stakeholders. We now look at each of these aspects in turn.

TABLE 4.1 *Representative CR inputs*

Issue	Resources Committed	Implementation
Community	Monetary Donations	Cause Promotions
Corporate Governance	In-kind Donations	Cause-related Marketing
Diversity	Hours Volunteered	Corporate Social Marketing
Employee Relations	Expertise	Corporate Philanthropy
Environment		Community Volunteering
Human Rights		Socially Responsible Business Practices
Product		

Source: (KLD Analytics) (Company reporting) (Kotler and Lee 2004)

CR characteristics

(Most) stakeholders are not passive receivers of CR information. Before they even learn about a CR program, they have ideas about what CR is and whether companies should be doing it. Moreover, the gamut of CR activities in which companies engage is very large. Rarely are two CR initiatives exactly alike. In order to distinguish among the many programs that are out there, stakeholders predictably look at certain characteristics of the CR in question. These categories help stakeholders make sense of a CR program and compare it to others, both at the company and at peer companies.

There are three characteristics to which most – if not all – stakeholders attend. These are:

- CR issue,
- CR resources,
- CR implementation.

The following discussion elaborates on each and Table 4.1 provides examples.

CR *issue*

The CR issue refers to the societal problem that the CR program is designed to address. One of the leading research organizations that rates companies' CR performance is KLD Research Analytics. This company categorizes all CR activities into seven broad and inclusive issues that are reasonably aligned with the way that most stakeholders categorize issues. These categories are:

- community,
- corporate governance,
- diversity,
- employee relations,
- environment,
- human rights,
- product.

Each of these represents an area that may be of interest to some stakeholders. Many companies will have CR programs dealing with each of these issues; notably, stakeholders may view each program very differently.

> By prioritizing the issues it addresses, a company signals whether or not it cares about the same things that stakeholders do.

For example, the Nestlé initiatives that are designed to reduce the environmental footprint of its manufacturing plants will have very different impacts on stakeholders, society, and financial performance than its efforts to expand access to nutrition for lower income people.[1] By addressing some issues over others, a company signals whether or not it cares about the same things that stakeholders do.[2]

TABLE 4.2 *Illustrative examples of CR implementation*

	Yoplait	Diageo	Microsoft	Home Depot
Implementational Form	Cause-Related Marketing	Corporate Social Marketing	Corporate Philanthropy	Community Volunteering
Description	Commitment to make a contribution to a cause based on sales	Support behavior change campaign	Direct contribution to a charity or cause	Support and encourage employees to volunteer their time to community organizations
Issue	Breast Cancer	Alcohol Education	Community	Homelessness / Poverty
Example Initiative	Consumers mail in specially marked Yoplait container lids. For every lid received, Yoplait donates 10¢ to Susan G. Komen for the Cure.	Diageo ran a TV advertising campaign throughout the UK to promote responsible drinking.	Microsoft provides grants to support community projects, the arts, civic responsibility, and other goals, with particular focus on organizations that use technology to achieve aims.	One hundred Home Depot employees built framing structures for 48 new homes in the Mississippi Gulf region.

Note: More information on these examples can be found at: Yoplait: www.yoplait.com/Sls1/default.aspx, accessed March 18, 2011; Diageo: Press Release, "Diageo Launches Drink Industry's First Nationwide Responsible Drinking TV Campaign," May 1, 2007, www.diageo.com/en-row/newsmedia/pages/resource.aspx?resourceid=337, accessed March 18, 2011; Microsoft: www.microsoft.com/About/CorporateCitizenship/en-us/our-actions/, accessed March 18, 2011; Home Depot: Press Release, "The Home Depot Foundation to frame more than 45 houses during Habitat for Humanity's Jimmy & Rosalynn Carter Work Project," May 8, 2008, available at www.habitat.org/newsroom/2008archive/, accessed March 18, 2011.

CR implementation

CR implementation is often the next thing stakeholders look at as they try to make sense of a company's CR engagement. CR implementation refers to *the way* that a company attacks a societal issue.

Table 4.2 shows examples of a number of different types of CR implementation.[3] To demonstrate the range, the reader will see that Yoplait, for instance, (left column) runs a cause-related marketing campaign, which contributes to Susan G. Komen for the Cure, a grassroots network of breast cancer survivors and activists that supports treatment and research for breast cancer. Diageo manages a Corporate Social Marketing campaign aimed at changing people's alcohol drinking habits through its education campaign. Microsoft, via its foundation, provides grants to organizations in an array of issues from health (including treatment of AIDS and malaria) to education (with an emphasis on increasing the high school graduation rate and preparing a new generation of students for college and beyond). Home Depot operated a Community Volunteering effort whereby it encourages and supports employees that build framing structures in the Mississippi Gulf.

Obviously, companies may address similar issues in different ways. Consider the issue of fighting AIDS in Africa. Emporio Armani does its part by teaming up with Product(RED). The global organization Product(RED) invites participant companies to use the "RED" brand on their products, giving a portion of proceeds to HIV/AIDS research and treatment.

Through this partnership, Emporio Armani markets a line of specially marked clothing and accessories, donating a portion of proceeds to AIDS treatment and research. People purchasing and wearing such clothing are able to make a visible statement about both their financial and their moral support of this important cause.

The same issue is approached very differently by Coca-Cola.[4] Through programs the company itself operates, it combines prevention, awareness, counseling and treatment for employees and other stakeholders, while keeping the individuals' identities confidential.

Stakeholders are interested in how companies implement programs for several reasons. For one, stakeholders believe that the nature of the program reveals a part of a company's *values*. They also look to CR implementation for clues about how the company solves problems, such as whether the company is innovative, and whether they go about CR in distinctive ways, vis-à-vis the competition. Moreover, stakeholders interpret CR implementation in light of what they already know about the company (e.g., its reputation). Ultimately, small differences in CR implementation can mean the difference in whether a stakeholder responds positively to a CR program or retreats from it.

Given this stakeholder interest, managers need to keep tabs on their CR implementation. The reality is that there are multiple ways of implementing CR. Two initiatives that address a very similar issue in different ways can sometimes lead to entirely different types of responses from stakeholders.

> Stakeholders use CR to make inferences about other, non-CR capabilities of the company.

Let's reconsider some of the examples in Table 4.2. Yoplait's cause-related marketing program is ideal for driving revenues because it encourages customers to purchase more products than they might otherwise. In contrast, Home Depot's pay-off for its volunteering efforts will probably be best measured primarily as an increase in employee retention.

CR resources

Companies differ substantially in the amount of CR resources that they devote to any given issue. Stakeholders realize this, and often use the resources committed as an indication of the company's commitment to improving societal welfare. Stakeholders pay attention not only to financial resources in these assessments, but also to a more *complex mixture of corporate resources that combines money, expertise and man-hours.*

Figures of these commitments are often available through annual company reporting.[5] For example:

- Walmart donated approximately $378 million to charities in 2008, making it the world's largest corporate donor of **cash**, according to Forbes.
- General Mills reports that in 2009 it donated about $16 million in **food donations** – equivalent to 17 truckloads per day – to America's Second Harvest, a hunger relief program.
- IBM recorded 10 million **hours of volunteered service** from more than 150,000 of their current and retired employees in its "On Demand Community" from its inception in 2003 to June 2010.

Not only do numbers of this magnitude make a statement about the company's values, but they also attract mainstream attention. Large donations are covered by the press, so they generate considerable awareness among many constituents (something we will explain in more detail in Chapter 8).

All things being equal, a larger commitment tends to drive more favorable outcomes. *However, all things are rarely equal,* and we do not wish to imply that larger programs are necessarily better; quite the contrary. That is why the amount of resources committed to CR is but one dimension in our framework. Unfortunately, many managers make the mistake of thinking that the larger a company's total commitment, the more favorably it will be perceived by stakeholders. In fact – and as we will explain in the coming chapters – stakeholders can sometimes be indifferent to large donations.

The lesson here is that managers need to broaden their conceptualization of what generosity means. Why should managers avoid relying on oversimplified yardsticks that yield single measures of CR resources? Because stakeholders do not think in oversimplified and single-measure ways. *Stakeholders, in fact, are more likely to gauge a company's generosity according to its means, favoring smaller companies that give a lot, relative to large firms.*

As we will see in the next chapter (see Chapter 5; section on CR efficacy), stakeholders also commonly assess how efficient and effective companies are in deploying their CR resources, punishing those that are wasteful and rewarding those that generate the best bang for the buck.

CR communication channels

When assessing CR activity at a company, stakeholders focus most closely on the three types of CR characteristics just described: CR *issue*, CR *implementation*, and CR *resources*. Most stakeholders, however, do not learn about CR characteristics from first-hand experience. It is far more common for stakeholders to receive CR information through an array of *communications channels*. These channels act as the conduit between the activity and the ears and eyes of stakeholders (see Figure 4.1). When these communication channels are effective, Understanding of the CR will be enhanced, but when they are ineffective as is often the case, Understanding often suffers.

> Stakeholders increasingly want a deeper and ongoing dialogue than that afforded by detailed annual reports.

Stakeholders are generally keen to learn about the social responsibility initiatives of companies, yet they often have difficulty in

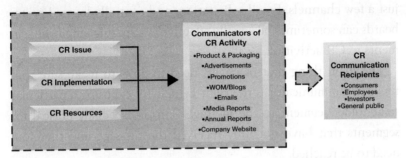

Figure 4.1 Communicating CR activity

getting the information they crave. *Managers must therefore develop and execute plans to get CR information into the eyes and ears of stakeholders.*

For many companies, annual CR reports detailing their activities play a large role in publicizing their good works. However, given that a relatively small number of people actually read these reports, managers must rely on other forms of communication. Readers of this book should think of annual reports as merely the tip of the iceberg when it comes to channels that are necessary to inform stakeholders of the CR activity. In fact, for many stakeholders, discussion of CR in annual reports may represent a form of communication that goes under the radar and is not seen at all, or at best just glanced over.

A broadening of CR communication

Leading companies are starting to use a very broad set of CR communicators, often resembling, in totality, the "integrated marketing communications" campaigns familiar to marketers. These communicators range from the simple to the complex, from the broadcast announcement to the highly targeted one-to-one marketing contact. For such marketing campaigns, companies routinely rely on product and packaging, branding, television advertisements, point-of-sale promotions, annual reports, and company websites to name just a few channels. Email solicitations and centrally located poster boards can sometimes be equally effective at exposing employee segments to CR activities.

The main thing that managers need to do is to make sure that the CR communicator is the right vehicle for exposing a particular stakeholder segment to the message. This is especially critical for segments that have not fully received the message and therefore need to be reached.

Examples of effective CR communication channels

> GE's ecomagination brand demonstrates the value of branding a line of business to increase the exposure and effectiveness of its CR message. These eco-friendly products have reached revenue levels of $17 billion by 2010 and are expected to drive revenues past the $25 billion mark in annual revenues by 2015.

Consider Yoplait's "Save Lids to Save Lives" campaign, which has practically become the "gold standard" of publicizing CR through product packaging. This campaign targets consumers directly at the *point of purchase*. Yoplait has pledged 10 cents to Susan G. Komen for the Cure for every specially marked lid that consumers mail in. The campaign has linked Yoplait closely with the breast cancer cause in many consumers' minds.[6]

To take another example, GE offers a whole line of environmentally friendly products under the "ecomagination" brand. GE has been running its ecomagination PR and advertising campaign touting its socially responsible practices and products since 2005. By *introducing and branding a line of business*, GE simultaneously increases CR exposure with customers, employees, investors, and the general public. This is a good example of a CR strategy that produces value for the triple bottom line: people, the planet, and profits.

The corporate website is yet another way to communicate a company's CR commitment. For example, BASF has dedicated *a major portion of its website* to its social responsibility commitments.[7] When we last looked at the corporate website it revealed *more visual space devoted to CR issues than anything else*. For example, most of the "cover stories" appearing on its homepage are CR related: "Ecology loves Economy," "Water Treatment in Africa," and "Children love Chemistry."[8] This website format exposes not only customers but also investors and members of non-governmental organizations – including activists – to the company's efforts.

Recent innovations

As CR becomes a mainstream phenomenon, managers face the daunting challenge of breaking through an increasingly cluttered CR communication landscape. As a result, companies are looking to new and innovative forms of communicators in an effort to capture the imagination of their constituent base.

One such example is Clorox, which is using "viral media" to integrate innovative promotional strategies with their CR communications strategies, in an effort to stand out (see Figure 4.2). Clorox is promoting its Green Works line of cleaning products by sponsoring performance art called "the Reverse Graffiti Project."

The artist at the heart of the campaign is Paul Curtis. Ask Curtis to describe his work and he says, "I make pictures by cleaning."[9] In essence, he cleans portions of dirty city walls to reveal negative images on the surface. The images at once provide striking evidence of the amount of pollution in the world and display the power of Clorox products to combat dirt build-up. Besides imagining what these agri-based cleaners can do to a dirty bathtub, stakeholders are likely to take away that Clorox is not an ordinary company, but an innovator designing products that are on the cutting edge.

Figure 4.2 The Reverse Graffiti Project "Powered by Clorox": a) The greenworks logo; b) Artists powerwash a wall; c) The end result

Other companies that are exploring these sorts of "guerilla" CR communications include McDonald's, which runs a CR blog called "values in practice." It connects people with the company and other stakeholders.[10]

Then there's MTV, which teamed up with Ogilvy & Mather to produce what it called a viral video to raise awareness and money for organizations fighting for human rights in Myanmar. This human rights issue was raised in the opening chapter as an example of how people form opinions based on what is often incomplete information, thus focusing the need for targeted communication.

Another innovative communication channel for CR is direct involvement in an issue-oriented TV program, as opposed to merely buying on-air advertising time. On American television, for instance, an example is the show *Extreme Makeover: Home Edition*, in which a needy family gets a custom home built for their specific needs. Sears is featured prominently in the episodes as it contributes appliances and home furnishings to the family that is the recipient of the network's generosity; other partner companies may supply a donation for scholarships or pay down the family's mortgage. This scenario is a win for the corporations and for the individuals who get a new home, while also engaging the audience.

The TV show *Undercover Boss* took another approach by having CEOs of well-known corporations pretend to be new hires – often in tedious roles – in order to get an inside view of what it's really like for their front line employees. Then they show social responsibility by addressing the significant issues that impact these individuals – something they would never have discovered from their proverbial ivory tower.

It is the impact at the individual level that is the focus. By signaling their desire to be involved in projects that affect their individual employees, these corporations have chosen a communication method that creates an emotional connection, making viewers (potential stakeholders) feel good about the company as well.

Potential negatives

Ultimately, a determination of which communication channels are employed must be based on the target recipient of CR communication and on the objective. But *managers should not think that they are the only ones with the ear of stakeholders*. Increasingly, third parties are commenting on corporate behavior, calling supporters or protesters to action. It is important for companies not to over-communicate or misrepresent their CR. The marketing adage "Tell, don't sell" is well advised here in order to avoid stakeholder suspicion.

> Increasingly, third parties are commenting on corporate behavior, calling supporters or protesters to action.

The website JustMeans addresses this very issue because the site is designed to "attract and ignite advocates for better business" by enabling communications between people around the globe. It is common in such communications for people to comment about individual companies. For example, a recent Kellogg campaign is criticized. Kellogg promotes breakfast as the most important meal of the day and pledges to donate money to children in food-insecure households. On the other hand, many of Kellogg's cereals contain high quantities of sugar, which is seen as irresponsible by JustMeans: "Put your flakes where your mouth is Kellogg, and come up with a CSR initiative that we can believe."[11]

Whether the amount of sugar in Kellogg's products is adequate or not is not as important as the larger lesson, that *stakeholders receive many messages and struggle to make sense of it all*. In the next chapter we delve into the mind of the stakeholder, explaining how stakeholders interpret all of this information.

Summary

A key message in this chapter is that what managers *think* they are saying may be quite different from what stakeholders *actually perceive*. As a result, astute managers need to be aware of what stakeholders look for, as well as the numerous ways in which they might get this information. Three aspects of CR that get stakeholders attention are: (1) the issue that is addressed by the company's CR (the social or environmental cause); (2) the program's implementation (the nuts and bolts of how the CR is executed); and (3) the resources committed to it.

Numerous communication channels are available, but some get the company's message across better. For example, annual reports are increasingly a rather diffuse means of reaching many stakeholders. Instead, an approach similar to integrated marketing campaigns is more effective. Examples of successful programs have included a point-of-purchase approach, where a portion of the cost goes to the sponsored charity. Others include branding a line of business; using the company's website or creating a blog for an interactive approach; partnering with a television show; or taking an artistic and innovative approach that demonstrates the value of a product while performing a task that impacts a community.

Finally, managers also need to be aware that they are not the only ones who get the stakeholders' ear. It is important not to oversell the company. This can lead to stakeholder suspicion about the company's motives or truthfulness and can lead to negative stakeholder reactions.

Endnotes

1 Nestlé, The Nestlé Creating Shared Value Report, 2008, available at www.nestle.com/Common/NestleDocuments/Documents/Reports/CSV%20reports/Global%20report%202008/Global_report_2008_English.pdf, accessed March 18, 2011.
2 As we elaborate in Chapter 7, many companies accomplish this prioritization via a "materiality matrix."
3 Implementational forms taken from: P. Kotler and N. Lee, *Corporate Social Responsibility: Doing the Most Good for Your Company and Your Cause* (Hoboken, NJ: Wiley & Sons, Inc., 2004); M.E. Drumwright and P.E. Murphy, "Corporate Societal Marketing," *Handbook of Marketing and Society* (2001), 183.
4 www.thecoca-colacompany.com/citizenship/pdf/tccaf_2006_hivaids_report.pdf, accessed March 18, 2011.
5 J.D. Margolis and J.P. Walsh, "Misery Loves Companies: Rethinking Social Initiatives by Business," *Administrative Science Quarterly*, 48(2) (2003), 268–305; M. Orlitzky, F.L. Schmidt, and S.L. Rynes, "Corporate Social and Financial Performance: A Meta-Analysis," *Organization Studies*, 24(3) (2003), 403–41.
6 Note that other companies have mimicked the Yoplait campaign. For example, Innocent drinks launched a campaign where customers could knit miniature hats and send them to the company. The hats were put on top of Innocent drinks bottles and the company donated 50 pence per hat

to a charity. 500,000 hats were sent and 250,000 British pounds was generated. More information can be found at www.innocentdrinks.co.uk/thebigknit/?Page=thebigknit_story, accessed August 31, 2010.
7 www.basf.com, accessed August 31, 2010.
8 "Ecology loves Economy" refers to solutions offered by BASF, e.g., to make cars lighter and consequently more fuel efficient. "Africa's water loves Treatment" addresses the problem of contaminated water in Africa and a water treatment product that BASF offers to solve it. "Kids love Chemistry" is an educational program that teaches chemistry and science to children. More information can be found at www.basf.com; accessed August 31, 2010.
9 www.reversegraffitiproject.com/index.html, accessed March 18, 2011.
10 www.crmcdonalds.com/publish/csr/home/_blog.html, accessed March 12, 2009.
11 Vijayaraghavan, Akhila (2011), "Share your breakfast with Kellogg: CSR or advertising?" JustMeans (accessed May 3, 2011, available at http://www.justmeans.com/Share-Your-Breakfast-With-Kellogg-CSR-or-Advertising/47257.html).

Further reading

Kellie A. McElhaney, *Just Good Business: The Strategic Guide to Aligning Corporate Responsibility and Brand* (San Francisco: Berrett-Koehler, 2008).

> The author argues that CR is a missed business opportunity if it is not as thoroughly branded as any other activity a company pursues.

Frank Buytendijk, *Performance Leadership: The Next Practices to Motivate Your People, Align Stakeholders, and Lead Your Industry* (New York: McGraw Hill, 2008).

> The book provides a practical leadership framework that enables managers to focus on stakeholders' behaviors within a company and beyond.

Nick Lakin and Veronica Scheubel, *Corporate Community Involvement* (Stanford: Greenleaf, 2010).

> This book is a practitioner's guide to improve corporate community involvement, e.g., by choosing the right partners.

FIVE

The psychological engine that drives CR reactions

Think back to the opening paragraphs of the book: you are a stakeholder, and you've heard something about a company's CR activity. Do you have an immediate and strong reaction? Would you take some action as a result of learning about a company's programs? And if so, under what conditions?

These kinds of questions are central to our research. We find that while it is tempting to assume that stakeholders respond to CR automatically and immediately once they learn something new about a company's efforts, in fact, it is rare that such information elicits in a knee-jerk reaction. Most responses unfold as each stakeholder interprets the CR activity, making a very personal determination of whether or not it "makes sense" and how it fits into his or her life.

The psychological process we are talking about may occur quite swiftly, or it may develop over a longer period of time, but all stakeholders process new CR information in a series of inter-related steps that we describe in this chapter. Ultimately, our approach recognizes the complex psychological process by which CR activity and information lead stakeholders to form relational bonds with companies.

The three levers that energize and move stakeholder reactions

The psychological engine that drives stakeholders' reactions to CR is made up of three factors that we call **The 3 U's**: *Understanding,*

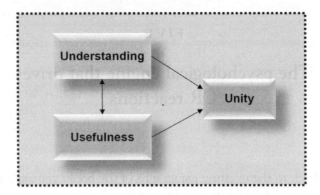

Figure 5.1 The three levers that drive returns to CR

Usefulness, and *Unity*. (See Figure 5.1 for a depiction of this process.) These three factors can be thought of as psychological levers that create the momentum needed to raise stakeholders' interest and produce the desired behavioral responses covered in Chapter 3.

Understanding refers to how a stakeholder interprets CR in light of what he already knows about the company. *Usefulness* is the stakeholder's appraisal of how beneficial it is to her. Finally, *Unity* expresses the stakeholder's assessment of the degree to which his or her goals and values are in unison with those of the company. Arguably, Unity is the most critical of the three and the primary determinant of stakeholders' behavioral responses to CR. Without this sense of Unity, the responses that accrue to the most successful CR actions of companies are less likely.

Since each component is complex in its own right, we next elaborate on the 3 U's more fully. The table below provides an overview of some major aspects of the psychological process we describe in this chapter. We also provide a sampling of the empirical evidence on which our assertions are based. Each of the studies we highlight supports our framework from a slightly different perspective.

The components associated with each of the 3 U's

Understanding	1. Awareness (knowledge of company's CR activities)
	2. Attributions (extrinsic and intrinsic)
	3. Efficacy (perceived social value created by company)
Usefulness	Stakeholder benefits
	1. Functional benefits
	2. Identity-related benefits
Unity	1. Identification (feeling in unison with company's core values)
	2. Trust (expectations of the company's future behavior)

The first lever: Understanding

Once they become aware of CR activity, stakeholders attempt to integrate this information with prior knowledge they may have about the company. They consider which aspects seem to dovetail with existing beliefs and which aspects appear to be in conflict. Stakeholders weigh new CR information in this way in order to construct a better *Understanding* of CR initiatives.

But the process is not simple. Our research reveals that Understanding is as multi-faceted as most CR programs, reflecting all the subjectivity and complexity inherent in the field. In determining why and how stakeholders react to CR, three facets of Understanding stand out as critically important.

The first is *awareness*, which pertains to the realization that the company has CR programs. The second is *attributions*, or what the stakeholder construes as the company's motivations for engaging in CR. The third is *efficacy*, or how effective a company's CR programs are at improving societal welfare. As we explain below, each of these facets is unique to the CR realm.

Awareness

Stakeholders may display a vague awareness of the general involvement of a company in CR, but we find that they rarely know even the most basic details about specific programs and activities. In too many cases, stakeholders lack even a simple awareness – a realization, perception, or knowledge – that the company is engaged in CR at all.

Stakeholders need to be exposed to a company's CR information through the communicators we outlined in the previous chapter. Yet, for any given CR program or set of programs, awareness will vary based on the *manner* by which stakeholders are exposed to the information. Equally important is the extent to which they are able and motivated to give their full attention to such information and thereby comprehend what is being offered.

So while some stakeholders might actively seek out information on CR initiatives, the overwhelming majority of stakeholders, given their busy lives, do not exert much effort to expose themselves to such information. For them, awareness is likely to occur accidentally, either from a company source, the media, or a friend, family member or colleague. Moreover, given that we tend to tune out most company and product-related information we are accidentally exposed to, awareness through accidental exposure, if any, is likely to be minimal.

So, the basic message from all our research regarding stakeholder awareness of CR activities is that, at least in absolute terms, it is low.

A sampling of study findings

A striking illustration of the awareness challenge is found in our research on the oral care program run by a consumer products multinational. In that study we conducted a series of focus groups and surveys among families whose children were enrolled in the program and others with similar demographic characteristics (matched for comparison purposes), but who were not enrolled in the program. While families enrolled in the program were, naturally, aware of it, only 13.9 percent of families from the same demographic and socio-economic group (i.e., potential beneficiaries and consumers of the brand) were aware of the program.

Many of our other studies find similarly low awareness. Our study of a $1 million gift to a child development center found that only 17 percent of those surveyed in the community were aware of the gift, despite a major campaign that included announcements in newspapers, websites, emails, flyers and even messages at the homecoming football game. In our study among yogurt consumers, only 20 percent of the respondents, who were regular consumers of these brands, showed even a reasonable level of awareness of their CR activities.

We also examined awareness among employees. Now, it might seem logical to assume that employees, because they are so embedded in the organization, would be highly attuned to their employer's programs, particularly since many of these are designed and implemented by the employees themselves. However, we found similarly low or limited awareness levels among employees. The following quote captures an all too common sentiment expressed by employees: "We actually do have a volunteer web site that gives you the organizations you could go to, but it's obviously not well-publicized. It's just sitting there on the 'L' drive."

A similar state of affairs was captured by a recent global employee survey conducted by a global consumer products company. This survey gauged employees' awareness and their involvement in the company's considerable CR initiatives. While awareness was higher than that of the general public, employee awareness of the company's umbrella CR initiative, as well as one of the flagship programs under that umbrella, a safe water drinking program for children, hovered at only about 50 percent.

> Communication is central to effective CR management.

Our research findings are echoed in a number of nationwide surveys. In 2003, Ipsos-MORI surveyed the British public on their reactions to CR.[1] They found that the general public is mostly in the dark about companies' socially responsible practices. While nine out of ten people surveyed wanted companies to communicate their CR activities to them, only about three out of ten people could even name a company they consider to be particularly environmentally and socially responsible. This finding led the study's director, Jenny Dawkins, to conclude: "Effective communication seems to be a missing link in the practice of corporate responsibility." When Ipsos-Reid did another study in 2006 there was barely any change.

> In a 2006 study, Ipsos-Reid polled members of their online panel, who were representative of the Canadian public. Only a third (33 percent) said they knew of any companies in Canada that have "made an explicit commitment to CR."
>
> A similarly low number (31 percent) were aware of any companies that have "formal policies in place that require companies to take on socially responsible activities and initiatives."
>
> About 38 percent said they knew of companies that have "created and carried out socially responsible activities and initiatives based on their policies."

Taken as a whole, we find that awareness of a typical company's CR activity is likely to be quite low even among those who are familiar with the firm's other activities. Thus, managers today are faced with a conundrum: Even as demand for CR appears to be increasing from virtually all stakeholder quarters, most of these stakeholders remain fairly unaware of what companies are actually doing in this domain.

In the words of Bob Langert, VP and Corporate Responsibility Officer at McDonald's: "The reality right now is that very few consumers possess an adequate level of knowledge of the things we are doing on the CR front."

Why might this be the case? This problem is particularly perplexing to companies in light of a growing and pro-active consumer interest in gathering CR information about companies. Specifically, a 2007 survey of American consumers conducted by the PR firm Fleishman-Hillard in conjunction with a consumer advocacy organization, the National Consumer League, reveals that a substantial and growing percentage of consumers (54 percent in 2007) say that they actively seek out information on the CR record of specific companies "all the time" or "sometimes."

So why is CR awareness so low in the face of both greater corporate communication and consumer interest in this domain? We argue that awareness depends on the *quality of attention* devoted to the CR information. Even when we expose ourselves intentionally to such communication, the enormous information overload we often experience in today's world can reduce the attention we are able to bring to CR communication.

The same dynamics may be at work in actually comprehending the CR material. Often we deem it sufficient to understand CR information at a cursory, surface level. We may acknowledge, for instance: "Yes, [Brand X] is helping kids." But many stakeholders are not motivated to process the CR information further; that is, at the deep, elaborate levels required to gain a full understanding of what the company is doing in its CR programs.

In sum, a complete, meaningful awareness of a company's CR programs requires stakeholders to be adequately exposed to such information, to pay focal attention to such information, and to comprehend it at a deep, elaborate level. Clearly, for some stakeholders, such as the beneficiaries of a particular CR initiative, this will be the case. For the rest, however, this process may be minimal or truncated, resulting in the low awareness levels evidenced in our and others' research.

In the final Part of the book, we will recommend ways that companies can raise awareness. For now, we continue by outlining how stakeholders make sense of CR activity once they become aware of it.

Attributions

When companies tout the benefits or features of their *products*, most stakeholders are comfortable with the fact that companies are doing so for one reason only: to make profits. As long as the product appeals to them, stakeholders – consumers in particular – are happy to consume it with the knowledge that they are also helping make the company richer.

When companies promote their CR *activities*, however, something interesting happens: stakeholders wonder about the company's *underlying motivation* for engaging in CR. Such attributional thinking (also known as "causal thinking") comprises questions such as "Why are they donating to this non-profit organization?" or, "Do they genuinely care about this issue?" And the answer greatly impacts how stakeholders judge the company, and ultimately how likely they are to respond favorably to the CR activity.

But where do these attributional beliefs come from? A great body of research in psychology suggests that as human beings, we engage in causal attributions routinely, particularly when we are faced with events or occurrences that seem out of the ordinary or unexpected. Given that today's business world presents more complexity, more ambiguity, more subjectivity, and more surprises than perhaps any era preceding it, it is reasonable that stakeholders, grappling with sometimes conflicting CR messages, will make their own attributions of a company's underlying motives for engaging in CR.

Consider for a moment the conflicting messages that stakeholders receive from Bentley's 2008 Green study.[2] The study's authors

Most Green Brands*	Reason**	Least Green Brands*	Reason**
1. Toyota	Hybrid cars	1. Exxon Mobil	Pollution and profits
2. Honda	Fuel efficient cars	2. Hummer	Gas guzzler
3. Whole Food	Organic foods	3. Ford	SUVs and trucks
4. General Electric	Alternative/renewable energy	4. General motors	SUVs and trucks/low gas mileage
5. Trader Joes	Organic foods	5. British Airways	Lack of concern for environment
6. BP	Green advertising	6. McDonalds	Waste
7. Ben & Jerry	Environmentally conscious stance	7. Wal-Mart	Llow prices, high pollution
8. Body shop	No animal testing	8. Shell	Pollution
9. Energy Star	Energy efficiency	9. Nike	Explotative labor practices
10. Timberland	Recycling	10. Apple	General
11. 7th Generation	Environmentally friendly products	11. General Electric	Pollution
12. Hewlett Packard	Recycling of Their products	12. Nintendo	Scored lowest by Greenpeace
13. Apple	Miscellaneous	13. Range Rover	Gas guzzler
14. Google	Miscellaneous	14. Chevrolet	SUVs and trucks
15. IKEA	Miscellaneous	15. BP	Pollution

*as perceived by Gen Y
**most frequently cited reason

Bentley Green study 2008

Figure 5.2 Conflicting messages, Conflicted feelings. Apple and BP appear on both the best and worst of the green companies listing

asked Americans which companies they thought ranked both the best and worst in terms of environmental conciousness. Surprisingly, the best and worst rankings shared two famous brands, Apple and BP (Figure 5.2). When either of these companies engages in CR, conflicting sentiments will lead many stakeholders to question the company's motives, no matter how pure their intentions.

The stakeholder's viewpoint

It appears that the key to a stakeholder's response lies in which of two kinds of attributions they make about the company. From the stakeholder's viewpoint, a company's CR motives are seen generally as either extrinsic or intrinsic. Extrinsic attributions include those that are made to the selfish interest of the company (i.e., increased profits). Intrinsic motives, on the other hand, are more about a company's desire to do good for society.

So, on the one hand, stakeholders that make *extrinsic* attributions chalk up the company's motives to *self-interest*, where the ultimate goal of CR is perceived to increase the brand's own welfare (e.g., increase sales/profits or improve the corporate image). Consider these responses, both from employees, taken from some of our qualitative research:[3]

> Just because a company supports a cause, doesn't mean that they care about anything but a profit. It's just a tax write-off.
>
> They are a company, and they are out for profits.

In a study of consumer reactions to cause-related marketing initiatives, Ellen and her colleagues[4] found that there are even different types of extrinsic attributions. Specifically, consumers further distinguish between strategic motives, such as gaining market share or sales, and highly egoistic ones, such as actually pocketing the donations.

On the other hand, *intrinsic* attributions refer to a stakeholder ascribing CR to *selfless* motives, where the ultimate goal of the company is to do good and/or fulfill its obligations to society (e.g., benefit the community or cause that is the focus of the CR initiative). For instance, stakeholders can ascribe a brand's efforts to improve the health of disadvantaged children in the US to its genuine concern for the cause. They do so because they perceive the company as wishing to respond to the clear needs of this group and thereby improve the children's lives. In the words of one of our focus group respondents: "I think they are interested in the community's health."

Just as individuals come up with various types of extrinsic attributions, so, too, can they perceive numerous intrinsic motivations. In the same study by Ellen and her colleagues,[5] consumers distinguished between intrinsic motives that were purely values-driven (e.g., "They feel morally obligated to help.") and those that were driven by a desire to be responsive to stakeholders (e.g., "They feel their customers expect it.").

> Individuals are usually tolerant of extrinsic movitations for CR as long as there is also evidence of intrinsic motivation.

Virtually all research to date points to intrinsic attributions as a primary driver of stakeholder evaluations of CR.[6] Individuals are tolerant of extrinsic motivations as long as there is also evidence of intrinsic motivations. Thus, extrinsic and intrinsic motives are not two ends of a single continuum, but rather operate separately as stakeholders attempt to make sense of a company's CR engagements. Since intrinsic and extrinsic attributions are independent of one another, they can co-exist. In fact, our research suggests that in today's CR landscape, stakeholders appreciate companies that find ways to simultaneously "do well and do good."

Let's take a look at the research supporting this idea. In our study of the oral care program, both program participants as well as members of the general population endorsed the dual motivations underlying the program:

> It's good because they are going to help us along with themselves.
>
> It's a form of marketing to get their products out but it also helps the community.
>
> They want to help the community but also to make a name for themselves and gain popularity.

These same kinds of attributions shed light on why General Electric's "Ecomagination" campaign has been generally well received by stakeholders. The company makes no secret of the fact that revenues from this branded line of compact fluorescent light bulbs, washing machines, aircraft engines, water desalination platforms, and wind turbines (among other eco-friendly products) are forecast to reach over $10 billion by 2010.[7] However, customers are enthusiastic about Ecomagination because the company appears to be genuine in its commitment to the environment.

> In today's CR landscape, stakeholders appreciate companies that find ways to simultaneously "do well and do good."

In fact, some of our research finds that consumers actually respond *more* positively to CR initiatives when they perceive *both* intrinsic and extrinsic motives. Creating "win-win" programs that purposefully mix intrinsic and extrinsic motives is not only tolerated, but often highly valued by people as an innovative approach to business. One of our focus group respondents put this best: "It's a two-way street."

Such attributions point to how CR initiatives can present an opportunity to go beyond win-win into the realm of consensus with a "win-win-win" in which everyone – the company, the stakeholder, and the social or environmental cause – all benefit.

Efficacy

As we laid out in the previous chapter, stakeholders tend to focus on certain characteristics of CR programs (i.e., what is the issue or cause, what is the channel or program through which it is implemented, and what resources will the company be providing for the program?). One reason that stakeholders will key in on these particular characteristics is that *they want to evaluate the extent to which CR efforts are actually bearing fruit in a recognizable way.* What we call efficacy, or the effectiveness of CR efforts, is an important facet of Understanding and has a number of consequential effects. When CR programs are highly effective at benefiting society, or at least perceived to be doing so, stakeholders will respond favorably. In contrast, programs that seem to have little bang for the buck are ultimately turn-offs for most people.

For example, CR efficacy often leads to positive attributions because it signals a company's genuine concern for societal/

community welfare. On the flip side, stakeholders are at least as sensitive to poor CR efficacy. When perceptions of efficacy become negative, such as when a company is embroiled in a scandal, stakeholders distance themselves from the company and sometimes even engage in destructive behaviors.

> One recent study by researchers Klein and colleagues (J.B. Klein, N.C. Smith, and A. John, "Why We Boycott: Consumer Motivations for Boycott Participation," *Journal of Marketing* 68(3) (2004), 92–109) found that the more consumers found a company's transgressions to be egregious, the more likely they were to join a boycott of the company's products. This finding illustrates that managers need to be aware of both sides of the coin as they explain corporate behavior to stakeholders.

More evidence

The notion of efficacy is still an emerging one in the study of CR, but we find clear empirical support for it in our research. For example, in our study of the oral care program, we asked participants in the program to rate how effective it was in improving their own and their children's oral health. Interestingly, we found considerable variance in respondents' perceptions of the program's efficacy. Moreover, people who perceived the program to be highly effective had significantly higher intentions to purchase (5 = very likely) this toothpaste brand than those who believed the program was not effective (Figure 5.3).

In a separate study, we surveyed a nationwide sample of frontline employees at retailers and restaurants. Employees who perceived their company's CR programs to be effective reported decreased intentions to leave their employer and increased intentions to deliver exceptional service to customers.

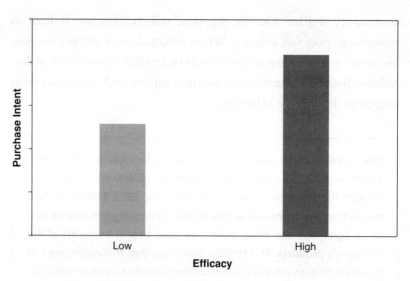

Figure 5.3 The effect of CR efficacy on purchase intent

That efficacy is compelling to stakeholders should make intuitive sense to managers. Nonetheless, there remains a tendency in CR reporting to underscore the "inputs" of their CR initiatives by citing statistics, such as the total amount of money donated, total hours volunteered, or the number of causes supported. This sort of reporting runs the risk of appearing abstract, dry, and meaningless to many stakeholders.

There is a place for reporting these inputs, but only when a clear link is made between spending and results, where stakeholders see that the company is getting a lot of societal "bang for the buck." As we will show below, this link can be made by providing evidence of an overall impact, or even by *telling stories of how individual people have been touched* by the company's efforts.

It is worth noting that no matter what a company does in the CR arena, stakeholders arrive at their own subjective understanding of what the company is doing, why it is doing so, and how well it is doing. This understanding can often be quite divorced from the company's actual CR efforts, which can work to the advantage – or disadvantage – of the company.

So, mere Understanding is not sufficient for CR value-creation. In order for the psychological levers to function effectively, CR must also be seen as personally Useful. We elaborate on this concept in our discussion of Usefulness, the second of the 3 U's, below. Efficacy, the final aspect of Understanding, also ties right in to Usefulness by contributing to the prestige of the company because it is successful in its endeavors; and this success is likely to make the program more Useful for many stakeholders, such as employees.

And so we move from Understanding, the first of our psychological levers that move stakeholder reactions, to the second lever: Usefulness.

The second lever: Usefulness

What do stakeholders expect or need from a company and its CR programs? A common thread in our research is that stakeholders cultivate relationships with companies, in part, as a means to improve their own condition. The second of the three psychological gears in our framework is related to the Usefulness of CR for stakeholders. Usefulness is multi-faceted and differs across stakeholders, but refers to how much CR succeeds in fulfilling key **stakeholder needs**.

> In order to function effectively, CR must be seen as personally Useful.

Over the course of our research, we have uncovered a hierarchy of benefits that CR can generate for stakeholders. These benefits range from the concrete and functional (e.g., lower incidence of diarrhea due to more frequent hand washing; fuel efficiency of an environmentally friendly hybrid car) to more abstract and identity related (e.g., self-esteem or work–home balance).

These needs of a higher order are related to a deep-seated desire to feel self-confident or socially accepted. Stakeholders want to "feel good" about associating with the company – and CR can provide a vehicle for them to lift their self-esteem through this connection. Likewise, many stakeholders consider it critical that they do not have to check their values at the door when they arrive at work in the morning; CR can help bridge this home–work gap as well.

CR can produce these same desirable effects even when the immediate Usefulness of a program is more functional, or concrete. In the oral care program for example, the participants (i.e., the children) received substantial functional benefits from the program in the form of healthier and cleaner teeth. In turn, this led to greater self-confidence and social acceptance from peers and helped fulfill their need for social connectedness and self-esteem.

CR benefits can be quite idiosyncratic, depending greatly on the circumstances under which CR is enacted; however, if done right, discovering which benefits are most compelling to stakeholders can be an informative exercise. (We explain how to do this in Chapter 7.)

Functional benefits

Functional benefits improve a stakeholder's condition in tangible ways. For example, in our study involving the oral care program, we asked parents whether the program resulted in any changes in their children. These parents consistently reported that the awareness, education and treatment program run by the company produced substantial functional benefits for their children in the form of healthier and cleaner teeth. Participants in the study had little difficulty relating good dental hygiene habits to these benefits, especially compared to non-program participants. As one of the participants put it: "It (dental hygiene) keeps your teeth free of cavities and takes care of your gums."

This increased awareness resulted in real, observable benefits for these stakeholders. We heard comments such as:

> For a long time I had problems with a tooth and I couldn't get it fixed because I couldn't afford it and they took care of it and left it looking like a normal tooth. Since it was a front tooth I felt very good about it.

> Even when the children do have a problem with their teeth, I am not as worried as before, because now I know there is a place to go at affordable prices.

> Some employees we spoke with were in charge of local CR programs, which exposed them to marketing, accounting, and general management challenges that they did not normally encounter in their work.
>
> Participating in such CR programs helped these employees perform better in their current job and opened attractive new career prospects for the future.

The benefits that CR program participants gain may seem somewhat obvious. To see whether CR generates functional benefits for those *not* directly targeted by CR, we interviewed employees in a Fortune 500 company. When we asked these employees whether they gained at all personally from the company's CR they named a number of functional benefits.

For example, some employees said that CR *provides opportunities to gain skills* that will help them advance in their career. Leadership, communication, and project management skills were among those cited.

In addition to these skills, many employees end up encountering other outstanding employees, pointing to the *networking and team-building benefits* that are frequently cited as contributing to a healthy workplace. Thus, employees sometimes make a clear connection between CR and their own career advancement.

Identity-related benefits

Identity-related benefits are much more abstract and relate to thoughts and feelings that people have about their self-image. In developing self-image, people have two important needs: for *self-esteem* and for *self-continuity*. These two concepts have been studied extensively and are known to be among the most fundamental of human needs. Our findings are consistent with theories of the self that suggest that we, as human beings, are generally interested in promoting "positive self-views" (that help us fulfill the need for self-esteem) and in maintaining a "consistent sense of who we are" (that help us fulfill the need for self-continuity).[8]

Empirical support

These ideas can be more clearly understood by looking at our research in the consumer and employee realms. Self-esteem refers to feelings of self-worth – in this case, a sense of self-worth that comes from their association with the company. We find that CR often improves stakeholders' self-esteem, or pride that they feel from being an organizational member. In the words of employees:

> If the company's doing good things as a corporate citizen... then I think you do feel better about yourself.
>
> I mean, it helps you be happy as a person...
>
> I'm proud to work [for the company], because we're working to use our profit to help others.
>
> It makes me feel good to be associated with the company that does that.

CR can also boost self-esteem by enabling employees to express their own sense of responsibility to their immediate or even larger community through their company's CR activities, a feeling that makes work highly rewarding. In the words of one employee: "For me personally, it encourages me to do more, and volunteer more and participate more. You take on that personal obligation that the company has taken on."

After hearing these clear indications that CR leads to self-enhancement, we tested the link quantitatively in a nationwide survey of frontline employees. We asked respondents to tell us their level of pride in working for the company (more formally known as organizational self-esteem). Figure 5.4a shows a comparison between respondents who were aware that their company engaged in CR and those who were unaware of any CR initiatives. Pride in the company was significantly higher for those who were aware. This relationship between CR awareness and self-esteem was robust enough to hold up statistically even after controlling for other factors such as age, tenure, personality, and support from supervisors.

But CR does more than just *raise* the overall level of self-esteem. It can also *protect* stakeholders' self-esteem from threats and thereby help employees to maintain a positive sense of self. For example, employees of large multinational companies sometimes find themselves in situations where they have to defend their company's reputation to hostile external stakeholders (e.g., in foreign countries where the local population and media have negative feelings towards the company). These geographic pockets of ill-will not only harm the company, they also hurt the self-esteem of its employees. As one focus group respondent stated: "You get outside ... and it is either no knowledge or a lot of negative knowledge, and it is a very painful thing, because we all know better inside the company."

CR helps such employees combat these negative external images by educating external audiences, and sometimes even themselves, about the company's core values and ethics. For them, CR provides a shield that protects the company's reputation in their minds and helps lessen the impact of negative sentiment found in their local communities. As such, CR offers a way to make stakeholders'

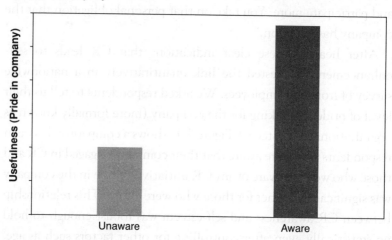

a) **Pride in company**

Usefulness (Pride in company)

Unaware   Aware

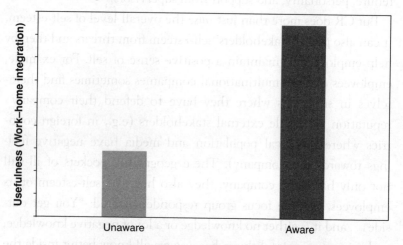

b) **Work–home integration**

Usefulness (Work–home integration)

Unaware   Aware

Figure 5.4 The effect of CR on two forms of Usefulness

opinions about the company and thus their own self-esteem resilient in both good times and bad.

> CR often improves stakeholders' self-esteem or the pride that they derive from being an organizational member.

Social psychologists assert that in addition to maintaining a *positive* sense of self, human beings need to maintain a *consistent* sense of self. In other words, having continuity in one's life is a fundamental psychological need. People become uneasy when they are not able to fully express themselves in all the various avenues of their life. So another benefit stakeholders want and need is self-continuity – the sense that their values and expression of who they are stay relatively consistent throughout the many spheres of life's activity.

Stakeholders find CR to be Useful when it provides them with such an opportunity to find greater continuity in their lives. By expressing the values that stakeholders hold dear, CR reaffirms to stakeholders that they are in the right place, and that associating with the company is merely an extension of who they are.

> Employees we have interviewed confirm that involvement in CR is a way to achieve greater work–home integration (i.e., continuity). Even when other aspects of their work are stressful, awareness that the company is "doing good" energizes them and reduces the stress they may feel.

The most striking evidence that CR can provide self-continuity comes from our multiple studies in the workplace. Employees simultaneously inhabit (at least) two life spheres: namely, work and home. Many employees look to integrate these two spheres in order to achieve continuity. Employees do not like to "check their morals at the door" when they arrive at work. Most prefer to have a seamless transition between their work and home lives, where work is a natural expression of how they see themselves as a person. This expression is not limited to work and home or family life, but also to the many other spheres in which people participate, such as community, spiritual life, and an array of self-enhancing activities that capture what matters to them.

CR helps employees feel more harmonious by balancing the often-competing needs of their work and personal lives. Consider the following quotes:

> One of the things that I've been putting a lot of thought into the last few years personally and trying to move more and more in the direction of, is trying to overcome this complete separation of work and non-work life.

> I don't want to leave here for them to say I have been selling soap. It is probably not quite what I am after. So, the better I can meet the personal purpose and pair it with my professional work, the more satisfied I am because then I see I can better combine the two. It is not the choice do one or the other.

> If you gave to my favorite charity or we did Habitat for Humanity... I would go home at night and I would sit down with my family and say, "you know what? I had a great day at work today and I don't feel like killing someone!"

Employees like these tend to interpret their employer's socially responsible behaviors as an indication that the company's values coincide with their own sense of the kind of lives – both work and personal – they want to lead. A contributing factor for such interpretation may be that companies' *CR programs often involve the employees' own social communities* (e.g., schools in which the employees' children study), thereby helping to integrate their professional and personal lives in an immediate and noticeable way.

On the other hand, *employees who work in remote locations often feel isolated* from what they perceive to be the literal as well as psychosocial center of the company (usually the corporate headquarters). For such employees, a company's *CR efforts provide a bridge to fellow employees who are scattered across multiple locations*. Involvement in such programs, and their additional corporate functions, helps employees interact with colleagues with whom they would not normally work. Such employees then develop a sense of oneness with the company through their involvement in the collective effort to make a difference in the world. A perfect example was a multinational company's company-wide relief efforts after the 2004 Tsunami in Southeast Asia. Consider the words of this employee who works in a regional sales office far away from headquarters: "The power of [the company] supporting what we want to do here in this community... wow, that makes me feel more connected to the company."

Just as we examined the link between awareness of CR and self-enhancement, we also re-tested the CR/Usefulness link in our nationwide study of frontline service employees regarding their feelings about work–home integration.

Figure 5.4b shows that aware respondents reported significantly higher levels of work–home integration than unaware respondents. As in the self-enhancement case, this difference held up even after controlling for a number of other factors such as tenure, personality, and the flexibility of the respondent's work schedule.

The upshot is that for most stakeholders, even those directly involved with a company's CR initiatives, *the primary Usefulness of CR lies in its ability to meet some of the more abstract identity-related needs they are trying to fulfill*. At the same time, as is clear from the reactions of employees to their employer's CR efforts, the Usefulness of CR in providing these higher-level benefits varies not just across stakeholder groups, but within a stakeholder group as well.

Therefore, managers would do well to learn more about what stakeholders find useful and communicate individual stories that represent some of the positive reactions. This can be an important step in creating a sense of Unity, the third and most critical lever that drives stakeholder response, both pro-company and pro-social.

The third lever: Unity

A fundamental insight from our research is that CR *value hinges on the extent to which CR actions cause stakeholders to form strong and enduring bonds with the company.* From the stakeholder perspective that we advocate in this book, this bond is best described as a sense of Unity with the company. Unity is important because it is the foremost determinant of the kinds of pro-company responses that companies seek.

Unity might be described as a stakeholder's overall appraisal of the quality of the relationship that he or she has with the company. Of the three "psychological levers" that we describe in this chapter, Unity is somewhat unique in that it is dependent on Understanding and Usefulness. Stakeholders develop a sense of Unity with a company based in part on how they Understand its CR activity and how much they find CR to be Useful. Like Understanding and Usefulness, Unity involves associations, perceptions, thoughts and feelings. It resides inside the mind of each stakeholder, so it is sometimes not apparent to others that Unity – or lack of Unity – is present until the stakeholder acts on these thoughts. (These actions are the subject of Chapter 7.)

While Unity can be tricky to assess, astute managers can uncover stakeholders' relationship appraisals if they (1) know what they are looking for, (2) engage in frequent dialogue with stakeholders, and (3) use some established market research techniques in recording the level of Unity.

Here we outline the two principal facets of Unity that managers need to look for: *identification* and *trust*. Below we will explain how to engage in dialogue effectively and apply market research techniques to the task of formally measuring Unity.

Identification

When stakeholders develop a good understanding of CR activity and are able to see how it improves their own condition, they begin to develop a sense that the company's values overlap with their own. After all, if the company shows that it is genuinely concerned with issues that are important to a stakeholder (Understanding) and they provide work–home balance (Usefulness), then the stakeholder is likely to feel that the company is aligned with what is important to him or her (Unity).

In extreme cases, the overlap between the stakeholder's values and those of the company may become so extensive that the stakeholder will feel part of a larger collective that is working towards "something that is larger than any individual." This is called *identification*, a stakeholder's sense of significant overlap between who they themselves are and what the organization, and its members, stand for.[9]

Stakeholders sometimes identify with companies to such a degree that they take on defining characteristics of the corporation. Consider Apple; for years, especially in the 1990s, it inspired such devotion from employees and consumers that they each thought that they were part of an ongoing struggle to take on Microsoft. In recent years, the company has successfully established a *lifestyle* image, depicting Apple as having the edge by being part of a hip, flexible, creative, and contemporary culture that resonates with the identity-related needs of its stakeholders.

Readers will know that their company has been successful in engendering strong identification if they hear people refer to themselves by organizational monikers such as P&Ger, IBMer, UPSer, or Harley–Davidson owner. People generally don't choose a Harley, for example, solely for its engineering, but rather for the perceived associations and identification with the company and other Harley-owners. And in response to the Apple ad campaign mentioned above, competing PC companies rolled out their own ads in an effort to engender wider identification and pride in the brand; these showed many different kinds of users, not just the conventional businessmen, stating, "I'm a PC."

> CR can contribute to stakeholders' sense that the company's values overlap with theirs.

Identification, however, is not a binary state of being where stakeholders are either completely devoted to the company or indifferent. Instead, identification should be viewed as a matter of degree. As a result, managers need not gauge the success of their CR activities by the proportion of highly committed members, but rather by *how significantly programs improve identification.* Measuring in this way, we find that CR very often results in a significant bump in identification with the company, even with those stakeholders who have no formal membership ties to the company.

The positive effect of CR on identification has proven to be extremely robust across our studies. We have substantiated this link between CR and heightened identification for companies selling yogurt, shampoo, laundry detergent, toys, printers, calculators, computers, financial services, civil engineering services, and more. We have also found that identification extends across various stakeholder realms including, but not limited to, consumption, employment, and investment.

Why might CR lead to identification? The reason is related to two types of associations that stakeholders have with regard to a company's identity. One type is *corporate ability associations*: the company's expertise in producing and delivering its products/services (e.g., industry leadership, technological innovation). The other is *CR associations*: the company's activities with regard to societal and environmental issues.[10] Of these two kinds of identity-defining associations, it is the company's CR associations that provide stakeholders with clearer insight into its "value system," "soul," or "character."[11]

Stakeholders often view CR activity as an expression of the company's character or soul.

A company's character as revealed by its CR actions is not only fundamental and enduring, but also often more distinctive than perceptions about its products or services. In fact, *a company's CR activities are likely to constitute the core, defining characteristics of its identity*, becoming the *primary* basis on which its stakeholders are drawn to identify with it. As stated by an employee of a multinational corporation we interviewed:

> Most people intertwine a huge part of their identity with what they do.... If the company's doing good things as a corporate citizen... [and] you intertwine your sense of identity with your work and that company, then I think you do feel better about yourself. It's kind of a daisy chain and that's where I can see it coming together.

Empirical evidence

Evidence for the CR-identification link is found in our study of multiple stakeholder responses to a $1 million donation by a large multinational company to a center for child development. The donation was announced and promoted through multiple communication channels in the city where the center is located. We surveyed three groups of stakeholders: (1) those who became *aware* of the gift and were able to identify the sponsor, (2) those who were surveyed before the announcement, and (3) those who were surveyed after the announcement but had not been exposed to information about the gift, and thus were also *unaware*. We then compared the responses of aware respondents to the other two unaware groups of stakeholders (pre- and post-announcement). We found that awareness of the gift resulted in heightened intentions to consume products, apply for jobs, and invest in stock of the company.

Further analysis[12] revealed that the aforementioned behaviors of aware stakeholders were driven by their level of identification with the company. Just how much identification increased as a result of awareness is shown in Figure 5.5. People who were aware of the gift identified significantly more than either group of unaware respondents.

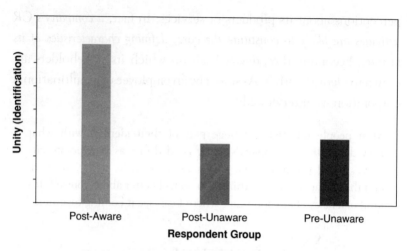

Figure 5.5 The effect of CR awareness on Unity

As we've noted earlier in the chapter, although awareness of the initiative was relatively low, those who did find out about the initiative were clearly drawn to the company.

Therefore, we advise companies to track such identification on an ongoing basis, as well as in relation to individual initiatives. (In Chapter 9 we will elaborate on how managers can measure stakeholder identification.)

Trust

Unity with a company is also often evident as an increase in *trust*. One can think of trust as a stakeholder's confidence in a company's reliability and integrity,[13] increasing his or her willingness to be vulnerable or take risks in interactions with that company.[14] In other words, trust is the lubricant that helps good relationships run smoothly. It reflects not only the expectation that the company will do what it says it will do, but also the perceived benevolence of the company.

The importance of building trust among stakeholders is well established; however, it may not be obvious why CR should generate such trust. *The main reason that CR builds trust among stakeholders is that social and environmental initiatives exhibit the company's munificence.* CR activity is an expression of the company's character or "soul." Stakeholders view this character as a template for how the company will act in the future. A trustworthy company is one that is expected to act fairly, benevolently, and in the interests of long-term joint gain.[15]

Trust is enhanced by CR because by engaging in it, the company indicates that it cares about its stakeholders and that it will not act opportunistically towards them, exploiting their vulnerability.[16] Thus, stakeholders see CR as a manifestation of the company's underlying benevolent disposition.

> Niamh Whooley, Senior Manager-CR at PwC says: "Promoting Corporate Responsibility builds trust, and this gives business a head start when dealing with customers, workers and regulators. It gives business the edge in attracting good customers and employees."

What the research shows

We have found a strong CR-trust link in our research. For instance, trust was increased after exposure to the oral care program. As one focus group respondent put it: "They are working on not the immediate, but long term results... They give us the trust to continue using their products."

In line with our qualitative data, our survey results showed significant increases in trust levels not only for participants in the program, but even for those in the general population who were merely aware of the program. Importantly, and as expected, the increases in trust and thus Unity were linked to greater levels of commitment (among both the participants and aware consumers) to reciprocate by purchasing products from the toothpaste brand and its parent company. In the words of a respondent: "It motivates you to buy their products because they are helping your community. So indirectly you are contributing to the community by buying their products and having them give back to the community."

Similarly, our research with employees in multiple companies revealed greater trust among those with particularly strong positive beliefs about the company's commitment to CR. There was a clear sense that this population was using CR to determine who the company is and what can be expected from it.

Consistent with our framework, we also found evidence that trust is driven in part by the Usefulness of any CR effort. *Trust is enhanced to the extent that CR initiatives are personally useful to the employee.* Take this employee in one of our focus groups: "Employees don't just automatically trust that [supporting a cause] is a good thing. So the more information that is released about it, and quite frankly even tying it into what it means for me the more likely I will want to be part of it."

It is worth noting that trust is qualitatively different from the attributions we discussed earlier in this chapter. *Trust* refers to expectations of the company *in the future*, while *attributions* (e.g., of genuine concern) are assessments of motivations for *past or current* behavior.[17] While distinct, the two ideas are often related causally; attributions drive trust. This occurs because – from the stakeholder perspective – a company's motivations today are predictive of its deeds tomorrow. Companies that are seen to have a genuine concern for others can be expected to generate heightened trust from stakeholders.

Summary

In this chapter, we have laid out the psychological process through which stakeholders interpret CR activity. The process includes a series of stages we call the 3 U's: Understanding, Usefulness, and Unity. Each serves as a lever that moves stakeholders to respond positively to the CR.

An important insight in our research is that stakeholders develop a sense of Unity with companies that provide good Understanding and Usefulness. As Figure 5.1 above suggests, the 3 U's interact with each other, but Unity plays a central role in driving CR value. Therefore, a company looking to create such value must not only continually seek to optimize the leverage provided by each part of the psychological process, but also make sure that they are working harmoniously, in a self-reinforcing way, towards fostering strong and enduring relationships with stakeholders. Companies that are able to achieve this sort of synchronized response to CR are those best positioned to encourage the sorts of behaviors that will benefit both them and their stakeholders.

Our framework shows that stakeholders routinely make determinations about how appropriate CR is for the company (Understanding), and how beneficial CR is for them personally (Usefulness) by continually updating what they know about a company's CR. Given the information overload so many people experience, the *quality* of the attention stakeholders bring to communications about CR is critical. Thus, communication should be seen as an ongoing dialogue between the company and individual stakeholders. The company attempts to communicate the logic behind their actions, and the individual assesses the degree to which the company belongs in his or her life (Unity).

More specifically, stakeholders make attributions about the company's motives as either extrinsic (focused on self-interested profit) or intrinsic (representing core values of a more selfless nature). Stakeholders understand that profit is part of business and will accept and even welcome this, but only if they also perceive an intrinsic motivation to help society or the environment through the CR.

Stakeholders sometimes get functional benefits, which are tangible, from CR initiatives. But equally or more important are the less tangible benefits related to one's identity: a sense of self-worth and self-continuity.

Moreover, identification with the company's values as expressed in its CR initiatives – and a corresponding sense of trust in the company's motives going forward – lead to a greater sense of Unity and therefore to pro-company behaviors. Unity is enhanced directly by the stakeholders' Understanding of the company's CR activity and by the perception that CR has personal Usefulness for them.

While the way that stakeholders interpret CR activity may be the root of CR value, such interpretations are highly idiosyncratic, dependent upon a host of contextual factors. Managers cannot accurately predict the impact of CR without taking the context into account. How the context influences the process is the topic of the next chapter.

Endnotes

1. www.ipsos-mori.com/researchpublications/researcharchive/poll.aspx?oItemId=849, accessed December 10, 2009.
2. P. Berthon and I. Cross, "Going Green for Generation Y," The Bentley Center for Marketing Technology (2008), available at www.prnewswire.com/news-releases/going-green-for-generation-y-new-bentley-college-study-reveals-perception-is-key-to-attracting-young-consumers-57280087.html, accessed March 18, 2011.
3. CB Bhattacharya and S. Sen, "Doing Better at Doing Good: When, Why, and How Consumers Respond to Corporate Social Initiatives," *California Management Review*, 47(1) (2004), 9–24; D. Korschun, When and How Corporate Social Responsibility Makes a Company's Frontline Employees Customer Oriented (Dissertation, Boston University, 2008).
4. P.S. Ellen, D.J. Webb, and L.A. Mohr, "Building Corporate Associations: Consumer Attributions for Corporate Socially Responsible Programs," *Journal of the Academy of Marketing Science*, 34(2) (2006), 147–57.
5. Ibid.

6 For example, Y. Yoon, Z. Gurhan-Canli, and N. Schwarz, "The Effect of Corporate Social Responsibility (CR) Activities on Companies With Bad Reputations," *Journal of Consumer Psychology*, 16(4) (2006), 377–90.
7 www.ge.com, accessed March 24, 2008.
8 D. Oyserman, H.M. Coon, and M. Kemmelmeier, "Rethinking Individualism and Collectivism: Evaluation of Theoretical Assumptions and Meta-analyses," *Psychological Bulletin*, 128(1) (2002), 3–72.
9 H. Tajfel and J.C. Turner, "The Social Identity Theory of Inter-Group Behavior," in S. Worchel and L.W. Austin (eds.), *Psychology of Intergroup Relations* (Chicago: Nelson-Hall, 1986); M. Bergami and R.P. Bagozzi, "Self Categorization, Affective Commitment, and Group Self-Esteem as Distinct Aspects of Social Identity in the Organization," *British Journal of Social Psychology*, 39(4) (2000), 555–77; J.E. Dutton, J.M. Dukerich, and C.V. Harquail, "Organizational Images and Member Identification," *Administrative Science Quarterly*, 39(2) (1994), 239–63; B.E. Ashforth and F. Mael, "Social Identity Theory and the Organization," *Academy of Management Review*, 14(1) (1989), 20–39; S.G. Scott and V.R. Lane, "A Stakeholder Approach to Organizational Identity," *Academy of Management Review*, 25(1) (2000), 43–62.
10 T.J. Brown and P.A. Dacin, "The Company and the Product: Corporate Associations and Consumer Product Responses," *Journal of Marketing*, 61(1) (1997), 68–84.
11 Ibid. See also S. Sen and CB Bhattacharya, "Does Doing Good Always Lead to Doing Better? Consumer Reactions to Corporate Social Responsibility," *Journal of Marketing Research*, 38(2) (2001), 225–43.
12 We conducted the mediation analysis proposed by R.M. Baron and D.A. Kenny, "The moderator mediator variable distinction in social psychological-research-Conceptual, strategic, and statistical considerations," *Journal of Personality and Social Psychology*, 51 (1986), 1173–82.
13 R.M. Morgan and S.D. Hunt, "The Commitment-Trust Theory of Relationship Marketing," *Journal of Marketing*, 58(3) (1994), 20–38.
14 D. Rousseau, S. Sitkin, R. Burt, and C. Camerer, "Not so Different after all: A Cross-discipline View of Trust," *Academy of Management Review*, 23 (1998), 393–404. C. Johnson-George and W. Swap, "Measurement of Specific Interpersonal Trust: Construction and Validation of a Scale to Assess Trust in a Specific Other," *Journal of Personality and Social Psychology*, 43 (1982), 1306–17.
15 D.J. McAllister, "Affect- and Cognition-Based Trust as Foundations for Interpersonal Cooperation in Organizations," *Academy of Management*

Journal, 38(1) (1995), 24–59; Johnson-George and Swap, "Measurement of Specific Interpersonal Trust."
16 S. Ganesan and R. Hess, "Dimensions and Levels of Trust: Implications for Commitment to a Relationship," Marketing Letters, 8(4) (1997), 439–48.
17 J.K. Rempel, J.G. Holmes, and M.P. Zanna, "Trust in Close Relationships," Journal of Personality and Social Psychology, 49(1) (1985), 95–112.

Further reading

Richard H. Thaler and Cass Sunstein, Nudge: Improving Decisions about Health, Wealth, and Happiness (New Haven: Yale University Press, 2008).

The authors of this book reveal that humans are fallible in many everyday decisions and suggest ways to nudge people in beneficial directions to make better choices.

Dan Ariely, Predictable Irrational: The Hidden Forces that Shape Our Decisions (New York: Harper, 2008).

This book shows that irrational behavior is human but that such behavior can often be predicted quite well, which brings opportunities to re-examine consumer choices.

SIX

How context influences the process

In the previous chapters, we laid out how stakeholders see CR, how they interpret CR information, and how they respond to CR. This straightforward multi-step process will – *all things being equal* – predict stakeholder behavior and help build the business case for engaging in CR activity.

But all things are rarely equal. That's why CR's ability to create value depends greatly on the context in which it is implemented. Knowing how context influences outcomes is critical to effective CR management, because only managers who build this knowledge into their decision-making can take full advantage of the opportunities, while also steering clear of the potential pitfalls.

The significance of context

This chapter presents some of the most important contributing contextual factors in stakeholder responses to CR. We call these *multipliers*. Multipliers magnify or dampen the effects of one part of our framework – and therefore its influence – on another part.

For example, the more a stakeholder feels Unity with the company (a significant contributor to stakeholder involvement, as discussed in Chapter 5), the more likely the stakeholder will be to purchase the company's products. But it's not quite that simple. The effect of Unity on purchase is dependent in part on another variable: the income of the stakeholder. Wealthy consumers are able to express their Unity with the company very freely, by paying a premium and purchasing frequently; but low-income stakeholders may be less likely to demonstrate their devotion to the company because they have more modest means. Thus, income can be considered a multiplier that influences an important link in the framework.

Numerous other conditions create a context within which stakeholder decisions and reactions occur. The wise manager will pay attention to these in order to maximize the value of the company's CR.

UPS and location

A good example of a company that is highly attuned to the context in which it enacts CR is UPS. The company has been extremely successful at soliciting participation in its United Way programs in the United States. UPS and its US employee base have collectively raised millions of dollars for the perennial charity. But when they decided to engage the thousands of employees located *outside* the US, it soon became obvious that rolling out the same programs in the same way would be far from optimal.

When it came to non-US employees, United Way not only suffered extremely low awareness but also failed to connect with employees at an emotional level. Recognizing that non-US employees would respond differently than their US counterparts, the company sought to tailor their CR initiatives to fit the new context.

> Companies can enhance the quality of the employee–company relationship by concentrating on CR issues that employees care about.

After a year of rigorous study, UPS chose the World Association of Girl Guides and Girl Scouts, an organization that engages about 10 million young girls in leadership programs and volunteer projects.

"That gave our employees, no matter where they were, the opportunity to connect to one organization [in a manner] similar to how we connected to the United Way in the United States," says Lisa Hamilton, President of the UPS Foundation.[1] The company integrates this signature initiative with others that are specifically tailored to the needs of individual countries.

By addressing issues that UPS employees care about, the company's CR activity accomplished three goals:

- It increased awareness of UPS's charitable giving,
- satisfied employees' needs, and
- enhanced the quality of the employee–company relationship much more than had it not considered these important contextual factors.

In other words, the success of this signature UPS CR initiative was contingent upon finding an organization that was known and supported by employees in countries outside the US. The clear lesson from the example above is that when it comes to CR, *companies need to be sensitive to the unique situation in which CR is enacted.*

This example may seem obvious in retrospect; however, in our experience too many companies roll-out CR programs with little or no consideration of the context. Some managers mistakenly presume that if a CR program is working with one set of stakeholders it will work just as well with another. Other managers are so keen to adopt the "best practices" of peer companies that they fail to make adjustments for their company's unique challenges and characteristics.

Going beyond "one size fits all"

Companies that want to maximize CR value need to understand which contextual factors influence the process. In other words, companies must go beyond a "one size fits all" approach, because the same

CR activities can produce dramatically different levels of Understanding, Usefulness, Unity, and consequently behavioral responses to CR depending on the context.

Although this should make intuitive sense to most managers, it can be extremely challenging to identify the situational factors that are most likely to improve the upside and reduce the downside of engaging in CR.

> Managers keen to adopt the "best practices" of peer companies may overlook necessary adjustments in light of their company's unique challenges and characteristics.

Our research showed that context is best understood by examining two categories of factors:

- The first category is related to differences among stakeholders (the stakeholder context).
- The second category operates at the organizational level, where differences in CR value can be attributed to differences among companies (the company context).

The discussion now turns to key factors in these stakeholder and company contexts. See Table 6.1 for a summary of examples that show how context influences the psychological process.

Stakeholder context

The stakeholder-centric approach, which this book advocates, requires managers to develop a deeper appreciation of just how heterogeneous stakeholders are. Each stakeholder is unique in the relationship they have with the company, the way they view CR, and who they are as a person. This stakeholder context can have profound influences on whether and how CR produces value for the company and society.

In analyzing the stakeholder context, we find three sets of factors that are most likely to influence how stakeholders interpret and respond to CR. These are:

- the stakeholders' **closeness** to a company and its CR,
- their **caring** about the issues at the heart of a company's CR efforts, and
- the personal **characteristics** of the stakeholder.

Closeness

Stakeholders vary in their closeness not only to a company's CR actions but also to the company itself. Some stakeholders, such as employees at the company's headquarters, are highly embedded[2] in the company, while others are more removed from the company's "core." Embedded stakeholders are active in the organization (i.e., the company), have easy access to other organizational members, can actually mediate the flow of resources or information in the organization, and have connections to other central organizational members.[3]

Employees are typically the most closely embedded group of stakeholders, while consumers and stockholders tend to see themselves, for the most part, as looking in from the outside. This obviously depends on the company and the specific stakeholders. Some customers, for instance, are highly involved in the company's operations (e.g., service customers), and some stockholders can be very active (e.g., stockholders with many shares).

Closeness to the company also varies even within each stakeholder group. While employees may be the most closely embedded group of stakeholders in a company overall, some employees will feel much closer to the company than others. For example, employees who work from satellite offices can sometimes feel disconnected from the rest of the company, and this can have great implications for which programs they find most useful. Therefore, *it is best for managers to gauge closeness on an individual level*, because this will be much more accurate than assuming that all stakeholder group members are alike.

Just as stakeholders can feel close to the company through these various relationships, so too can they feel closeness to the company's CR. This closeness to a company's CR can be described and measured. At one end of the spectrum, there is a complete lack of participation in the CR domain; at the other end, a stakeholder has strong and sustained involvement in a company's CR programs. In the latter situation, these involved stakeholders often co-create CR with the company, helping develop, support and sustain activities in this domain. (See Chapter 10 for further elaboration on how to measure the stakeholder's sense of closeness to the company's CR.)

> Employees who work far away from corporate headquarters sometimes feel disconnected from the rest of the company; targeted, relevant CR can help bridge that divide.

Closeness as a multiplier

Consider the framework that was described in detail in Chapter 5. It explains the three psychological levers that drive stakeholder reactions to CR: namely, the degree of Understanding, Usefulness, and Unity. *Closeness – whether to the company or its CR efforts – amplifies the effects of each individual lever in shifting stakeholders' interpretation of CR activity.*

Here is a closer look at how this works. By definition, closeness increases stakeholder knowledge of a company's CR initiatives. As a result, it enhances the stakeholders' broader Understanding of the company's CR, potentially leading them to make more desirable attributions and have more accurate estimates of the efficacy of the programs.

Notably though, this greater emphasis and scrutiny on efficacy can actually lead to adverse consequences if closer stakeholders uncover unfavorable evidence about the company. So managers need to take into account the very real potential for negative reactions and be prepared to address pertinent issues.

Closeness, as already suggested, can also enhance the Usefulness of a company's CR to its stakeholders because such Usefulness can often hinge on actual participation in the life of the company, especially in the CR domain (e.g., employee involvement in specific programs).

Finally, closeness is likely to magnify the likelihood of Unity with the company's values as expressed in its CR programs. In fact, our thinking on Unity[4] implicates stakeholder *embeddedness in the company as one of the prime facilitators of Unity*.

> The more stakeholders are able to co-create CR activities with the company, the more they find such activities to be highly Useful.

With a feeling of closeness, the individual stakeholder not only knows more about the initiatives, but is also more likely to engage in an effort to co-create the CR program with the company and identify with both the program and the company, thus reaping more personal benefit (Usefulness) and a greater sense of shared values (Unity) with the company.

A deeper look at the studies

A number of our studies provide evidence for the influence of closeness when it comes to Understanding of the company's activities. For instance, our research on employee responses to CR produced clear findings that mirror the earlier discussion on location: Those who are physically closer (i.e., where they work or reside) to corporate headquarters, or to where CR is enacted, are more likely to develop an Understanding of the company's CR actions than stakeholders who live and/or work farther away.

Specifically, data from our studies of employees at both headquarters and branch offices revealed that the farther away employees were from company headquarters or the CR program location, the worse was their Understanding of what the company was doing. While many of our respondents had a general sense that the company was doing something, specifics about the company's commitments and accomplishments were few and far between.

Take, for example, these employees, who – despite their strong interest in CR – found it difficult to stay abreast of CR developments at their company:

> We are a branch office so I don't see all the good they do. I read about it every once and awhile... and there are all these drives and fundraisers there. At [my former company] you got to see it. You witnessed it even if you didn't get a chance to do everything.

> They give five, ten, fifteen thousand dollars to various organizations. I mean, that goes blind to everybody except those who are in that department who have contributed to it.

Among employees we interviewed, those based far away from headquarters expressed frustration that the company did not adequately keep them abreast of developments in their CR activity. Consider these comments:

> 80% of the people on the [factory] floor have no clue of any of the stuff that we talked about.

> For a marketing company, we do a piss poor job of marketing anything internally.

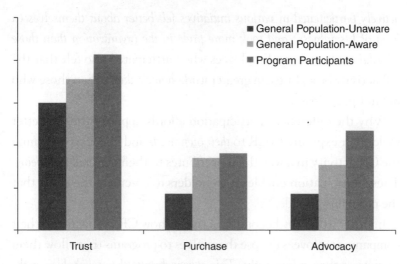

Figure 6.1 The influence of closeness on reactions to CR

Based on findings in our study of the oral care program, closeness was indeed a multiplier because it helped improve the sense of Unity (measured as trust). Closeness also led to improvements in stakeholder responses to CR (purchase intent and advocacy behaviors). Responses for both purchase intent and advocacy behaviors were least favorable to the company for unaware non-participants, elevated somewhat for aware non-participants, and highest for aware participants. Figure 6.1 illustrates these findings.

Just as closeness can influence CR activity's effect on Understanding, it can also impact how Useful CR is to stakeholders. Consider results from our focus groups with a cross-section of employees at a global consumer goods company. As with Understanding, examining the level of Usefulness (to the stakeholders) of the company's CR programs we found considerable disparity in people's opinions.

Upon closer examination, we found that this variance was linked to *how involved the stakeholders were to* the CR activity. *Those who actively participated in various initiatives felt better about themselves (a form of Usefulness) and took more pride in the organization than those who did not participate.* Employees who participated also felt that the CR activity brought them greater *work–home balance* than those who did not participate.

Why the difference? Participation affords opportunities to better mold their exposure to CR to *their own needs* and hence to customize the CR activity in a way that contributes to their *personal well-being.* Thus, participation enables stakeholders to co-create the value that the programs provide.[5]

In other words, by becoming active in how CR is enacted at their company, employees expose themselves to programs that allow them to express themselves fully. *This approach puts the stakeholder in the driver's seat, giving them a sense of involvement and accomplishment.*

Having recorded this phenomenon qualitatively, we decided to replicate the findings in a nationwide quantitative survey of frontline employees in the retail and hospitality industries. In that study, we asked 539 respondents at various companies to describe how much CR helped them marry their work and home lives (i.e., its Usefulness to them) and how much they participated in CR at their company.

> The Usefulness of CR is significantly greater for those who participated in the initiative frequently versus those who did not because such participation allowed them to mold the experience to their own needs.

By comparing responses for employees who participated a great deal to those who participated only infrequently, it became clear that participation was enabling some people to extract value that wasn't there for non-participants.

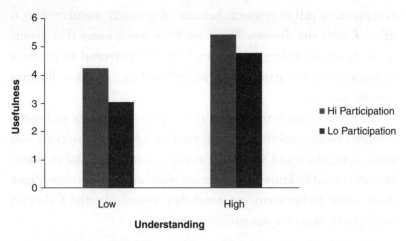

Figure 6.2 The influence of participation on reactions to CR

Figure 6.2 confirms that an Understanding of CR is beneficial for companies. (Such benefit is evidenced by the jump in Usefulness when Understanding of CR goes from low to high.) But perhaps more interestingly, the Usefulness of CR is significantly greater for those who participated versus those who participate infrequently. Thus, participation (and hence closeness) can help stakeholders get more out of CR, even when Understanding is relatively low.

Caring

Not all CR initiatives are equally compelling to stakeholders. *The extent to which CR is effective in reaching company goals depends on a stakeholder's personal support of the issue or issues involved in CR, or what we call caring.*

Stakeholders each have unique and personal preferences for some causes over others. A stakeholder may believe very strongly, for instance, that climate change is the most important issue facing society today. Another stakeholder may be particularly committed to supporting AIDS research because of a family member who is afflicted with the disease. There are even some issues that generate such strong feelings that they have the potential to create a chasm within a company's stakeholder base (e.g., abortion, firearms regulation).

The bottom line is this: Issues that capture the hearts and imaginations of some stakeholders will produce lukewarm reactions – or worse, a negative and visceral response – from other stakeholders. Managers need to know that there are stakeholders who clearly care about social rather than environmental issues, like the following employee from one of our studies:

> In terms of what the company has offered, I've always had a soft spot for the Boys and Girls Club. I like working with kids. Role models for the less fortunate, that's always been a soft spot for me... [But] environmental recycling... doesn't really appeal to me. I recycle and am conscious with the earth, but it's not something I get into.

The research points to this conclusion: Knowing what excites stakeholders is important, because the more stakeholders care about the issues addressed by a company's CR programs, the more likely they are to find such initiatives to be personally Useful.

For example, *when an employee sees her employer address issues that she cares about, it helps her marry two otherwise distinct spheres of her life: home and work.* High levels of caring help bridge the gap between work and home, and thus help her lead a more coherent existence where she can express herself fully.

Likewise, a consumer who learns a company is focused on a societal problem that he cares about will feel particular pride through his association with that company. Thus, *caring can help improve a stakeholder's perception of Usefulness.*

Study findings indicate that caring can also help maximize the Unity that is felt between stakeholders and a company. In that regard, Unity can blossom from addressing issues that a stakeholder cares about, signaling that the stakeholder and the company share the same values. Since CR can be seen as an expression of a company's soul, stakeholders use CR as a means to assess the extent to which the company's identity matches their own. This Unity (i.e., overlap of values) is much more likely to be sensed when CR tackles an issue that is of paramount importance to a stakeholder.

Studies on caring

There is considerable evidence in our research that caring influences the ways that stakeholders interpret and respond to CR. For example, caring strongly impacts how stakeholders build relationships with companies.

Consider the study involving the purchase of calculators, printers and computers.[6] We asked consumers about their sense of Unity under a variety of scenarios. In some scenarios, the company performed admirably (e.g., supports diversity, abolishes sweatshops), while in others the company was a poor CR performer (e.g., ended diversity programs, runs sweatshops). As part of the research, we also measured respondents' caring about the issue in their respective scenario. Results were quite telling:

- For respondents who *did not care* about the cause (i.e., diversity or sweatshops), there was only a modest advantage in terms of Unity for companies that performed well in their CR.
- In contrast, consumers who cared about the cause responded more strongly.
- Those who cared deeply about an issue in the negative scenario took this as a signal that the company shared no traits with them; and these respondents distanced themselves from the company considerably.

Thus, the effect of moving from a negative to a positive scenario with high caring individuals was much stronger than it was for the low caring individuals. In sum, *high caring individuals reward good behavior more and punish bad behavior more harshly than their low caring counterparts.*

Characteristics

Each of the company's stakeholders has a unique situation and personal history that determines their needs and colors the way they see the world. Thus, we find that the multi-faceted profile of an individual is often a strong influence on how he or she interprets and ultimately responds to CR. These traits, what we call characteristics, can range from *demographics* to *cultural* attributes of an individual. *Characteristics influence how stakeholders interpret and respond to CR because they are often closely associated with the needs and preferences of stakeholders.*

Demographics

The demographic segment to which a stakeholder belongs may have accepted norms of behavior and preferences that may lead to CR making a company a more or less attractive target for Unity. For example, *higher income* individuals and those with advanced levels of *education* are often drawn quite strongly to CR activity.

There is also evidence that *gender* plays a role in employee responses to CR. While many beliefs are essentially equivalent across gender, females are more likely than males to be actively involved in environmentally friendly behavior but score lower than men when asked whether technology can be used to solve ecological problems.[7]

Likewise, employees – who have a relationship based on a contractual agreement with the company – will look for different things from a company's CR than consumers do. And employees with a long *tenure* at a company are likely to develop a more nuanced Understanding of its CR than new employees.

Cultural differences

The studies also demonstrate a range of differences that correlate with the stakeholder's culture. Not surprisingly, some cultures believe more strongly than others that CR is appropriate for companies to engage in. Less obvious is the finding in one study that Unity and other outcomes depend on the degree to which a stakeholder has *acculturated* into American society.

Specifically, in the study of the oral care program, as discussed in Chapter 5, both physical and psychosocial Understanding changed as a result of participating in the program. But the influence of acculturation among participants in focus groups became especially apparent in the results. We asked Spanish-speaking parents living in the US about their Understanding of the company's CR and regarding dental hygiene. Interestingly, this change in Understanding was stronger among our *less* acculturated respondents, those who had immigrated more recently and who had not yet fully adapted to the values and norms of the US.

We found that as relative newcomers to the country, these respondents were eager to adopt beliefs and behaviors that enabled them to adapt to the host country. More acculturated individuals are less motivated to adopt new beliefs because they are already well established culturally.

We confirmed these qualitative observations in a follow-up survey of a separate sample of beneficiaries in the same program. Comparing the Understanding of participants against a control group (non-participants with the same demographic profile), the research showed that program participants had a better Understanding that good dental hygiene leads to both *functional* benefits (e.g., helps prevent

TABLE 6.1 *Examples of how context influences the process*

	Description	Example of the Influence of Context
Stakeholder Context		
Closeness	Stakeholder embeddedness in the organization.	Employees at headquarters feel closer to the company and respond positively to CR, while employees located in satellite offices can feel alienated and thus more skeptical of CR activity.
Caring	Stakeholder support of the societal issue addressed by CR programs.	Consumers feel more Unity with companies that address societal issues that they care about personally.
Characteristics	Demographic or psychographic profile of stakeholders.	Females are more likely than men to behave in environmentally friendly ways, but are less likely to favor the use of technology in addressing climate change issues.
Company Context		
CR	The type of CR program and the way it is communicated.	Consumers tend to prefer distinctive CR programs that differentiate the company from competitors.
Core business	Reputational perceptions of the company (e.g., product quality, CR positioning of brand).	Companies with high quality products gain a greater advantage from engaging in CR than companies with poor quality products; the latter companies are viewed with more skepticism.
Characteristics	Demographic profile of the company.	Small, local, and family owned businesses (respectively) are generally viewed more favorably than large multinationals.

cavities) and *identity-related* benefits (e.g., gives more self-confidence) for their children.

Digging deeper, though, we found that while both types of beliefs were substantially stronger among the whole participant group as a result of the program, the *improvement was significantly greater for the less acculturated respondents*. Thus, the level of Understanding that stems from a company's CR initiatives depends on the *social and cultural context* that the individual brings to their interpretation of CR.

Company context

Aspects of the CR environment pertaining to the company itself, the industry it belongs to, and the competitive arena in which it operates make up what we call the *company context*. Within this company context, some factors are critically important for managers to know about.

These factors fall into three basic categories:

- those pertaining to the CR itself,
- aspects of the company's core business, and
- key characteristics of the company.

Because stakeholders interpret and respond to CR based in part on how they make sense of it within the wider landscape – comprising the company and its competitors – CR value can develop in idiosyncratic ways.[8] As with stakeholder factors, managers need to adapt to the company context, fine-tuning CR strategy to maximize the desired outcomes.

How stakeholders interpret CR activity varies greatly depending on the characteristics of the programs themselves. *The difference between programs that generate Understanding, Usefulness, and Unity and those that do not can be largely chalked up to the type of CR program and the communication about such efforts.* CR type refers to characteristics of the CR initiative itself, while *communication* refers to the way in which stakeholders are told about the company's CR.

CR type

Stakeholders characterize the type of CR activity by weighing (1) how distinctive CR is, and (2) how closely it fits with what the company does.

Let us look at each of these briefly.

Distinctiveness

The distinctiveness of a company's programs – how innovative or unique they are – can set apart the company's CR activity from competitor's CR in much the same way that distinctive products can provide advantages when selling to customers.

Consider the example of Product(RED) which has been mentioned in Chapter 4. Product(RED) has gained widespread awareness and strong appeal thanks in large part to its innovative approach.

Such distinctive CR programs are likely to catch the attention of stakeholders more than their ordinary counterparts. *In an era where consumers and other stakeholders are increasingly bombarded with CR-oriented messages, novel programs "break through the clutter" more effectively than programs with which stakeholders are already familiar.*

Distinctive initiatives can also be highly effective in generating positive responses from stakeholders because they set the company apart as a pioneer. Moreover, distinctive programs are often given attention by the news media, adding to stakeholders' Understanding of CR.

The importance of "fit"

The second way that stakeholders characterize the *type* of CR activity is the degree to which initiatives "fit" with what the company does or stands for. *This fit refers to how much stakeholders perceive a link between the issue addressed through CR activity and the company's product line, brand image, position, and/or target market.*[9]

Examples of high fit programs are Home Depot working with Habitat for Humanity, or Revlon working with a group preventing domestic violence. In contrast, a Revlon homelessness program or a Home Depot domestic violence campaign would be considered low fit.[10]

A close fit reinforces people's perceptions of what the company stands for. In contrast, when fit is not obvious, stakeholders struggle to make sense of why the company is involved in the CR activity, attenuating their response.

In one recent study, researchers Becker-Olsen and colleagues[11] conducted an experiment that randomly presented respondents with high fit or low fit CR initiatives. (For example, they were told that Home Depot was running either a homelessness or domestic violence initiative.) Respondents were then asked for their thoughts about the program and the company. The researchers counted these thoughts and rated them in terms of their valence (i.e., positive–negative).

In the low-fit condition, respondents listed more thoughts related to the company's motives, and the thoughts were quite negative. In contrast, in the high-fit group people listed fewer thoughts; however, these were significantly more positive than comments from those who saw the low-fit pairing. In short, their findings demonstrate that fit contributes to stakeholders' Understanding of a company's CR efforts.

Communication

There is a second aspect of CR factors that will influence the relationships in our framework. That is, CR value is also impacted considerably by the *communication* of such efforts.

> Companies need to work harder and smarter to communicate their CR activities to key stakeholders so that Understanding, Usefulness, and Unity are fully realized.

This should be encouraging to managers, because how and where CR activity is communicated is something that is under managerial control for the most part. However, our experience shows that companies need to work harder and smarter to communicate their CR activities to key stakeholders so that Understanding, Usefulness, and Unity are fully realized.

Awareness is a critical ingredient in stakeholders' reactions to CR; a minimum amount of publicity is needed if value is to be maximized. Companies need to pass this threshold of awareness if they are to see any business or societal return on investment. However, more publicity is not always better.

Looking at the downside

Stakeholders are generally receptive to CR but are wary of companies that appear to be leveraging their CR opportunistically. Suspicion can become especially strong when the proportion of resources allocated to promoting CR reaches unacceptable levels relative to spending on the initiative itself.[12] Thus, whether communications are directed at internal audiences of employees or external audiences such as customers, *companies must be wary of over-promoting CR*; otherwise stakeholders will become mistrusting of the company and may even withdraw from an existing relationship.

Stakeholders evaluate not only the quantity but also the quality of communication, distinguishing between communication channels they see as more or less credible. Not surprisingly, the sources deemed most trustworthy for CR information tend to be third parties.

Publications such as *Business Ethics* or CR ratings by independent organizations (e.g., *Fortune*) that take a neutral stance on companies' CR status are perceived as credible sources of CR information. Of course, getting cooperation from the media can be highly challenging, which is why many companies rely on corporate advertising as a reliable – albeit expensive – means of getting their CR message out. Unfortunately, *company-generated communications do not engender the same trust as third-party sources since the company has a stake in the reactions of the audience.*

> Stakeholders can become resentful when initiatives are designed, executed, and promoted from the proverbial ivory tower.

Finally, along with quality and quantity of communication, the extent to which CR leads to desirable stakeholder responses depends on *whether the company communicates CR in a bottom-up way or as a top-down directive*. We find that the *top-down* approach can dilute the corporate benefits of even the most well-intentioned CR initiatives. The reason is that stakeholders (in particular employees) can become resentful when initiatives are designed, executed, and promoted from the proverbial ivory tower.

In contrast, we find that *a bottom-up approach encourages stakeholders to contribute to programs that are the most relevant for them personally*. The bottom-up approach asks for input on CR matters at every stage, resulting in an *ongoing dialogue with stakeholders* that will steer CR efforts on a path that is most consistent with the corporation's values.

As a result, stakeholders who are involved in shaping the initiatives feel that they are a part of CR rather than simply a target of a promotional campaign. This does not mean that top-management commitment to CR is dispensable. Executives need to lead by example and act as brokers to impart their company's CR philosophy to employees.

Core business

Stakeholder reactions to CR are dependent upon the core business of the company sponsoring such efforts. By core business, we mean not only the class and quality of products the company makes, but also its reputation in the marketplace. Both our own research and the work of others shows that stakeholders respond to CR based on two major facets of core business:

- the corporation's ability to make innovative and high quality products, and
- the market position of the company.

Firm market value study

Author CB Bhattacharya along with researcher Xueming Luo studied the influence of core business from a higher-level perspective. The study examined business value (measured in terms of stock market value) as a function of CR activity. They used secondary data from sources such as the Fortune 500 ratings and COMPUSTAT.

Largely consistent with other experimental findings, the effects of CR on business value depended substantially on other aspects of a company's core business (including product quality and market position).

Product quality

An aspect of core business, namely product quality, yielded some intriguing results in the study involving a technology company. In that experiment, subjects told us their intent to purchase computer printers after they read one of four randomly assigned blurbs about the company's CR activity and its product quality.

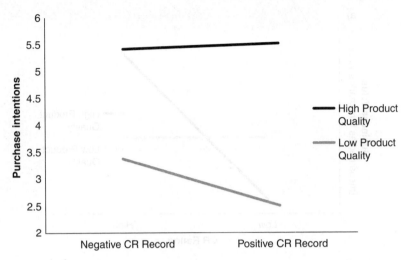

Figure 6.3 The influence of Product Quality on reactions to CR

For CR activity, subjects either read a description that the company had an excellent CR record (i.e., positive) or a very poor CR record (i.e., negative). For product quality, subjects read third-party ratings of the company's printers. (The company name was disguised so as not to influence the evaluations.)

Overall, subjects did not differ much in their responses to the negative versus positive CR activity condition. *Differences only became evident once the company's core business was factored in.* Analysis revealed that the impact of a company's CR on consumers' purchase intentions varied with product quality.

Figure 6.3 shows that when product quality was high, purchase intentions rose slightly based on the company's CR record (negative versus positive). However, *when product quality was low, consumers were actually less favorable towards the positive CR record company than the company with a negative record.*

The reason for this reaction is that these consumers perceived that the company was spending on CR rather than developing high quality products, *a trade-off they considered to be unacceptable.* This

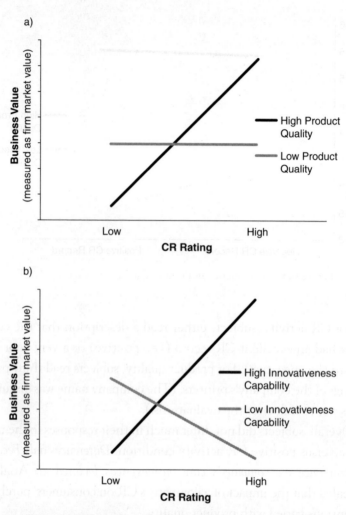

Figure 6.4 The influence of core business on business value

finding underscores a basic premise of this book: that stakeholders expect a company to "do good" and also to "do well" – not trade one for the other.

Similar findings have been documented at the market level as well. For example, in a study conducted by one of us (Bhattacharya) and Xueming Luo, as shown in Figure 6.4a, companies with high product quality saw significant improvements in business value as a result of their CR activity, while companies with low product quality saw little to no benefit. Similarly, CR *produced greater business value for companies with high innovativeness capacity than it did for their less innovative peers* (Figure 6.4b).[13]

The clear lesson from both these studies is that companies with high quality products and services have a lot to gain from engaging in CR, while companies with low quality products may be better off focusing on product development before engaging fully in CR.

> Companies with high product quality stand to gain more from CR than peers with low product quality.

Marketing strategy

The second aspect of core business is the marketing strategy of the company conducting CR, including its positioning and branding strategies and allied product, price, promotion and distribution strategies. Marketing strategy is important because as stakeholders learn about CR activity enacted by the company, they not only respond directly to it, but also attempt to place the behavior within their pre-existing notions of what the company does and what it stands for.

For instance, we find that a stakeholder's knowledge of a company's positioning strategy can have a substantial impact on their reaction to its CR. While a company's CR can, in general, draw stakeholders into enduring and resilient relationships with it, *the pull of CR is greatest for companies that do not just engage in CR but are actually positioned as CR brands.*

Why do CR brands have this built-in advantage?

- First, CR initiatives promoted by companies positioned on a social dimension are likely to gain extra awareness because they tend to

have more explicit and sustained communications regarding the activities.
- Second, when companies that are positioned on quality or other product/service dimensions engage in CR, stakeholders are more skeptical of the motives behind such actions (i.e., make more extrinsic attributions). On the other hand, CR-positioned companies engender little skepticism when they engage in such activity; in fact, it is entirely consistent with who they are and what they stand for.

Thus, by engaging in CR activity, CR brands present a coherent and consistent face to the world relative to non-CR brands. In the process, such brands attract a segment of consumers that care more about CR.

We tested this notion in our yogurt study. Recall that this survey compared consumer responses to three brands: Stonyfield (a CR-positioned brand), Dannon and Yoplait (non-CR positioned brands). We found that as a result of CR activity, Unity (measured as identification) was enhanced across the board. However, as shown in Figure 6.5, Stonyfield saw greater rewards in terms of customer loyalty and advocacy than either of its competitors, which were not positioned as CR brands (5 = high loyalty/advocacy).

In the case of Stonyfield, its CR activity is seen as integrated with the company's core business, thus revealing Stonyfield's essence or soul as a company. As a result, *consumers felt more Unity with Stonyfield, both in terms of trust in the brand and their identification with it.*

Company characteristics

Just as the characteristics of stakeholders matter in determining stakeholder responses to CR, so, too, do the characteristics of the company. Reputation, demographics and culture are such factors.

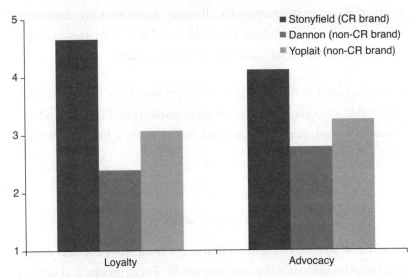

Figure 6.5 The influence of CR Positioning on reactions to CR

Reputation

One very important characteristic is *the company's reputation*. Companies with strong reputations will reap greater rewards from CR activity than those with poor reputations because stakeholders will carry goodwill into their evaluation of the CR.

Not only are stakeholders likely to be more aware of what companies with strong reputations are doing, but they are also more likely to make favorable attributions regarding such companies' CR actions, leading to a heightened sense of Unity.

On the other hand, companies with poor reputations or those belonging to industries that already breed some mistrust (e.g., oil, tobacco, and alcohol) often find that the effect of CR initiatives is dampened because many stakeholders cannot get beyond the cynical attributions they already hold. (This would, of course, be an example of a negative multiplier.)

There is a limit, however, to how much a prior reputation can help foster Understanding, Usefulness and Unity. Our research in the context of corporate–non-profit alliances shows that for companies with strong positive reputations, additional CR activities may not create much additional value due to ceiling effects.

> Stakeholder Understanding and Unity based on CR are more favorable for companies that are small rather than big, local rather than national, and family-owned rather than a big impersonal conglomerate.

Company size and demographics

In addition to the effects of reputation, a company's size and demographics also influence the response to CR. Focus groups and surveys we conducted as part of our research into yogurt consumers' responses to CR revealed clear positions. Namely, stakeholders are more likely to have a favorable Understanding and strong feelings of Unity when the company engaging in CR is *small* rather than big, *local* rather than national, and a *family-owned* operation rather than a big impersonal conglomerate or multinational. As one respondent put it:

> Recently many formerly socially responsible companies, such as Stonyfield Farms and Boca have been consumed by other multinational corporations, such as Dannon and General Foods. I feel that if the parent company is not socially responsible in all of their product lines, this strongly diminishes the validity of any gestures in their other product lines. Therefore, I do have mixed feelings about Stonyfield although I am very glad that they make it possible to get organic yogurt in a regular market.

Organizational culture

Finally, the culture of the organization can also contribute to the effects of CR. *Companies that pride themselves on a corporate culture of serving others – whether customers or society at large – stand to benefit more than competitors.*

In our study of frontline employee responses to CR, we found – as one would expect – that feelings of Unity increased as a function of perceptions that the company is socially responsible. Interestingly, however, this effect was *significantly stronger* for companies that had a *company-wide philosophy of customer service* and weaker for companies that took an "us against them" attitude towards customers.

This reaction is understandable because *customer-centric companies view CR as a natural extension of the company's commitment to helping others*. In contrast, CR engagement at otherwise internally focused companies arouses suspicion because it seems to be at odds with the internal orientation that is dominant in other aspects of the business.

Summary

We have argued throughout the book that managers need to do more than simply "do good." In this chapter we provided empirical evidence that the next steps in successful CR should not embrace a one-size-fits-all approach, which is likely to lead to missed opportunities. Rather, managers should look at the contextual factors that make the company's situation unique.

Consider some of these key points:

- If all things were equal, the psychological levers described in Chapter 5 (Understanding, Usefulness, Unity) would likely predict stakeholder reactions to a company's CR. However, the effect of these levers depends critically on the context. Some aspects of context can serve as "multipliers" by enhancing or detracting from other factors that influence stakeholder reactions. Therefore, managers need to understand how context impacts reactions.
- A stakeholder's closeness to the company – and to its CR – is a big factor in the degree of Understanding, Usefulness, and Unity the stakeholder perceives. Employees in remote locations, for instance, are less driven by these psychological levers, unless managers adjust their approach in order to interest and involve them.

- Caring about the chosen CR issue is a multiplier for most stakeholders and can help bridge the gap between work life and home life; conversely, not caring about the cause is likely to decrease involvement and the corresponding degree of benefit from the CR.
- Company context factors include the reputation of the company and how good a fit the CR initiative is with the core business. A company with a negative reputation is likely to have difficulty overcoming this obstacle as suspicions may arise about its motives for engaging in CR.
- Companies with an organizational culture of serving others have a built-in advantage compared to companies that stakeholders perceive as only interested in the bottom line.
- Stakeholders appreciate a bottom-up approach in which they are involved in and co-create CR, as opposed to only having directives come down from a corporate ivory tower. Innovative programs are also more likely to break through the clutter of information and capture the attention not only of stakeholders, but also of the media.
- A company is likely to be rewarded for its CR to the degree that it has its "house in order." A company that has low product quality but spends a lot of money on CR is likely to disappoint stakeholders who do not see this as an appropriate trade-off. Similarly, stakeholder reactions to CR activity are most favorable for companies that already have a history of success and innovation with their products and services.

The stakeholder-based CR management approach proposed in this book demands that managers be aware not only of whether CR favorably impacts the business and its varied constituents, but also of the conditions under which CR is likely to produce the most favorable results. Just as important, companies that do not adapt their efforts to the demands of the marketplace run the risk of their CR efforts seriously backfiring, damaging relationships with key stakeholders and harming corporate performance.

So far, we have delineated the value created by stakeholder reactions to CR actions, articulated the psychological engine that drives stakeholder reactions and produces such value from the CR inputs, and laid out both the stakeholder and company determinants of the success of CR.

Now it is time to discuss the *implications* of this framework. The next chapter will provide advice for managers on how to configure, implement, and evaluate CR activity.

Endnotes

1 Business Week video of Lisa Hamilton, UPS, available at http://feedroom.businessweek.com/index.jsp?fr_story=11323caab1c36773a1af66531340d7734edf30d9, accessed February 15, 2009.
2 S.G. Scott and V.R. Lane, "A Stakeholder Approach to Organizational Identity," *Academy of Management Review*, 25(1) (2000), 43–62; M. Granovetter, "Economic Action and Social Structure: the Problem of Embeddedness," *American Journal of Sociology*, 91(3) (1985), 481; H. Rao, G.F. Davis, and A. Ward, "Embeddedness, Social Identity and Mobility: Why Firms Leave the NASDAQ and Join the New York Stock Exchange," *Administrative Science Quarterly*, 45 (June) (2000), 268–92; for review, see, T. Dacin, M. Ventresca, and B. Beal, "The Embeddedness of Organizations: Dialogue and Direction," *Journal of Management*, 25 (1999), 317–56.
3 K. Faust, "Centrality in Affiliation Networks," *Social Networks*, 19 (1997), 157–91.
4 CB Bhattacharya and S. Sen, "Consumer–Company Identification: A Framework for Understanding Consumers' Relationships with Companies," *Journal of Marketing*, 67(2) (2003), 76–88.
5 C.K. Prahalad and V. Ramaswamy, "Co-opting Customer Competence," *Harvard Business Review*, 78(1) (2000), 79–88; S.L. Vargo and R.F. Lusch, "Evolving to a New Dominant Logic for Marketing," *Journal of Marketing*, 68(1) (2004), 1–17.
6 S. Sen and CB Bhattacharya, "Does Doing Good Always Lead to Doing Better? Consumer Reactions to Corporate Social Responsibility," *Journal of Marketing Research*, 38(2) (2001), 225–43.

7 W. Wehrmeyer and M. McNeil, "Activists, Pragmatists, Technophiles and Tree-huggers? Gender Differences in Employees' Environmental Attitudes," *Journal of Business Ethics*, 28(3) (2000), 211–22.
8 K. Basu and G. Palazzo, "Corporate Social Responsibility: A Process Model of Sensemaking," *Academy of Management Review*, 33(1) (Jan 2008), 122–36; A. Nijhof and R. Jeurissen, "Editorial: A Sensemaking Perspective on Corporate Social Responsibility: Introduction to the Special Issue," *Business Ethics: A European Review*, 15(4) (Oct 2006), 316–22.
9 K. Becker-Olsen, A. Cudmore, and R.P. Hill, "The Impact of Perceived Corporate Social Responsibility on Consumer Behavior," *Journal of Business Research*, 59 (2006), 46–53; R. Varadarajan and A. Menon, "Cause-Related Marketing: A Co-Alignment of Marketing Strategy and Corporate Philanthropy," *Journal of Marketing*, 52 (July) (1988), 58–74.
10 Example from Becker-Olsen, Cudmore, and Hill, "The Impact of Perceived Corporate Social Responsibility on Consumer Behavior."
11 Ibid.
12 Y. Yoon, Z. Gurhan-Canli, and N. Schwarz, "The Effect of Corporate Social Responsibility (CSR) Activities on Companies With Bad Reputations," *Journal of Consumer Psychology*, 16(4) (2006), 377–90.
13 CB Bhattacharya and X. Luo, "Corporate Social Responsibility, Customer Satisfaction and Market Value," *Journal of Marketing* 70(4) (2006), 1–18.

Further reading

David Vogel, *The Market for Virtue: The Potential and Limits of Corporate Social Responsibility* (Washington, DC: Brookings Institution Press, 2006).

Vogel argues that a market for virtue does exist but that it is limited by the high costs of responsible behavior.

Minu Hemmati, *Multi-Stakeholder Processes for Governance and Sustainability: Beyond Deadlock and Conflict* (London: Earthscan, 2002).

Hemmati explains how companies can use multi-stakeholder processes to solve complex issues and advance sustainable development.

Aron Cramer and Sebastian van der Vegt, *Raising the Bar: Creating Value with the United Nations Global Compact* (Sheffield: Greenleaf, 2004).

This book describes the United Nations Global Compact and what it means for companies to implement its principles.

PART III

Putting insight into action

Throughout this book, we have argued that CR value is derived in part by the stakeholder route, whereby stakeholders react to CR based on the information to which they are exposed. For this reason, we recommend that companies work hard to develop an appreciation of how stakeholders interpret and ultimately respond to CR activity. In Part I we described the link between CR activity and stakeholder responses to CR (i.e., CR value); and in Part II we outlined the psychology behind such responses.

But what is a company to do with these insights? In this part, we discuss the implications of our approach. We do this by highlighting three ways that companies can maximize CR value and maintain this value over the long term.

To that end, Chapter 7 shows how companies can empower stakeholders so that they become co-creators of CR – a process that draws them closer to the activities for better Understanding, ensures that programs are optimally Useful, and enhances Unity, the stakeholders' sense that the company shares their values. Chapter 8 articulates the important role of communication; that is, how companies can get their message out in ways that draw stakeholders closer to the company. Chapter 9 provides guidance on how to quantify key components in our framework and discover linkages between them so that companies can calibrate CR activities on a long-term basis. Chapter 10 empirically validates the framework. Finally, in Chapter 11 we look ahead and outline a few key areas that merit further investigation for companies wishing to leverage CR's potential fully.

PART III

Putting insight into action

SEVEN

Co-creating CR strategy

Co-creating CR initiatives: Some background

In Chapter 5, the discussion focused on the importance of Usefulness, Understanding, and Unity as psychological levers that drive stakeholder reactions to CR; then Chapter 6 elaborated on closeness and other key stakeholder variables that help yield and magnify the desired CR outcomes. It is not a given, after all, that the outcome is always positive, as some variables can magnify a negative reaction, such as when a stakeholder feels cut off from the core of the company. This chapter, therefore, takes the next critical step, examining how to enhance Usefulness and Understanding and achieve a sense of Unity, with a special eye to *involving stakeholders in the process of co-creating a company's CR initiatives to maximize the benefit to all.*

> In spite of the stakeholder involvement rhetoric, most companies continue to develop, implement, and manage their CR as an essentially top-down process.

In today's environment, there is demand for co-creation. Our research, presented in the following pages, shows quite convincingly that both employees and consumers are not content to be passive recipients or even "enablers" of the program. They want to be "enactors" who are actively engaged in co-creating CR initiatives with company personnel. Through co-creation, stakeholders become part of the solution, thereby reducing the gap between their expectations and the firm's response.

Co-creation is not a new idea. As thinking on CR has evolved over recent years, meaningful stakeholder engagement has become one of the driving forces guiding CR action. Much has been said about why and how different stakeholder groups must come together in the design and implementation of CR for it really to achieve its goals, both through process and outcome.[1] And more and more companies are taking a multi-stakeholder approach in their CR.

For instance, Telefónica has been exploring various ways, such as online discussions on specific topics, to engage in ongoing, two-way dialog with the stakeholders most relevant to their business. This type of ongoing communication allows the company to respond directly to stakeholder interests when developing strategy.[2]

Similarly, according to the Indian company, Godrej: "co-creation and collaboration are sometimes essential to make CR activity more meaningful and participative. We follow a partnership approach so that a wider set of relevant stakeholders are involved. This ensures that implementation is done effectively and with a wider outreach."[3]

Yet, most of this discussion and action has centered on the need to engage the diverse sectors of society – particularly NGOs, the government, the media, and other civil society groups. Less has been said and done about *engaging the company's primary stakeholders, such as employees and consumers*.

In other words, in the rush to do CR right, and in the hope of gaining social legitimacy as a consequence, many a company seems to have reached out to get the ears of a wider set of stakeholders while not paying a lot of attention to how deeply it can – and, in fact, needs to – connect with its fewer but more proximal and significant stakeholder groups. For instance, a mere glimpse of CR in the employee domain reveals a clear chasm between the sense of the company from the viewpoint of the senior management and the feelings of its employees regarding the appropriate source and ownership of its CR.

Our research findings show that in spite of the stakeholder involvement rhetoric, most companies continue to develop, implement, and manage their CR as an essentially top-down process. In other words, it is senior management that decides what causes/issues to support and how. As one of our in-depth interview respondents (a female in the Toys and Sporting Goods industry, located at the company headquarters) put it:

> As I said, every CEO we've had for the past couple of years has had a focus in the community and has made the company sort of take it on. The two CEOs and the one before that were into blood drives. So what is one of the things that we had to do on every one of our sites? Blood drives!

In other words, while the stakeholder-psychology approach to CR points to greater ownership of a company's CR initiatives by its most important stakeholders, both anecdotal evidence and our own research reveal that more often than not, this is far from the case. Employees, in fact, are typically passive executors of top management's CR decisions. Importantly, however, at the same time this research shows that employees yearn to play a greater leadership role in their employers' CR initiatives; as co-creators of market value, they also want to be co-creators of CR value.

In a recent study produced by the Wharton School and the UN Global Compact concerning CR ownership, 71% of the 400 companies surveyed indicated that their CR policies and practices were developed and managed at the CEO level, 57% at the Board of Directors level, and 56% at the senior management level. (The UN Global Compact, "UN Global Compact Annual Review" (2007), 10, available at http://www.unglobalcompact.org/docs/news_events/8.1/GCAnnualReview2007.pdf, accessed August 4, 2011).

While surveying worldwide employees of a multinational corporation, we found that 80 percent of its employees the world over deemed it important that the company provided them with opportunities to participate in their CR programs. In the words of a focus group respondent:

> If we are looking to energize employees... there's going to be a natural tendency to say, "we're going to empower you through charitable giving in some capacity." I have half dozen organizations that I work with, and I'd love to be able to extend that reach through [the company].

Thus, matching gift programs, where the company matches employee charitable donations dollar-for-dollar, are popular with employees because they give the individual the freedom to decide which charity to support yet also leverage the resources available through the company. Employees are very responsive to this sort of effort because it demonstrates in very clear terms that the company's values match their own.

In reality, however, besides the example of matching gifts, it is more common that companies and employees – who comprise one of their most immediate and important stakeholder groups – often don't see eye-to-eye on who really is making the difference through CR. *Most of the power is held by the company, leaving many of the employees feeling unempowered, unmotivated, and sometimes even disenchanted and disengaged.*

> Employees yearn to play a greater leadership role in their employers' CR initiatives.

Analogously, in the *consumer* context, recent research by Rosen, Irmak, and Jayachandran makes this same point. When consumers are able to choose the cause in a cause-related marketing campaign, they perceive higher co-creation of value, which in turn enhances their purchase intentions.[4] Interestingly, the ability to co-create value with the company even mitigates the negative impact that other contingent factors (described in Chapter 6), such as low support for the cause or low perceived fit between the company and the cause, would otherwise have on consumers' purchase intentions. These authors see a need for further research that examines other means by which consumers' perceptions of value co-creation can be enhanced. Specifically, *getting consumers involved* in more complex aspects of program design can achieve this goal.

Getting the needed involvement

What do companies need to strive for, then, to ensure that their employees and customers participate in their CR initiatives in a way that maximizes the 3 U's of Understanding, Usefulness and Unity? Going back to our discussion of closeness in Chapter 6, the answer lies at least partly in companies *involving their stakeholders in a manner that embeds them within the social folds of the company.*

In other words, the company needs to ensure that its two closest stakeholder groups – consumers and employees – as well as colleagues responsible for CR management all participate in such a way that brings them closer to the center of the social network embodied by the company.

> When consumers are able to choose the cause in a CR initiative, they perceive higher co-creation of value, which enhances Usefulness.

As mentioned in the beginning of this chapter, involving and embedding employees and consumers is best achieved through the *co-creation* of the company's CR strategy and actions. Consistent with the individual-level approach that this book takes, marketing researchers Prahalad and Ramaswamy say that "the co-creation experience depends highly on individuals. Each person's uniqueness affects the co-creation process as well as the co-creation experience. *A firm cannot create anything of value without the engagement of individuals.*"[5]

Thus, our recommended approach for formulating and implementing CR initiatives diverges significantly from approaches that generate potential CR programs mainly through internal discussion and debate among a handful of employees or managers. Instead, the co-creation-oriented, stakeholder-centric approach initiates *dialog* with stakeholders and *incorporates representative stakeholder input as early as possible into the formulation process*.

In this way, companies can not only work on creating additional value for stakeholders through the co-creation process itself, but also can be assured that a full range of relevant programs and issues are considered. Then, whatever is ultimately chosen has been in part created by the relevant stakeholder groups.

Managers should also be aware that an unavoidable consequence of bringing in diverse stakeholder perspectives while formulating CR strategy is the introduction of a multiplicity of responses, which can lead to conflict. However, such conflict can often be constructive and lead to superior solutions. As Svendsen and Laberge note in their co-creative model of stakeholder engagement, when companies and stakeholders recognize that *interdependence* is required for sustainable outcomes, they are motivated to overcome competing perspectives and needs in order to make innovation possible.[6] For example, Scandic, a Swedish hotel chain, co-created such a solution when it invested $150,000 to engage employee participation by showing them how to save water, energy, and waste.[7]

Four steps to successful CR formulation

The next section focuses on four key steps – *articulation, generation, distillation,* and *selection* – that we recommend for formulating

CR programs. While articulation and distillation are more reliant on managerial input, generation and selection actively engage key stakeholders.

Articulation

We have argued in this book that companies need to tailor their CR strategy to their situation. Since every company has a unique set of circumstances under which it operates, the objectives of CR may differ substantially across and even within industries. In fact, views may even differ across colleagues responsible for CR within a particular company. That is why managers need to articulate exactly what the goals of CR are for that company, given its unique situation.

Indeed, in a 2008 survey of 238 executives, McKinsey[8] found variability in how respondents viewed CR as benefiting their company. For example:

- The majority saw CR as a way to improve the company's reputation in the marketplace.
- Some, however, expected CR to help them attract, motivate and retain talented employees.
- Others viewed CR as a means to reduce the cost of capital.

Thus, the first and arguably *most critical task* for those engaged in formulating CR strategy is *determining the kind of CR value that needs to be created* and *formally articulating the objectives* of CR activity in a particular instance. Only after that can CR managers determine the most appropriate stakeholder groups to target for involvement.

It is extremely difficult to determine the means to achieve CR value unless the ends are clear. CR strategy may differ substantially based on the desired goal; for example, *the goal of enhancing corporate reputation and brand equity requires a much broader stakeholder focus than the goal of attracting and retaining employees.*

Whatever the goal, the company's motivation for exploring CR activity to produce value must be articulated and justified in such a way that creates executive "buy-in." There are two main reasons why articulation and buy-in are important:

1) Initial support from corporate leadership is needed to procure the necessary resources that must be invested in these activities.
2) Ongoing support is needed to insure that the CR strategy can be implemented and sustained long enough to obtain results.

A valuable way to better co-create CR goals with fellow employees (as well as to get broad-based internal buy-in) is to build shared understanding among colleagues by *learning from knowledgeable others in the business*. Consider Aramark, a leading provider of food services, facilities management, and uniforms. In 2006, executives at the company reviewed their CR activity finding that while substantial and beneficial, the fragmented nature of its efforts was wasting potential opportunities to create CR value. In their bid to revamp their CR strategy, company executives reviewed archives and research studies at the Center for Corporate Citizenship at Boston College, attended conferences and classes, and learned about best practices and execution challenges by meeting with various executives from companies such as Starbucks, Verizon, and Reebok who had launched successful CR initiatives.[9]

> A critical task for those engaged in formulating CR strategy is determining the objectives of CR activity.

Managers need to decide on the primary objectives of their programs. Then, in light of the objectives of the CR activity, managers can take the next step: determining which stakeholder groups are most attractive to target to achieve those aims. For example, after all their research and internal brainstorming, the Aramark team settled on two primary objectives for its CR. First, it wanted CR to strengthen bonds with employees. Second, the company wanted to improve its reputation among opinion leaders in local communities. Based on these twin objectives, Aramark finally decided on (i.e., selected) a signature program called Aramark Building Community, which was designed to be highly Useful to these two groups (i.e., employees, community opinion leaders).

Generation

How do ideas get generated for CR projects? While many CR initiatives have come from CEOs, Boards of Directors, or upper management levels, the reality is this: The world is moving towards an "involve me" culture in which stakeholders want to partner with organizations.[10] By creating a participative culture, the gap between stakeholder expectations and company actions can be lessened or eliminated. Stakeholders themselves then become part of the solution.

In the spirit of co-creating CR solutions with relevant stakeholder groups, we recommend following this sequence; namely that:

1) once the objectives have been decided, and
2) the relevant stakeholders identified, then
3) companies should engage and interact with members of those stakeholder groups to generate a portfolio of CR initiatives that are in line with the objectives.

> The benefits of a particular CR program can differ greatly among stakeholders, even within a particular stakeholder group.

Engaging individual stakeholders

To take one example, PepsiCo uses its Pepsi-Refresh project to engage its stakeholders. Individuals, NGOs and social businesses can upload proposals online. Site visitors vote for their favorites. The winners receive grants in the amount of $5,000 to $250,000. Overall, PepsiCo grants more than $1,000,000 per month.

The need for dialoging with multiple individuals is critical because research shows that individuals are often not alike, even within a particular stakeholder group. For example, we find that benefits of a particular CR program can differ greatly among employees of the same company. While some employees may look to CR to fulfill a need to feel closer to others at the company, other employees may view the same CR program as an opportunity to learn new skills.[11]

Being able to match the underlying psychological needs fulfilled via specific CR initiatives at the individual level is very important. It greatly enhances (a) the ability to focus on those segments most likely to be receptive to particular initiatives, and/or (b) the ability to market the programs differentially to different segments, thereby greatly enhancing the chances of the 3 U's being maximized.

Many companies do not go the distance in this regard. For example, though PNC Bank surveyed its employees to find out that early childhood education was a cause that resonated with many employees, they did not dig deep enough into the specific psychological benefits that different employees derived from participating in the program. It is possible that engaging in such an exercise would have produced a program that encouraged greater employee participation compared to the "Grow Up Great" program.

An important question when it comes to generating ideas for CR programs is: How do companies go about co-creating CR programs that make use of the three psychological levers of the framework?

To accomplish this goal, the program needs to 1) help stakeholders develop greater Understanding, 2) make it likely that stakeholders find it personally Useful, and 3) engage stakeholders enough for them to perceive stronger Unity with the company. Some additional answers lie not only in having stakeholders be part of the process of generating ideas, but also in how managers go about soliciting that input and probing for more detail.

Marketers have long been concerned with tapping into the mind of consumers in order to match product features with their consumer benefits. Taking that idea further, the simplest technique to adapt from marketing research is to conduct qualitative research with key stakeholders. The purpose of such research is to uncover material issues of interest to them and thereby generate ideas.

For example, research firms conduct semi-structured interviews with representatives of stakeholder groups specified by the client. As these questions are typically qualitative rather than quantitative, and because of the nature of the subject, discussions often range freely. As a result, a range of issues emerge, which are often presented to the client in the form of a materiality matrix. (This kind of matrix is discussed further below.) Such a process generates ideas and choices that might not have come from a strictly top-down approach. And the stakeholders tend to feel more involved.

Laddering

Although simply asking stakeholders about which CR issues they believe the company ought to be involved in is a possible approach, digging deeper produces better results. For instance, one of the fundamental ways by which benefits are linked to features in the product context is a technique called "laddering." Laddering goes deeper than simply asking which features are most important to consumers. In this technique, the researcher identifies key product features and keeps probing the respondent to articulate the *functional* and *psychosocial benefits* that the features provide and finally the *values* these benefits help fulfill.

However, this product-focused method is just a starting point. We suggest that in contrast to this question-and-answer technique – and similar to an approach suggested by Jeffrey Durgee in his book

Creative Insight[12] – it is more effective to engage the stakeholder through *interactive dialog*. Such dialog leads naturally to being able to "ladder down" from the general CR context, values, needs, and benefits to the specific kinds of CR initiatives these stakeholders feel would help fulfill those needs.

Keeping in mind that the co-creation process itself ought to be of value, at the outset it is helpful to "warm up" stakeholder participants and make them feel like partners by assessing the broader psychological context in which they evaluate CR. This process might entail asking about:

- their views of CR in general,
- their views of CR within the industry and within the focal company,
- their expectations of the company,
- the attributions they make about the company's current actions, and
- the rewards stakeholders provide to companies they deem socially responsible.

Broadly speaking, this initial phase provides an opportunity to get stakeholder input before delving deeper into the psychological process; that is, the 3 U's that comprise the basic framework of the approach this book takes on enhancing CR value. Once the general context has been assessed, researchers can probe stakeholders about the kinds of psychosocial and identity-related needs they are looking to fulfill and the benefits they are looking to receive from CR initiatives of the given company. These typically include benefits to the self (i.e., both how individuals relate to others and how they view themselves) as well as benefits to society.

Discussion of our research in previous chapters revealed two main psychological benefits related to a sense of oneself – benefits that being affiliated with a socially responsible company can provide to a stakeholder – namely: self-esteem and self-coherence. CR can enhance both.

How do these kinds of benefits come about?

First, CR *can improve a person's perception of self-worth, through his or her association with the company.* For example, it is quite common to hear stakeholders claim that buying from a socially responsible company makes them feel good, or that they have great pride in working for a good corporate citizen.

Second, CR can *bring greater coherence to a stakeholder's life by making interactions with the company a natural expression of how they see themselves.* For example, someone who feels that it is important to help the homeless may find it extremely fulfilling to associate with a company that addresses this through their CR. Then, by continually reinforcing who they are, each interaction with the company provides the stakeholder with a sense of self-coherence and continuity with their values between the sometimes-conflicting realms of work and home life.

Having determined the *psychosocial and identity-related benefits* desired by stakeholders, what direction does a marketer or manager take next? Laddering down from these benefits, the next step is to establish the *functional* benefits that would be received by the direct beneficiaries of the program. Functional benefits are those that improve the stakeholder's well-being in tangible ways. For example, "better oral hygiene" is a functional benefit received by the participants of the previously discussed oral care program. Similarly, improved "school readiness" is a tangible benefit received by participating children in the PNC Bank's "Grow Up Great" campaign.

But functional benefits can occur in surprising ways. In our studies of employees, for example, people often indicated that they picked up management skills and other valuable work-related skills through participation in CR programs – a considerable functional benefit. By taking leadership of a volunteer initiative, for instance, employees can learn how to supervise others. Thus, participating in CR activity can become a training ground for some stakeholders.

Note that even very *different functional benefits* that a CR initiative provides often also lead to satisfying *very similar psychosocial benefits* and values, because most if not all individuals aspire to achieve these self-related benefits in their lives. In that sense, the higher order psychosocial benefits and values will be more likely to supersede any single stakeholder role or functional benefit because they are related to more universal human needs. (See Exhibit 7.1 at the end of this chapter for an example of psychosocial and functional benefits in the context of the oral care program.)

In sum, managers and researchers can best determine how to co-create CR initiatives with specific stakeholder groups by first uncovering the psychosocial and identity needs these stakeholders are looking to fulfill. The next steps involve progressively starting to "ladder-down" or do "reverse laddering" from such psychosocial needs to uncover the *functional* benefits of such a program. In this way, by understanding how to help stakeholders enhance their sense of self, managers have a firmer footing for coming up with a successful initiative. And then – finally, rather than initially – it is essential to get respondents to discuss which types of programs would deliver these benefits.

Once some skeletal programs have been articulated, interviewers can also "ladder up" from the proposed initiatives to the benefits. This process of laddering up and down the chain between features and benefits will generate a set of possible initiatives and vastly improve managers' understanding of how stakeholders stand to gain from the company's CR activities.

Distillation

Having generated a set of CR initiatives collectively with stakeholders, managers need to "distill" or prioritize these initiatives in line with the core competencies of the company and identify what the company is able to deliver best. In other words, even the best CR initiative will be a wasted effort if the company is hindered in implementing it. For example, in the PNC Bank "Grow Up Great" case, employees had to obtain clearance certificates from state authorities in order to volunteer and teach pre-school children, which proved to be a possible drag on the volunteering rates.

> While articulation and distillation are more reliant on managerial input, generation and selection actively engage key stakeholders.

A practical approach at this distillation phase is to create a "materiality matrix" in which CR initiatives can be plotted in terms of two dimensions:

- the importance or attractiveness to stakeholders, and
- the importance to the company in terms of the likely influence of the initiative(s) on business success.

In an effort to avoid the kind of problem suggested by the PNC Bank program, AT&T views the latter dimension as a composite of two criteria: not only the importance of the CR issue to the company, but also the company's *ability* to act on the issue in a meaningful way.

Similarly, the consulting company AccountAbility refers to the two key dimensions of the materiality matrix as external (i.e., reflecting stakeholder priorities) and internal (i.e., reflecting company priorities).[13] Although this is a simple and elegant classification, it reveals an underlying problem: Companies need to remember that employees are not really "external" to the company. And of course, that is the whole point of improving the feeling of closeness and involvement for this group of stakeholders.

Overall, the distillation phase filters the co-created set of alternatives from the generation phase to a reduced set that can be implemented successfully by the company.

Selection

In the final selection stage, managers need to select the signature initiative with which to go forward, as well as identify the specific stakeholder segments to target. After all, certain segments may find certain initiatives to be more Useful (e.g., because they care more about the issue), have better levels of Understanding about a particular initiative (e.g., because they make more intrinsic attributions) and/or provide higher levels of Unity with the company (e.g., because they perceive a stronger identity overlap). All of these factors would be helpful for managers to explore before selecting and implementing a particular initiative.

Creating partnerships

A key co-creation partner in the selection stage is the non-profit firm (or sometimes multiple firms) that will implement the initiative. As a result of going through the aforementioned steps of articulation, generation, and distillation, managers should have a reasonably good idea of the broad parameters of the kind of initiative they want to select and implement. Companies and NGOs need to find "common ground" that entails a number of steps from building new operating standards to building long-term partnerships based on co-creation, whereby the company becomes a key part of the NGOs' ability to deliver value and vice versa. As Brugmann and Prahalad note, such co-creation ventures deliver a lot of benefits to both parties, not the least of which is *added social legitimacy for the for-profit and expanded market impact for the non-profit.*[14]

In order to select an initiative from among alternatives, the "development team" (comprising both company and NGO representatives) can think of a CR initiative as a bundle of features such as:

- the cause (e.g., school readiness, dental hygiene, AIDS),
- the implementation of the cause (e.g., cause-marketing program, volunteering),
- proposed non-profit partners, and
- the proposed type and level of stakeholder engagement.

Once the short-listed programs are described, with the underlying features that create CR initiative "concepts," it is time to target the stakeholder groups to be brought into the co-creation process. These stakeholders then would help to identify the most attractive program. This is typically accomplished through quantitative marketing research.

Creating experiments and looking at research results

Exhibit 7.2 (at the end of this chapter) provides examples of concept initiatives we have created and tested with consumers as part of our research program. (Note that for a variety of reasons, the company may or may not want to reveal its name at this point, but instead choose to describe its identity in terms of the products and services it provides.)

To gauge the relative attractiveness of competing CR initiative concepts, one method is to draw equivalent random samples from pre-defined stakeholder target groups (e.g., managerial employees who have been with the company from five to fifteen years) and show one particular concept to each sample. In technical parlance, this kind of study is called a "quasi-experiment" with a "between-subjects design."

It is good practice also to have a "control group" who won't see a CR concept, but will respond to questions on company reputation, brand loyalty, etc., that can provide a "baseline" comparison point to establish whether the proposed CR initiatives are likely to create any business value. Companies will typically have access to employee information electronically, and the availability of Internet panels (e.g., Zoominfo) has also made it convenient for such research in the customer sphere to be conducted online.

Once stakeholders have been exposed to a concept, the next step is to seek their reactions. This is achieved by asking a variety of follow-up questions that essentially pertain to the constructs of the model presented in Chapter 5 – based on the 3 U's.

To elaborate, there should be questions on:

(1) *psychological aspects*, such as attributions, perceived effectiveness, likely engagement, functional and psychosocial needs likely to be fulfilled by the program, including trust and identification;
(2) *outcome measures*, such as corporate reputation, brand/company loyalty, advocacy; and
(3) a variety of relevant *stakeholder characteristics*, such as demographics, level of caring for the issue, and perceived fit between the company and the cause.

More details of the specific questions to ask in this exercise will be provided in the Calibration Chapter (Chapter 9).

Interpreting the results of this experiment is a key step in the selection process. Although overall attractiveness of each CR initiative is an important yardstick, managers may benefit from looking at segment-specific responses (i.e., broken out by demographic and psychographic characteristics). For example, older consumers tend to care more about Alzheimer's, whereas younger ones care more about AIDS. Researchers can create a matrix of initiative by segment to understand better whether different initiatives are preferred by different segments in the market. If this is the case, managers will need to decide which initiative/segment combination to move ahead with for their program.

Finally, pilot-testing the CR initiative before launching it full scale is a great idea. Often, a variety of problems only surface when the initiative is actually launched. Keeping this in mind, Aramark piloted the "Aramark Building Community" initiative in three markets – Houston, Chicago, and Philadelphia. The goal was to acquaint themselves better with their partner "Neighborhood Centers Inc." (NCI) and learn about mutual strengths and weaknesses. Only after completing two successful projects and with plans for future collaborations underway, was the Aramark–NCI partnership publicly announced.

The pilot enabled Aramark to learn that each local relationship is unique and "just because something worked well in Houston did not guarantee that it would work the same way in Chicago or Philadelphia."[15] Going forward, the Aramark Building Community team adopted a *flexible approach in each market* and agreed that although program activities might look different at the market level, the underlying mission would unite stakeholders around the globe.

Overall, the formulation phase seeks to engage stakeholders and co-create CR initiatives that are both desired by stakeholders as well as attractive to the company in terms of likely social and business value. Once managers have identified the initiatives with which they want to forge ahead, they must implement them in a way that maintains and maximizes the 3 U's over the long term. We turn to implementation now.

Implementation

One of the most important lessons to emerge from our research is the need for companies to put their employees and even consumers at the *center* of their CR efforts, empowering them as co-creators of effective CR strategies. This means that it is not sufficient to engage these stakeholders in the formulation of the CR strategy. Companies need to follow through to the implementation stage by ensuring that these groups are actually the primary enactors of CR, bearing primary responsibility in the execution of the CR strategy as well.

Based on both our research and our conversations with companies, we have identified three factors that drive the success of the CR implementation strategy. These are (1) whether the stakeholder is an enactor or merely an enabler, (2) whether the connection with others in the company and its program is primarily horizontal or vertical, and (3) whether management keeps the process of evaluating the program Formal or Informal.

Enactor versus enabler

CR is a top-down rather than a co-created endeavor in most companies because the former approach is easier. Such an approach may provide efficiencies in terms of visibility and scope, but the research suggests that it will not only end up disaffecting key stakeholders but also miss out on creating additional value for companies because participants would derive social and psychological value from the co-creation experience.

How, then, might a company implement a co-created approach to CR instead? Let's look at different contexts for the answers.

In the employee context, for instance, to have CR be truly effective, companies need to *make their employees the primary enactors in social responsibility programs*. Employees see themselves as closer to their community than company executives and therefore feel more qualified to implement CR at the ground level.

Importantly, shifting the primary responsibility for their CR programs to employees does not absolve the company of its responsibility to be an effective enabler. For a truly successful, co-created CR experience, a company must support the employees' efforts in several specific ways.

- First, the company must maintain clear, open, continuous, two-way communication with its employees in the CR domain, facilitating the interchange of ideas both vertically and horizontally (across employee groups).
- Second, and more generally, the company must provide the requisite guidance and resources to its employees so that they are able to implement their CR plans effectively. This includes going beyond merely allowing CR involvement on company time

to – ideally – working with employee groups to help them fully integrate their CR efforts into a coherent, complete job-product.

Needless to say, such enabling presupposes the company's provision of adequate financial and material resources to allow employees to make a difference in their chosen CR domain.

> Companies need to make their employees the primary enactors in CR programs.

Corporate social marketing initiatives[16] are particularly attractive from this perspective because in their synergy with the company's core competencies, they represent a win-win strategy. Not only do they allow the company to reap returns from its CR investment through its employees, but they also provide returns to the stakeholder group that is the target of the CR effort.

Finally, companies interested in a co-created CR experience must also recognize and reward employees for their CR successes in ways that are not extraneous to but rather fully integrated with the reward structure implicit in their job-products. For instance, Shell bases employee bonuses on individual and corporate performance. Environmental and social aspects make up 20 percent of how employee performance is measured.

Consumers are also an important group in this regard. Although they are not as close to the company as employees, many of the above guidelines apply to the consumer realm as well. To maximize the co-creation experience, companies should also *communicate* clearly with consumers, *offer guidelines* for implementation, and *reward* them appropriately. For instance, Disney recently launched the program "Give a Day. Get a Disney Day." In this program, consumers can volunteer a day of service at a participating organization and then (contingent on that service being completed and verified), they would receive free admission to a Disney theme park for a day.

Additionally, researchers Schau, Muniz, and Arnould propose a set of twelve practices that help co-create value for brand community members.[17] Many of these practices would enhance the consumer co-creation experience in the CR context as well. These practices fall into four major categories: (1) social networking, (2) impression management, (3) community engagement, and (4) brand use. While an exhaustive description of these practices is beyond the scope of this book, a few illustrative examples make the point clear.

For instance, "badging" and "documenting" are two ways of solidifying community engagement. Continuing the Disney example above, Disney might think of creating T-shirts or other visible symbols to "badge" those consumers who have volunteered ten, twenty-five, or fifty days of their time.

Similarly, consumers could be encouraged to keep blogs or post updates on social networking sites such as Facebook or Twitter to "document" their volunteering experience and share stories with other similar people. By making consumers feel more like enactors and satisfying higher order needs such as self-continuity and self-esteem, the astute manager can employ such practices to intensify the feeling of Usefulness among consumers, and in turn strengthen Unity.

Horizontal versus vertical

Implementation of CR needs to happen horizontally, not vertically, and in a way that not only empowers consumers and employees to be the enactors, but also *connects them to each other* in meaningful ways. This practice helps create a "community of virtue."

Embedding stakeholders in the company network means not just bringing them closer to the company, but also connecting them to others who are important/central members of the network. In other words, by definition, networks are comprised of people, and embedding involves bringing stakeholders into the company network, helping them create strong, enduring, and meaningful ties with other network members.

Such connections over time transcend the company to spill over to other realms of the stakeholder's life, providing the coherence and integration that many crave, creating a thread running throughout their personal, professional, and social lives. This is why, based on their brand community work, Schau and her colleagues conclude that "value is manifest in the collective enactment of practices, which favor investments in networks rather than firm-consumer dyads."[18]

What better way to create such value than by having these connections and networks be based on a common, higher purpose? CR provides just that: mutuality of purpose and intent among all stakeholders. It helps create "social capital" – which is generally viewed as the glue that facilitates collective action and helps create a successful community of virtue.

Social capital can broadly be described in terms of the trust, mutual understanding and shared values and behaviors that bind members of human networks and communities and make cooperative action possible.[19] Specifically, such social capital created in communities of virtue increases willingness of community members to share information, follow group norms and rules, put the collective purpose ahead of self-interests, cooperate on joint projects, and help others reach their goals.

> CR creates "social capital" – which is generally viewed as the glue that facilitates collective action and helps create a successful community of virtue.

An interesting example of such a network is the Earthkeepers community started by Timberland. Earthkeepers encourages all of us to "learn," "connect," and "act." In the true spirit of co-creation, Timberland says:

We'll be incorporating your feedback as we develop Timberland's CSR strategy. We'll begin by asking a question that corresponds with one of our four CSR pillars: energy, product, workplace, and service. We hope you'll join the conversation by posing questions and comments and providing suggestions for how to approach opportunities and challenges. Let your voice be heard – join the conversation…

Building on the brand community literature, we assert that practices such as "welcoming" new members and "empathizing" with fellow members help solidify such horizontal network connections and promote cooperative behaviors.[20] Embedding stakeholders within such communities not only creates social value, but also enhances their Understanding of the company's actions and strengthens Unity with the company, in turn creating business value via pro-company behaviors.

Formal versus informal

Informality has been a trend in many ways as businesses look outside the box and seek innovative solutions. For example, these comments suggest that giving power to employees can be successful, and their approach seems to have an informal flavor:

> What if we gave a little power to the employees, hey, if you can find savings in one area of the company, we'll contribute it to your favorite cause or do something that saves us money and makes us more productive. I think retention is a big thing. When you have happy people they want to stay. I'm not saying if you gave to my favorite charity or we did Habitat for Humanity that I would feel like I wanted to stay for ten more years. But I would go home at night and I would sit down with my family and say "You know what? I had a great day at work today and I don't feel like killing someone." That maybe is not measurable in percentage points, but it's measurable (return on investment), if you get up the next morning at 5:30 and get on email and you're not angry that [company X] is eating into your personal time, because now in your personal time you're doing something that is also part of [company X].

Yet, while it is easier for companies to let the stakeholder co-creation process be informal, as the above quote exemplifies, formal processes can often foster more effective co-creation among employees. Research findings corroborate this:

- Overall, our research suggests that companies should put specific systems in place. These include organizational monitoring, evaluation, and reward systems. These allow for co-creative implementation to happen effectively in both the employee and consumer realms.
- Other researchers also find that formal structures work better. For example, Prahalad and Ramaswamy report that their key learning – from thousands of executives the world over who had begun to explore value co-creation – was that every organization needed a systematic approach to engage not only its customers, but also employees, partners and other stakeholders at large, both to unlock value co-creation opportunities and execute them.[21]
- Similarly, Svendsen and Laberge suggest that companies develop a set of written principles that emphasizes respect, the inclusion of all voices, a valuing of diversity and a commitment to openness, transparency, and maximum information sharing.[22]

Operationally, we urge companies to monitor and manage their stakeholder contributions formally in the CR realm. The process can range from defining stakeholder roles and tasks to integrating such roles and tasks into company operations and obtaining stakeholder feedback to improve the process over time.

Formalizing these processes increases the likelihood that stakeholders will find the company's CR initiatives to be more Useful as they realize that their efforts are not in vain. The results of formalizing the process should also impact Understanding as stakeholders will likely make more positive intrinsic attributions about the company's CR when they observe the effort put in by the company to put appropriate structures in place to monitor, manage, and reward stakeholder contributions.

Ultimately, the positive impact that such formal structures for co-creating CR strategy have on Usefulness and Understanding should translate into stronger levels of Unity.

Summary

So far, Part I of this book introduced the underlying concept that stakeholders can add enormous value to CR; and that the needs of individual stakeholders are best seen as a range of desires, all of which are important for managers to understand. Part II delved into the mind of the stakeholder to see what drives stakeholder reactions and what variables influence or magnify those responses. Now Part III, beginning with this chapter, calls for action. It entails using the framework laid out in the previous chapters with a special focus on moving from mere rhetoric about involving stakeholders to truly engaging them. And of course, action requires strategies. Each chapter in this section discusses strategy for different purposes.

In this chapter, we presented the concept of how a company can co-create the formulation and implementation of their CR strategy with relevant stakeholder groups. Examples and data from research studies back up the importance of the strategy. While co-creation in itself is not a new idea, it has not been systematically used in the CR arena and we believe that the concept has significant potential. Systematically engaging and embedding stakeholders in the formulation process helps managers maximize the 3 U's as well as key variables such as caring and closeness, all of which go towards simultaneously creating more business value and more social value. Some major points to take away from this chapter include:

- Key stakeholders – especially employees and often consumers – respond best to being directly involved. Moreover, embedding

stakeholders in CR programs helps create a "community of virtue" that in turn enhances a sense of Unity with the company.
- Areas in which stakeholders can best contribute to developing CR programs, and thus feel embedded in them, are in generating ideas and selecting causes of greatest interest. The areas of responsibility in which management still plays the key role are distillation of the ideas and implementing them.
- Companies need to determine the primary objectives of their CR and then target the relevant stakeholder groups to co-create their programs, coming up with a portfolio of possible initiatives.
- Through the established technique of "laddering," managers can do qualitative research with targeted stakeholders, starting with a focus on the more universal psychosocial needs that stakeholders hope to satisfy and moving from there to more functional benefits to arrive at specific social causes and program ideas.
- The best approaches to CR co-creation allow stakeholders to be enactors rather than enablers, to have their connection be primarily horizontal or in the form of a network rather than vertical, and for the program itself to be managed in a formal rather than informal manner in order for the company to demonstrate its commitment to the program as well as a clear method for giving rewards to the involved stakeholders.

In the next chapter, we discuss what managers can do to communicate their CR initiatives effectively to their key stakeholders.

Endnotes

1 J. Brugmann and C.K. Prahalad, "Cocreating Business's New Social Compact", *Harvard Business Review* (February 2007) 80–90.
2 Boston College Center for Corporate Citizenship, "How Virtue Creates Value for Business and Society," (2009), available at commdev.org/files/2426_file_Boston_College_McKinsey_31909.pdf, accessed March 22, 2011.

3 S. Srivastava, "For the Betterment of Society," available at http://timesascent.in/index.aspx?page=article&sectid=21&contentid=20090414200904141450376302 17abad0, accessed June 9, 2011.
4 S. Rosen, C. Irmak, and S. Jayachandran, "Value Co-Creation in Cause-Related Marketing: How Letting Consumers Choose the Cause Enhances Consumer Support," Working Paper, Moore School of Business (2009).
5 C.K. Prahalad and V. Ramaswamy, "Co-creating Unique Value with Customers," *Strategy & Leadership*, 32(3) (2004).
6 A. Svendsen and M. Laberge, "A New Direction for CSR: Engaging Networks for Whole System Change," in J. Jonkers and M.C. de Witte (eds.), *The Challenge of Implementing Corporate Social Responsibility*, (London: Palgrave McMillan, 2005).
7 www.mkg-worldwide.com/Site_web/htr/dossier/Scandic%20Hotels_csr.pdf, accessed September 1, 2010.
8 "McKinsey Global Survey Results: Valuing Corporate Social Responsibility," *McKinsey Quarterly*, March, 2009.
9 Aramark, "Aramark Building Community," Case Study, available at www.aramark.com/ServicesandIndustries/CaseStudies/BuildingCommunity.aspx, accessed March 22, 2011.
10 P. Katsoulakos and Y. Katsoulakos, "Corporate Responsibility and Sustainability Management," 4CR Working papers, 4CR Part B, 4CR B1.3, (July, 2006), available at www.csrquest.net/uploadfiles/4CR%20B1.3.pdf, accessed March 22, 2011.
11 CB Bhattacharya, S. Sen, and D. Korschun, "Using Corporate Social Responsibility to Win the War for Talent," *MIT Sloan Management Review* (January 2008), 36–44.
12 J. Dugree, Creative Insight: The Researcher's Art, Copy Workshop (Chicago: 2005).
13 AccountAbility, "The Materiality Report," November 2006, available at www.accountability21.net/uploadedFiles/publications/The%20Materiality%20Report.pdf, accessed December 11, 2009.
14 Brugmann and Prahalad, "Cocreating Business's New Social Compact."
15 www.causeconsulting.com, accessed December 11, 2009.
16 P. Kotler and N. Lee, *Corporate Social Responsibility: Doing the Most Good for Your Company and Your Cause* (New Jersey: Wiley, 2005).
17 H.J. Schau, A.M. Muniz Jr., and E.J. Arnould, "How Brand Community Practices Create Value," *Journal of Marketing*, 73(5) (2009), 30–51.
18 Ibid.
19 D. Cohen and L. Prusak, *In Good Company: How Social Capital Makes Organizations Work* (Boston: Harvard Business School Press, 2001).

20 Schau, Muniz, and Arnould, "How Brand Community Practices Create Value."
21 Prahalad and Ramaswamy, "Co-creating Unique Value with Customers."
22 Svendsen and Laberge, "A New Direction for CSR," pp. 131–47.

Further reading

David Jones, Chelsea Willness, and Shannon MacNeil, "Corporate Social Responsibility and Recruitment: Testing Person-Organization Fit and Signaling Mechanisms," *Academy of Management Proceedings*, (2009) 1–6.

This article examines why some people are particularly interested in working for responsible companies.

Judy N. Muthuri, Dirk Matten, and Jeremy Moon, "Employee Volunteering and Social Capital: Contributions to Corporate Social Responsibility," *British Journal of Management*, 20(1) (2009), 75–89.

The article investigates the contribution of employee volunteering to CR in three case studies from the UK.

Jane Collier and Rafael Esteban, "Corporate Responsibility and Employee Commitment," *Business Ethics: A European Review*, 16(1) (2007), 19–33.

The authors draw on existing research to identify factors that impact employee motivation and employee commitment to CR.

Exhibits

Exhibit 7.1 Examples of benefits to stakeholders as a result of an oral health initiative

Although the laddering technique was not used in its formulation, the oral health program is a case that illustrates both functional and psychosocial benefits. The initiative's goal is to improve the oral health of over 50 million American children by providing education, oral care tools, and access to dental care. The table below shows that the beneficiaries of the CR program (i.e., the children in the program) received substantial functional benefits from the program in the form of healthier and cleaner teeth. Due to their cleaner teeth, the beneficiaries, in turn, felt greater social acceptance from peers, as well as greater social connectedness and self-esteem.

Not surprisingly, this CR initiative provides no functional benefits to consumers at large (i.e., those who are not beneficiaries of the initiative). However, based on their perceptions of the initiative, even nonparticipants gain psychosocial benefits through their purchases of the brand that sponsors the initiative, including helping others in need and a sense of well-being and contentedness. Investors, on the other hand, receive functional benefits through their ownership of stock in the company if the initiative is successful in generating profits through heightened purchase; this is manifested in increased stock returns and lowered risk. These outcomes, in turn, may yield psychosocial and identity benefits of financial and professional advancement, as well as a sense of achievement and self-esteem.

	Program Beneficiaries	Consumers	Investors	Employees
Psychosocial and identity benefits	• Social acceptance • Self-esteem	• Altruism • Well-being	• Financial success	• Work-home integration
Functional benefits	• Healthy teeth		• Stock returns • Lower risk	• Professional skills

Exhibit 7.2 Examples of CR initiative concepts

These two (fictitious) versions of CR concepts, and the instructions preceding them, were presented to two roughly equivalent groups of individuals. The differences between the two initiatives include the non-profit agency chosen to partner with as a beneficiary, the amount of money set aside for the project, and the media venue. The research seeks to understand whether, why and how the differences in "stimuli" drive different consumer reactions to the company as well as to the non-profit.

The following is an excerpt from a recent *Wall Street Journal* article about the pharmaceutical company X's recent alliance with company Y. Please read it carefully.

Last month, the pharmaceutical company X announced a partnership with company Y, an international non-profit agency dedicated to AIDS prevention and supporting the developing world. This alliance is particularly noteworthy given company X's sterling corporate reputation. Company X has made it to the top 10 list of *Fortune*'s annual survey of the world's Most Admired Companies (by far the most visible and frequently cited source of corporate reputational data) 14 times in the last 15 years – the best reputational performance by any company. These rankings are based on *Fortune*'s reputation index, constructed from a variety of criteria including its financial performance, product quality, treatment of employees, community involvement, environmental performance and organizational issues, such as diversity and high ethical standards. Out of a maximum of 100 on the reputation index, company X has consistently scored in the high 90's.

As part of its alliance with company Y, company X has not only pledged $10 million to subsidize AIDS-related medication, including its drug Crixivan, in the developing world, but also agreed to form a joint task force with the non-profit. The financial subsidy, made through the X *Foundation*, will help procure medication for roughly a million HIV positive individuals for one year. More importantly, the X *Foundation*, which brings together some of the top managerial talent at company X and company Y, will seek to leverage the marketing expertise of company X. The team will conduct marketing research in developing countries to identify the most pressing challenges in both the prevention of HIV infections as well as the care of people with HIV/AIDS, and develop action plans to improve the delivery and effectiveness of medical and social services in the different high-risk communities.

The following is an excerpt from a recent *Business Week* article on company X. Please read it carefully.

Last month, the pharmaceutical company X announced a partnership with AIDS International, an international non-profit agency dedicated to reducing the incidence of the AIDS epidemic in the developing world. This alliance is noteworthy because company X has an excellent corporate reputation. In fact, *Fortune's* annual survey of the world's Most Admired Companies is by far the most visible and frequently cited source of corporate reputational data – and X has made it to the top 10 on this list 14 times in the last 15 years – the best reputational performance by any company. Typically, company reputation is an index constructed from a variety of criteria including its financial performance (e.g., profitability, earnings growth), product quality (e.g., better quality, more innovative products), treatment of employees (e.g., better pay, employee stock ownership), community involvement (e.g., charitable contributions, employee volunteer programs), environmental performance (e.g., better history of environmental accidents, fines, permit violations) and organizational issues (e.g., diversity, high ethical standards). A company has to be excellent on all these dimensions to make it to Fortune's top 10 in terms of reputation; in fact, out of a maximum of 100 on the reputation index, X has consistently scored in the high 90's.

As part of this alliance with AIDS International, X not only pledged $3 million to subsidize HIV/AIDS medication in the developing world, but also agreed to form a joint task force with the non-profit. The financial subsidy, made through the X *Foundation*, will help procure medication for roughly 30,000 HIV-positive individuals for one year. More importantly, the task force, that brings together some of the top managerial talent at company X with AIDS International personnel, will seek to leverage the marketing expertise of company X. Specifically, the team will conduct marketing research in developing countries to identify the most pressing challenges in the care of people with HIV/AIDS and subsequently develop action plans to improve the delivery and effectiveness of medical and social services in the community.

EIGHT
Communicating CR strategy

Getting the message out

The basic take-away from our stakeholder-centric research is as simple as it is powerful: CR strategies need to *bring consumers and employees closer to a company's CR*, and ultimately to the company. The proximity of stakeholders to a company's CR actions ranges from a complete lack of awareness of any such activities, to a central, driving role in the company's CR strategy. A fundamental goal of a company's CR strategy, then, must be to move the most important and/or valued stakeholder – employees and consumers – up this proximity continuum, from utter unawareness to complete involvement.

The previous chapter focused on both the importance of co-creation of such an endeavor as well as how a company can formulate and implement its CR programs in a way that maximizes the likelihood of effective co-creation. However, this is only part of the story. Clearly, co-creation is restricted, almost by definition, to those most valued stakeholders whose needs and welfare matter the most to the company.

A program such as the previously discussed oral care program run by a large multinational, for example, can be co-created with select stakeholder groups, such as employees, the disadvantaged communities it aims to benefit and its public sector partner(s), such as the Boys and Girls Club of America. But such actions, while essential, are incomplete. For a company to create maximal stakeholder-based value through its CR efforts, it needs to *cast a much wider net*, ensuring desired levels of Understanding, Usefulness, and Unity among as many stakeholders as possible. While this is virtually impossible to do through co-creation alone, companies *can* achieve these goals through communicating effectively with the broader stakeholder set.

In short, companies need to inform employees and consumers, both current and (no less important) *potential*, about their CR programs. And they need to do so in a concrete, clear, coherent, and consistent manner.

This is easier said than done; while more and more companies are seriously focusing on communicating with their stakeholders about CR, there remains a surprisingly high degree of ignorance, confusion, doubt, and – critically – even suspicion (just think "greenwashing") among stakeholders, including one's own employees, about what exactly a company is doing and why it is doing it.

> Effective communication needs to include both the rationale behind the CR engagement and the specifics of how the programs operate.

Thus, effective communication needs to include both the *rationale* behind the CR involvement, if any, and the *specifics* of the programs, their operations, the amount of company resources devoted and the challenges faced, and most importantly, their successes. Many companies, for example, are starting to be successful at communicating their CR commitments to their shareholders (e.g., CR reports); some of these same lessons can be applied to communicating with employees and consumers. For instance, Shell sends out its CR report to 2 million people including its 120,000 employees. Companies like Patagonia are going further by increasing their transparency to consumers. Consumers can go online at Patagonia's "footprint chronicles" website, check the footprint of each of Patagonia's products, and engage in a discussion.

At the same time, companies need to realize that both employees and consumers can learn about a company's involvement in specific CR (and the lack thereof) and their motivations for doing so from multiple sources (e.g., blogs, online chat rooms, media), many of which are external to the company and, therefore, not controllable by it. As a result, the credibility of such sources can often be high as they are seen to be more "objective" than internal press releases.

> There remains a high degree of ignorance, confusion, doubt, and even suspicion among stakeholders as to what a company is doing and why exactly it is involved in CR.

Thus, companies must aim for high credibility in their communications so as to offset any stakeholder cynicism, particularly since that is likely to increase with the volume of communication. This can be done through the involvement of credible and influential internal sources (e.g., in company online communities such as IBM's On Demand Community) and by reporting objective information rather than "feel good" rhetoric. While the latter is undoubtedly important in inspiring employees and customers to get involved and feel part of a greater cause, by itself it can come across as empty PR.

The remainder of this chapter provides more detail about how a company can communicate with its stakeholders to optimize the 3 U's.

Communicating to optimize the 3 U's

It is a self-evident fact that if stakeholders don't know about a company's CR activities, there is no way they will be able to react to these actions in any manner, favorable or unfavorable. Thus, at a bare minimum, to elicit favorable reactions from their stakeholders, companies must ensure that their stakeholders have an accurate and clear sense for what the company is doing CR-wise. Of course, companies realize this, and more and more companies are trying to reach out to a broad swath of their stakeholders with their CR message.

The primary target of such messages has traditionally been the investors; in fact, many companies, including most on the Fortune 500 list, today routinely link a well-produced, detailed CR report to their annual reports, mailing it to key audiences and posting it on their websites. More recently, companies have started communicating directly with other external stakeholder groups through the general media, mass and personal, and not a day goes by without advertisements in the mainstream press describing the CR actions and achievements of companies both large and small. This is reflected on more and more company websites as well, which highlight the CR of the company in the lead pages.

Yet, as we mentioned in Chapter 4, most consumers and even employees continue to remain in the dark about what most companies are doing in this arena. This is due largely to the fact that most companies today, while experts at communicating about their products and services to the public, are still quite skittish about publicizing their CR actions in a sustained and carefully coordinated manner to their stakeholders.

At the heart of this hesitance lies the widespread, persisting and not entirely erroneous belief that even as CR actions become ubiquitous, proactively telling people about a company's CR poses a set of risks that is unique to this domain of company action. Foremost among these risks is the concern that (in contrast to communication surrounding products and services) CR communication can produce heightened skepticism about the company's intentions and even actions, causing it, at least under certain situations, to backfire on the company, in terms of negative stakeholder reactions.

To elaborate, when a company advertises its products and services, consumers typically don't ask why a company is doing so: As we mentioned, everyone expects a company to work hard to tell people about what they have to offer. On the other hand, when a company tells consumers about its CR actions, one of the first questions many of them still ask is: "Why is the company telling me this?" And as we discussed in Chapter 5, such queries can lead the consumer to make attributions about the company – whether intrinsic (i.e., company has community's best interests at heart) and/or extrinsic (i.e., company only cares about money) – with the latter resulting in negative thoughts and feelings about the company, particularly if it is to the exclusion of the former (e.g., greenwashing).

Such skepticism can block new understanding. It can persist in, and, in fact, often color, consumers' view of the information contained in the communication, becoming a closed loop or type of self-fulfilling prophecy, where the same information can be interpreted as purely self-serving rather than at least partially other-serving, confirming their original suspicions about the company's intent.

> A fundamental goal of a company's CR strategy must be to move key stakeholders up the proximity continuum, from complete unawareness to extensive involvement.

This basic risk in communicating about CR is exacerbated by companies' need to communicate their CR information to multiple stakeholder groups of varying importance, with varying expectations, needs, and involvements. Moreover, for companies that have a diverse product portfolio or where a corporate branding strategy is not used to represent the whole organization, it is unclear how the corporate CR message could be communicated maximally to benefit all the brands produced by the company. For instance, stakeholder knowledge and awareness about the oral care program will clearly benefit the brand if it results in the right kind of Understanding, Usefulness, and Unity. However, how the parent company might communicate about the oral care program to benefit the entire company (i.e., its entire family of brands), needless to say a very desirable outcome of CR communication, is not entirely apparent.

In the face of this complexity, our stakeholder psychology perspective suggests that *companies need an integrated, targeted, long-term communications strategy, incorporating the various elements of the communications mix* (e.g., the CR Audit and Report; CR Manual; Advertising and PR; personal "selling") to achieve *three hierarchical goals* in the minds and hearts of their stakeholders:

- appropriate **Understanding** of the company's CR,
- maximal **Usefulness** of the CR; and, in part as a result of these,
- high **Unity** based on the CR.

Specifically, our framework suggests that in trying to optimize stakeholder reactions, companies need to have the following CR communication goals: (1) increase awareness, (2) assure credibility, (3) convey effectiveness, (4) clarify usefulness (i.e., the benefits to the stakeholders), and (5) make the company identity salient.

Next, this chapter fleshes out how these goals might be achieved through the two key elements of a company's CR communication strategy: the message (i.e., what to communicate) and the media (i.e., where to communicate), in a coordinated and optimized manner.

What to communicate: message

Today, there is no question that companies need to get out their CR message to as many stakeholder groups as possible; by definition, what a stakeholder doesn't know about a company's CR actions cannot help the company; in fact, as the CR clamor continues to grow, silence can actually hurt a company. At the same time, a company needs to remember the simple logic that what it tells stakeholders is the basis, largely, for their reactions. That is why much thought and planning needs to go into the CR message put out by the company.

To give one example, researchers Menon and Kahn examined consumer reactions to CR messages that differed in their *focus* – either on the *CR issue* (e.g., social cause) or on the *company's specific involvement* with it. For instance, in its initiative on wildlife, Johnson & Johnson can focus directly on the issue of the dangers of extinction of certain wildlife species and try to persuade consumers to support the World Wildlife Fund's efforts to save those endangered species, using simply the company logo to identify it as the sponsor in an understated manner. Alternatively, the company can demonstrate its specific involvement by featuring its baby shampoo predominantly and promising a 10 cents donation to the World Wildlife Fund for every purchase.[1]

Interestingly, the researchers found that when the CR message is predominantly about a social issue (versus about the company or its products), consumers are actually more likely to be suspicious of ulterior motives on the part of the company because such advertising does not fit their perceptions of marketers. Namely, consumers see marketers as a group whose communications have one and only one goal: to sell their products (i.e., "schemer schema"[2]).

How then might a company best communicate its involvement with various CR issues? There are several factors that the company can emphasize in its CR communication to achieve the goals we laid out above, such as its *commitment* to a cause, the *effectiveness* (i.e., impact) it has on the cause, why it engages in a *particular social initiative* (i.e., CR motives), and the *congruity* between the cause and the company's business (i.e., CR fit).

Commitment

A key way for a company to achieve many of its basic communications goals is to convey its sustained commitment to a CR issue as explicitly as possible. This process should include how exactly this commitment is expressed, whether through donating funds, making in-kind contributions, and/or dedicating other corporate resources such as marketing expertise, human capital (e.g., employee volunteering), and research and development capability to the issue.

There are several additional aspects of commitment to consider. These include:

- the amount of resources devoted,
- the length and durability of the association, and
- the consistency of the commitment.[3]

For example, in its 2007 corporate responsibility report, Target talked about its signature Take Charge of Education (TCOE) program by stating: "Target . . . donates a percentage of purchases made on Target credit cards to K-12 schools that cardholders designate. Since we launched the program in 1997, we've donated more than $246 million to schools."[4] Here the company emphasized *all three aspects* of its commitment: the substantial *amount* of input (i.e., $246 million) as well as the *durability* (i.e., since 1997) and *consistency* of support (i.e., one percentage of purchases made on Target credit cards).

> Researchers Webb and Mohr found that longer-term commitments were more likely to be seen as driven by a genuine concern for increasing societal/community welfare, while shorter term campaigns were more likely to be viewed as a way to exploit the cause for the sake of profit.

By conveying clearly its commitment to a CR issue, a company achieves several objectives. As seen in the Menon and Kahn research,[5] such an approach represents an honest effort to communicate the company's desire to make a meaningful difference on the focal CR issue while at the same time helping itself, which stakeholders are increasingly coming to accept and even, in some contexts, expect.

In other words, when stakeholders learn about a company's specific commitment to a CR issue, they are more likely to make intrinsic attributions (i.e., ascribe sincere motives to the company) while at the same time making extrinsic attributions that, because they make sense, do not offset the intrinsic ones. Thus, companies have no need to hide their market motives if through their messages they can convince stakeholders that they are also, at the same time, genuinely interested in contributing to the CR issue.

This finding is corroborated by researchers Webb and Mohr, who found that the durability of support for a cause was used as a cue for judging a firm's motives: longer-term commitments were more likely to be seen as driven by a genuine concern for increasing societal/community welfare, while shorter-term campaigns were more likely to be viewed as a way to exploit the cause for the sake of profit.[6]

> The extent of a company's commitment to its CR programs is a primary input into consumers' Understanding of the company's CR motivations.

At the same time, knowledge of the company's commitment level can signal to the stakeholder what the company's potential actually is to make a real difference or impact (also see below) on the CR issue of choice. German chocolate producer Ritter Sport, for example, has been staunchly supporting a project to produce organic and fair-trade cocoa in Nicaragua since 1990. Such long-term commitment not only engenders the desired mix of attributions but also increases the potential usefulness of the company's involvement to those stakeholders who can benefit directly from the CR issue.

Effectiveness

One of the key components of the lever we call Understanding in our model of stakeholder reaction was the stakeholders' need to understand the effectiveness of a company's CR initiatives. There is a clear and direct implication of a program's effectiveness for CR messages: Instead of focusing on the input side of its involvement in a CR issue, companies need to convey clearly, meaningfully, and accurately the *output* side of their CR endeavor; that is, the societal impact, or the actual benefits that have accrued, or will accrue, to the issue/people at the heart of specific CR actions.

> Creating social value is a prerequisite to creating business value.

For example, a press release by the National Institute of Child Health and Human Development (NICHD) on various corporate partners' support for the "Back to Sleep" campaign in the fight against Sudden Infant Death Syndrome (SIDS), estimated that the lives of about 3,500 American babies were saved by 2002 thanks to corporate support.

> Pampers has launched a social initiative in partnership with the United Nations Children's Fund (i.e., UNICEF). The "One Pack = One Vaccine" program gives tetanus vaccines to expectant women in developing countries and thus saves their newborns from a disease called newborn tetanus. For each specially marked Pampers pack sold, the company makes a donation to UNICEF equal to the cost of a tetanus vaccine. Since the program was launched in Great Britain in 2006 it has expanded to many other countries, mainly in Europe and America. The North America campaign alone has provided funding ($11 million) for more than 45 million tetanus vaccines. *The title of this program clearly communicates the societal impact* of the program *and the impact of consumers' purchase* of the Pampers' products designated for the social program.

Our research suggests that while stakeholders may be impressed, at least initially, by a company's CR inputs, what really matters, ultimately, is the extent to which they feel that the company has actually made a difference. In other words, *emphasizing the actual difference the company has made through its CR endeavors is an effective communication strategy because it is a key component of what determines stakeholder reactions to such actions.* At the same time, by being factual, a company can avoid giving the impression that it is "bragging".[7]

Furthermore, stakeholders' knowledge about a company's social impact also serves as a diagnostic cue with regard to its underlying CR motives. For instance, our research with Shuili Du clearly documents the positive associations between the perceived societal impact of a company's CR initiative and consumers' intrinsic attributions and, consequently, consumers' behaviors toward the company.[8]

Communicating such effectiveness is easier said than done. The importance of being effective applies not only to the CR effort, but also to the communication itself; that is, it is essential to *communicate effectively.*

To do so, companies need to present output information that is concrete yet understandable, comprehensive yet not overwhelming. Many companies today rely on standardized, widely adopted performance metrics (e.g., global green standards such as ISO 14001) to communicate their successes. While this is an important and necessary first step in enabling consumers to gauge what a particular firm has achieved in not only absolute terms but also relative to other companies engaging in similar actions, many times the detail and jargon inherent in such measures, particularly in the environmental context, can confuse the stakeholder rather than edify.

Thus, in communicating CR effectiveness information, companies must address it at the right level of knowledge for the targeted stakeholder group, ensuring that the performance metrics actually mean something to the reader. Certainly this would be a more useful method for communicating, say, with managers or with knowledgeable investors, which are groups that may be more interested in that level of detail, than with many employees or consumers.

The same applies for third-party certifications, which reflect the stamp of approval on a company's CR performance by independent appraisal agencies. While such stamps are significant in that they help legitimize a company's CR efforts in terms of certified outcomes, they are often not understandable by consumers and employees who are not familiar with the specific criteria used by the certification agencies.

Notably, communicating effectiveness does not just mean focusing exclusively on one's *successes*; companies also need to acknowledge their *failures*, relative and/or absolute. For instance, in its 2008 Corporate Responsibility Report, the Dutch transportation company TNT devotes an entire chapter not just to its accomplishments but also its challenges.[9] Stakeholders understand that companies will not always achieve their intended CR goals. Like any other endeavor, the success of CR strategies is based on a complex confluence of favorable forces, planned and unplanned. As a result, the reporting of failures, unless they are massive and sustained, can actually build trust and contribute to the right mix of attributions.

In other words, by providing an honest, realistic context in which to interpret a company's performance, the acknowledgement of failures can actually enhance the credibility of the successes the company has had, allowing it explicitly to reformulate its goals and strategies in light of the failures, making these common knowledge. Failure to do so, on the other hand, can arouse stakeholder suspicion, and contribute to perceptions of what in the environmental space has been termed greenwashing.

> Honestly acknowledging failures in CR performance can enhance the credibility of a company's successes.

Motives

As is amply clear by now, conveying the appropriate motives for one's CR actions is one of the primary objectives of CR communications. Thus, in addition to communicating commitment and effectiveness, a company's communications should also explicitly address its motives.

As stated earlier, a key challenge in CR communication is to reduce stakeholder skepticism. In light of this, should companies only emphasize altruistic, intrinsic motives, denying business-related motives in their CR communication? Or should they be honest and acknowledge business motives underlying their CR initiatives?

A study of businesses' CR communication at their websites finds that companies vary as to the types of CR motives they communicate to stakeholders.[10] Some stress the intrinsic motives for their CR activities. For example, PNC Bank states at the company website, "Giving back is a bedrock value at PNC." Alternatively, other companies stress the business case for its engagement in CR. For example, Carrefour explains the rationale for its environmental initiative as follows: "Consumers are increasingly attentive to everything that has to do with safety and environmental health. Safeguarding the environment is a criterion they will increasingly consider."

To reiterate, research on CR attributions shows that consumers often perceive multiple motives and they understand that companies often seek to achieve certain business goals through their CR initiatives.[11] According to Forehand and Grier, acknowledgement of extrinsic, firm-serving motives in its CR message will actually enhance the credibility of a company's CR communication and inhibit stakeholder skepticism, which underlies the potential boomerang effect of CR communication.[12] Therefore, a company should emphasize the convergence of social and business interests, and frankly acknowledge that its CR endeavors are beneficial to both the society and itself.[13]

> As long as a company is genuinely committed to making a difference in the social arena, there is little need to hide profit seeking motives.

In other words, if a company is successful in communicating how effective it has been in creating social value via its CR initiatives, there is much to be gained then from the company doing the same for their economic value as well. Stakeholders are likely to find the combination of motives more believable, realistic, and deserving of their trust.

While a pure focus on economic value will clearly elicit cynicism, a focus just on social value can, in many cases, generate suspicions regarding the company's motives. In particular, if the company knows it has certain key swaths of stakeholders who view a company's CR efforts as a way to cover its problems in its core business (e.g., dropping profits, a lack of strategic focus), they may react negatively to such information, viewing it as a particularly poor use of the company's time and resources. For these stakeholders, or even the growing masses who are increasingly convinced of the need for companies to create both social/environmental and economic value from CR rather than just one or the other (i.e., do good *and* do well), information about effectiveness on both fronts, and critically, how each enables the other, enhances their understanding of a firm's motives and successes.

Fit

Implicit to the notion of joint value is the need for companies to engage in CR that is completely congruent and wholly integrated with their overall business strategy. Therefore, another way to assure credibility through CR communications is to *convey this congruence between a company's CR issues and its identity*, or CR fit. As we saw in Chapter 4, stakeholders don't necessarily feel a sense of Unity with a company's CR actions; this sense of Unity develops based on a perceived congruence or fit between their own values and what they perceive to be the company's values.

Stakeholders often expect companies to focus only on those CR issues that have a high fit, or a logical association, with their core corporate activities as well as their values.[14] CR fit may result from common associations that the brand shares with the cause, such as product dimensions (e.g., a herbal products brand sponsors the protection of rain forests), affinity with specific target segments (e.g., Avon fights breast cancer), or corporate image associations created by the brand's past conduct in a specific social domain (e.g., Ben & Jerry's and the Body Shop's activities in environment protection).[15]

CR fit is a key driver of stakeholders' CR attributions.[16] Research by Gilbert suggests that stakeholders will at first, almost automatically, attribute CR activities to the company's intrinsic motives (i.e., selfless), and then "correct" this inference, if they think a bit more about the company's motives, considering alternative, contextual factors (e.g., competitive pressure, financial motivations).[17]

Low CR fit, due to the lack of logical connection between a social issue and a company's business, is likely to increase such "second-thought" thinking on the part of the stakeholder, making them more likely to make purely extrinsic attributions (e.g., attracting customers for profit or market share), thereby obstructing their positive reactions to a company's CR activities. Therefore, a company should highlight the CR fit of its social initiative if there is congruence between the social issue and its business pursuit.

By elucidating the underlying link between the sponsorship and its core business (and/or its values), the company is able to create a perceived high fit and hence enjoy greater business returns from its CR activities. Sometimes these values are quite apparent from the company's CR actions, as in the case of Wainwright Bank, for whom a progressive social agenda is an integral part of its identity. Its key values have been influenced by the 1960s' civil rights movement and their CR initiatives include (among others) support for the gay community, civil liberties, and affordable housing.[18] *Other times, stakeholders may be confused as to what a company's CR actions specifically say about the company, beyond the general sense that they are trying to "do good."* In such instances, the company actually needs to *spell out the implications* of its CR actions for its identity, making it easier for stakeholders to assess the extent to which affiliating with this identity satisfies their own identity-related needs (e.g., to understand themselves better and to feel good about themselves). For example, DenTek Oral Care, a sponsor of the American Diabetes Association, includes in its sponsorship communications the information that diabetes can lead to tooth decay, bad breath, dry mouth, and gum disease.[19] Because many people may not know about diabetes-related dental problems, the sponsorship might otherwise seem to be a bad fit. Without this step, that coveted sense of Unity is likely to be harder to achieve.

On the other hand, it is necessary to keep in mind that communicating extremely high fit can backfire, particularly if the issue doesn't seem to make sense in light of the company's core business. For instance, some research shows that anti-smoking and anti-drinking campaigns run by cigarette and alcohol companies, while fitting well with their core business, actually strains the limits of credulity for stakeholders trying to make sense of why a company would engage in a particular CR issue.[20] Not surprisingly, these days, many alcohol producers (e.g., Diageo, Budweiser) urge us to "drink responsibly!" In short, a CR campaign that serves to undercut a company's core business, while of high fit, just doesn't make sense to stakeholders. Thus, even if the company believes in the importance of such campaigns, they need to be handled delicately, through communications of effectiveness, commitment and perhaps explicitly addressing the motives and how the campaign makes sense.

Where to communicate: media

There are a variety of communication channels through which information about a company's CR activities or record can be disseminated. A company can communicate its CR activities through official documents, such as an annual corporate responsibility report, press releases, and a dedicated section of its official corporate website to CR. It can also use TV commercials, magazines or billboard advertisements, and product packaging to communicate its CR initiatives.

In fact, research shows that corporate responsibility reporting has gone mainstream: Nearly 80 percent of the largest 250 companies worldwide issued corporate responsibility reports in 2008, up from about 50 percent in 2005.[21] In addition to corporate responsibility reporting and dedicating a section of its corporate website to CR, companies also use traditional advertising channels to communicate their CR activities. For example, Diet Coke has been running TV commercials on its CR initiative to help raise women's awareness about heart disease, and the brand has also set up a website, www.dietcoke.com/reddress, to communicate the brand's involvement in the cause and various ways for consumers to get involved. Companies can also use product packaging to communicate CR initiatives. For example, Stonyfield prints messages on the lids of its 6oz cup yogurt to communicate the company's involvement in a wide variety of health and environmental initiatives to stakeholders.

There are many communication channels for CR, and these are likely to vary in the extent to which they are controllable by the company. A counterpoint to such company-controlled CR communication channels described above is the large and increasing number of *external* communicators of CR (e.g., the press, customers, monitoring groups, consumer forums, blogs and social networks) that are *not* entirely controlled by the company. A company can control the content of CR messages through its own *corporate communication channels* (e.g., that Walmart is a good steward for the environment), but obviously it has little control over how its CR record is *communicated in the media* (e.g., that Walmart provides insufficient healthcare for its employees).

Similarly, a company can exert greater control over the content of CR communication by members of its value chain (e.g., employees, channel members) than by those who are not part of the value chain (e.g., monitoring group, customers). Moreover, there is likely to be a trade-off between the controllability and credibility of CR communication; the less controllable the communicator is, the more credible it is, and vice versa. Stakeholders will likely perceive the company as more self-interested when they learn about its CR primarily through company sources compared to non-corporate sources. And since individuals are often more critical of messages from sources they perceive as biased or self-interested,[22] CR communication via corporate sources will trigger more skepticism and have less credibility than non-corporate sources. For example:

- Research by Syzkman, Bloom, and Blazing found that consumers viewing an anti-drinking and driving message that was sponsored by a beer company (versus a non-profit organization) inferred more self-serving motives of the sponsor.[23]
- Similarly, research by Yoon et al. showed that consumers reacted more positively to a company's CR activities when they learned about these activities from a neutral source (e.g., an independent organization that provides unbiased evaluations of corporate activities) than from a corporate source.[24]

These examples are not different from the dynamics of communication about a company's product and services, except that the likelihood of skepticism is generally greater in the CR realm. Therefore, although getting media cooperation is often difficult, companies benefit most from positive media coverage from independent, unbiased sources, such as editorial coverage on TV or in the press. It would greatly enhance a company's CR reputation if it were reported positively by specialty publications such as *Business Ethics*, or if it receives a good CR rating by independent organizations such as the *Dow Jones Sustainability Index* and *Fortune* magazine.

> Companies need to encourage word-of-mouth about their CR activities, because informal communication channels are often more trusted than messages sent by the company.

Also of importance, companies should try to encourage informal yet credible communication channels such as *word-of-mouth by stakeholders*. For example, Dawkins emphasized that companies should not underestimate the power and reach of employees as CR communicators. Dawkins' research on employee advocacy showed that about a third of employees have advised someone to use their company because it had acted responsibly.[25] Since employees typically have a wide reach among other stakeholder groups through their social ties, and they are often considered a credible information source, companies should "tune up" their internal CR communication strategy and find ways to engage employees in a manner that can turn them into their CR advocates.

> The challenges of communication in the era of online/social media can be exemplified with the case of Nestlé and palm oil. In spring 2010, Greenpeace started a campaign against the company for sourcing palm oil from unsustainably managed forests and thus contributing to deforestation and the loss of living space for orang-utans in Indonesia.
>
> Greenpeace launched a fake Kit Kat commercial online (1.5m views) and organized an email protest (200,000 emails). The campaign was also taken to Nestlé's fan page on Facebook, where users usually discuss and celebrate their favorite Nestlé products. Protesters started to use distorted company logos as profile pictures and attacked Nestlé for its unsustainable behavior. A Nestlé online administrator replied to the protesters, writing "... we welcome your comments, but please don't post using an altered version of any of our logos

> as your profile pic – they will be deleted." This was understood as an attack on freedom of speech and increased public attention and criticism even more.
>
> Just a few weeks after the campaign had been started, Nestlé gave in. It came up with a comprehensive "zero deforestation" policy and developed a plan to identify and remove any companies in their supply chain with links to deforestation.

Like employees, consumers can also serve as an informal yet highly credible CR communication channel. In particular, the power of consumer word-of-mouth has been greatly magnified given the popularity and vast reach of Internet communication media such as blogs, chat rooms, and social media sites (e.g., Facebook). Companies like Stonyfield and Ben & Jerry's have been benefiting from consumer ambassadors who raved, in the virtual world, about their social responsibility endeavors.

For example, one consumer wrote enthusiastically about Ben & Jerry's butter pecan ice cream and its support for an educational foundation, "... besides the great flavor that the Ben & Jerry's Butter Pecan Ice Cream offers you, a portion of the proceeds go to the Tom Joyner Foundation... (that) provides financial support to students attending historically black colleges and universities."[26] Companies can be proactive in utilizing social media to engage consumers to be their CR advocates. To cite an earlier example, Timberland, a company that is known for its environmental stewardship, launched the Earthkeeper campaign in 2008 to recruit one million people to become part of an online network designed to inspire real environmental behavior change. As part of the Earthkeeper program, Timberland launched an innovative global network of online social networking tools, including a strong Facebook presence, a YouTube Earthkeeper Brand Channel, and a richly populated Earthkeeper blog, as well as an

Earthkeeper product collection which serves as the paramount expression of the company's environmental commitment.[27] Through this campaign, Timberland not only effectively communicates its sustainability initiative, but also engages consumers to spread the word about this initiative and, importantly, the company's involvement in this initiative.

In sum, companies need to find the optimal balance in their CR communication strategies between *controllability* and *credibility*, harnessing both traditional and new media to drive communications through both company-controlled and non-company-controlled channels. In doing so, companies would do well to chart out a longer-term communication strategy that varies over time. Specifically, companies might want to target their initial communications to key opinion leaders, who then become highly credible and persuasive non-company sources of communication for disseminating CR information to the broader public.

Such a strategy has been adopted by Nestlé, for instance, which actively participates in CR conferences and targets CR thinkers in both academia and industry, not only with follow-ups that update their CR activities, but also with invitations to participate in Nestlé-sponsored CR forums. This approach integrates vertical communication, from company to stakeholders, with horizontal communication, among stakeholders, to ensure the optimization of the three internal drivers at the heart of our stakeholder-centric model of CR.

The key role of education

A basic thread underlying our discussion of stakeholder Understanding of CR is that there is not a lot of it: Stakeholders' understanding of what companies are doing and why is, in general, rather sparse. While we have focused so far on stakeholder perception of the company's actions, the same often applies to stakeholders' understanding of the CR issues themselves.

In other words, apart from a still relatively small segment of the public, most people today are generally aware but still relatively uninformed about many of the pressing social and environmental issues facing not just their local communities but also the broader global landscape. In their eagerness to come across as good citizens, many companies lose sight of this basic gap in stakeholder understanding, focusing instead on communicating in detail what they themselves are doing. However, if stakeholders don't understand the importance of these issues at a specific, meaningful level, then they are more likely to perceive the company's involvement as a move to "jump on the CR bandwagon" rather than effect change where it really matters. If stakeholders don't appreciate the CR issue, they are hardly likely to appreciate a company's efforts to engage with it.

It is important, then, for companies to educate stakeholders on the CR issues they are involved with. In particular, companies need to clarify to the stakeholders why a particular issue is worth focusing on, with a clear emphasis, if possible, on the Usefulness of such engagement not just to the environment or society in abstraction, but more specifically to the stakeholder as well. For instance, as part of its sustainability efforts, Air France, in conjunction with the French Ministry of Ecology, launched an environment education program in 2006, which focused on raising awareness among certain customer groups of the environmental problems facing their communities. More recently, Océ UK Ltd., an international leader in digital document management and delivery solutions, has run a "Go Green" campaign to help raise the environmental awareness of all Océ employees, including staff based at the head office in Brentwood. The company held a range of activities throughout the week including daily newsletters providing employees with environmental information and facts. In other words, depending on the knowledge levels of the stakeholders with whom it is communicating, it is essential for a company to "connect the dots" for them in terms of the specific ways in which the company's CR actions can help them.

In many instances, the company may find that the stakeholder is confused about the CR issues at stake, not because they are under-informed, but actually over-informed. Because of the sheer volume of often confusing and even contradictory information stakeholders are exposed to on a regular basis, they may either tune out or be quite at sea as to what really are the key issues and facts and why these matter. In such situations, it is important for the company's CR communication to cut through the clutter, not just physically but substantively as well, presenting the CR information in a simple, concise and clear manner that conveys persuasively the issues at stake for the company, the world, and most importantly, the stakeholder.

Summary

Effective communication is a critical part of CR. Because companies need to deal with the perceptions people have and attributions they make about a company's motives behind being involved in CR in the first place, it is important to tread lightly – neither overstating nor misrepresenting – and find a balance among the various factors to which stakeholders react. For example:

- Among these factors is the spectrum of control and of credibility. Companies have control over their own internal communication paths, but far less, if any, control over external media, including the press, and more significantly in this decade, social media and other less formal means of communicating.
- As a result, it is ever more important to turn stakeholders into potential advocates for both the cause and the company. This happens, first of all by having a program that is a good fit for the company's core mission, and then by providing clear and specific,

though concise, information about what the company is doing in the CR realm and how everyone benefits.
- A formal statement by the company in its annual report or on its website may give the needed information, but it can also run the risk of being less credible due to "tooting one's own horn." However, providing specific numbers and also acknowledging the benefit of CR to the company itself – instead of presenting CR as entirely a good-will venture – comes off as realistic and acceptable to stakeholders.
- Similarly, informal word-of-mouth can have either an enormously helpful or deleterious effect. Partnering with a beneficiary and with key stakeholders produces the most positive attributions and therefore the best results, serving as a buffer against negative attributions.
- Companies should focus on *what* to communicate, *how much*, and *where* to place that information. The "what" includes information to help the public connect the dots – including the company's commitment (with specifics such as dollar amounts or numbers of volunteers), its motives (being honest about the program also benefits the company), how good a fit the program is (by demonstrating the link and rationale), and how effective the program is (providing specific data on what the company has been able to achieve in the social realm in a concise way). This kind of communication should make the company's identity stand out and also state goals and values with which stakeholders can identify (thereby increasing both Usefulness and Unity).
- The "where" should take into consideration the vast range of new and social media, including interactive methods such as blogs, from which millions of people get information.
- When possible, getting coverage by third parties, especially prestigious organizations or journals, such as *Fortune*, provides a sense of objectivity, which can shield the company from negative impressions that stem from overstating or "greenwashing" their motives.

Endnotes

1. S. Menon and B.E. Kahn, "Corporate Sponsorships of Philanthropic Activities: When do they Impact Perception of Sponsor Brand?," *Journal of Consumer Psychology*, 13 (2003), 316–27.
2. M. Friestad and P. Wright, "The Persuasion Knowledge Model: How People Cope with Persuasion Attempts," *Journal of Consumer Research*, 21 (1994), 1031.
3. F.R. Dwyer, P.H. Schurr, and S. Oh, "Developing Buyer-seller Relationships," *Journal of Marketing*, 51 (1987), 11–27.
4. "Target Corporate Responsibility Report", 2008, available at http://sites.target.com/images/corporate/about/responsibility_report/2008/full_report.pdf?ref=sr_shorturl_responsibilityreport2008, accessed December 2009.
5. Menon and Kahn, "Corporate Sponsorships of Philanthropic Activities: When do they Impact Perception of Sponsor Brand?"
6. D.J. Webb and L.A. Mohr, "A Typology of Consumer Responses to Cause-related Marketing: From Skeptics to Socially Concerned," *Journal of Public Policy and Marketing*, 27 (1998), 226–31.
7. S. Sen, S. Du, and CB Bhattacharya, "Building Relationships Through Corporate Social Responsibility," in D.J. MacInnis, C.W. Park, and J.R. Priester (eds.), *Handbook of Brand Relationships* (Armonk, NY: M.E. Sharpe, 2009), pp. 195–211.
8. S. Du, CB Bhattacharya, and S. Sen, "Maximizing Business Returns to Corporate Social Responsibility (CSR): The Role of CSR Communication," *International Journal of Management Reviews*, 12 (2010), 8–19; and S. Du, CB Bhattacharya, and S. Sen, "Reaping Relational Rewards from Corporate Social Responsibility: The Role of Competitive Positioning," *International Journal of Research in Marketing*, 24 (2007), 224–41.
9. TNT Corporate Responsibility Report 2008, available at: http://group.tnt.com/Images/tnt-corporate-responsibility-report-2008_tcm177-427051.pdf, accessed March 22, 2011.
10. I. Maignan and D.A. Ralston, "Corporate Social Responsibility in Europe and the U.S.: Insights from Businesses' Self-presentation," *Journal of International Business Studies*, 33 (2002), 497–514.
11. P.S. Ellen, D.J. Webb, and L.A. Mohr, "Building Corporate Associations: Consumer Attributions for Corporate Socially Responsible Program," *Journal of the Academy of Marketing Science*, 34 (2006), 147–57.
12. M.R. Forehand and S. Grier, "When is Honesty the Best Policy? The Effect of Stated Company Intent on Consumer Skepticism," *Journal of Consumer Psychology*, 13 (2003), 349–56.

13 M.E. Porter and M.R. Kramer, "Strategy & Society: The Link Between Competitive Advantage and Corporate Social Responsibility," *Harvard Business Review*, 84 (2006), 778–92.
14 Cone Evolution and Environmental Survey (2007), available at: http://www.coneinc.com/content1091, accessed May 19, 2008; and: E. Haley, "Exploring the Construct of Organization as Source: Consumers' Understanding of Organizational Sponsorship of Advocacy Advertising," *Journal of Advertising*, 25 (1996), 19–36.
15 Menon and Kahn, "Corporate Sponsorships of Philanthropic Activities."
16 Ibid. See also C.J. Simmons and K.L. Becker-Olsen, "Achieving Marketing Objectives Through Social Sponsorships," *Journal of Marketing*, 70 (2006), 154–69.
17 D.T. Gilbert, "Thinking Lightly About Others: Automatic Components of the Social Interference Process," in J.S. Uleman and J.A. Bargh (eds.), *Unintended Thought* (New York: Guilford Press, 1989), pp. 189–211.
18 www.wainwrightbank.com/html/wia/index.html, accessed October 27, 2010.
19 Simmons and Becker-Olsen, "Achieving Marketing Objectives Through Social Sponsorships."
20 Y. Yoon, Z. Gurhan-Canli, and N. Schwarz, "The Effect of Corporate Social Responsibility (CSR) Activities on Companies with Bad Reputations," *Journal of Consumer Psychology*, 16 (2006), 377–90. See also Simmons and Becker-Olsen, "Achieving Marketing Objectives Through Social Sponsorships."
21 KPMG International Survey of Corporate Responsibility Reporting (2008), available at: www.kpmg.de/docs/Corp_responsibility_Survey_2008.pdf, accessed March 22, 2011.
22 J.L. Wiener, R.W. LaForge, and J.R. Goolsby, "Personal Communication in Marketing: An Examination of Self-interest Contingency Relationships," *Journal of Marketing Research*, 27 (1990), 227–31.
23 L.R. Syzkman, P.N. Bloom, and J. Blazing, "Does Corporate Sponsorship of a Socially-oriented Message Make a Difference? An Investigation of the Effects of Sponsorship Identity on Responses to an Anti-drinking and Driving Message," *Journal of Consumer Psychology*, 14 (2004), 13–20.
24 Yoon, Gurhan-Canli, and Schwarz, "The Effect of Corporate Social Responsibility (CSR) Activities on Companies with Bad Reputations." See also Simmons and Becker-Olsen, "Achieving Marketing Objectives Through Social Sponsorships."
25 J. Dawkins, "Corporate Responsibility: The Communication Challenge," *Journal of Communication Challenge*, 9 (2004), 108–19.

26 Associated Content, Ben and Jerry's butter pecan ice cream (2008), available at: http://associatedcontent.com/article/1227799/ben_and_jerrys_butter_pecan_ice_cream.html?cat=22, accessed March 2009.
27 CSRWire, "Call all Earthkeepers: Timberland Earthkeeper Network Inspires Consumers to Take Real Eco-action" (2008), available at: www.csrwire.com/News/12339.html, accessed March 2009.

Further reading

Mette Morsig and Suzanne C. Beckmann, *Strategic CSR Communication* (Copenhagen: Djof Publishers, 2006).

> Mette Morsig and Suzanne Beckmann's book explores the challenges managers might face if they engage in a stakeholder dialogue about how to communicate their CR initiatives.

Nigel Middlemiss, "Authentic not Cosmetic: CSR as Brand Enhancement," *Journal of Brand Management*, 10(4/5) (2003), 353–61.

> This article addresses the question how to communicate CR successfully and concludes that the credibility of programs has a key importance.

Diane Holt and Ralf Barkemeyer, "Media coverage of sustainable development issues – attention cycles or punctuated equilibrium?," *Sustainable Development* (2010), available at http://onlinelibrary.wiley.com/doi/10.1002/sd.460/pdf, accessed March 22, 2011.

> This article examines the increasing media interest in sustainability related topics and illustrates its observation with a sample of more than 100 newspapers.

NINE

Calibrating CR strategy

Once CR programs are put into motion, it is essential to monitor whether they are generating enough value to warrant the investment. It is also essential to understand *how* value is generated so that this knowledge can be disseminated throughout the company, improving other programs and enhancing stakeholder relationships in the process.

But many companies still concentrate primarily on the direct route to CR value; that is, the extent to which it is directly tied to an immediate financial gain in an obvious way, such as via cost savings (see Chapter 2). As a result, some managers lack the expertise to truly understand how stakeholders think and behave based on their exposure to CR activity.

This chapter, therefore, provides guidance on how to go about calibrating CR programs based on active and ongoing measurement of stakeholder reactions to CR. The following pages outline techniques for quantifying CR value and ways to turn these measurements into actionable knowledge that can be disseminated throughout the company.

The fundamental principles of conducting research are consistent with those with which marketers are already familiar. The goal here is *not* to review basic market research techniques, but rather to highlight how the framework presented in this book can be applied in practice; and, to highlight ways that researching in the stakeholder realm is different from much research done with the consumer segment.

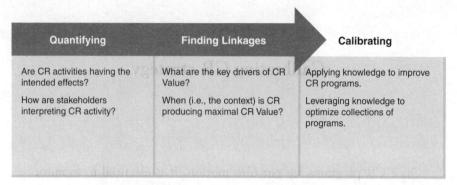

Figure 9.1 Calibrating CR activity

Evaluating CR programs involves three processes (see Figure 9.1): quantifying, finding linkages, and calibrating.

- *Quantifying* requires collecting data that can be numerically coded in a form that is amendable for analysis;
- *Finding linkages* involves analyzing that data in order to develop an understanding of how variables in the framework relate to one another; and
- *Calibrating* means using the knowledge to improve relationships with stakeholders.

All three steps are important if managers are truly to leverage CR in ways that improve corporate performance.

STEP 1: Quantifying stakeholder perceptions and CR value

The familiar adage "You can't manage what you can't measure" is as true in the CR realm as it is in other disciplines. If managers are to optimize CR activity, then stakeholder reactions – both behavioral responses and psychological interpretations – must be recorded. *Putting numbers onto hunches is the only way to reliably know how strongly held and pervasive the thoughts and actions of stakeholders are.*

In quantifying stakeholder reactions to CR, we rely upon a number of well-proven methods and techniques. These involve both surveys and experiments conducted in the field as well as in the lab. The research also involves a varied set of stakeholder segments such as employees, consumers, and business-to-business customers. But the common theme is clear: *Even the deepest thoughts or the most obscure behaviors should be measured whenever possible, if it is thought that they might impact CR value.*

The framework described throughout the book, and especially in Chapter 5, is designed to identify which thoughts and behaviors are the most important drivers of CR value. This framework points to two overarching questions that should be answered in CR-related research.

- **The first question is whether CR programs are having their intended effects.** Managers need to know that their CR programs are really generating value.
- **The second question (related to the first one) is how stakeholders are interpreting CR activity.** This speaks to the underlying reasoning stakeholders engage in deciding whether they want to approach or withdraw from the company. Below is a discussion of these questions.

Addressing Question 1: Are CR programs having the intended effects?

As we have argued throughout this book, much of the value that CR generates is derived from the behaviors of stakeholders. Clearly then, in evaluating CR programs, it is essential to quantify this value, and when possible, even put a dollar value on behaviors. In this way, managers can gauge *how pervasive* these responses are and *how beneficial* they are to the company.

The first step in evaluating CR programs is to set goals. These goals may be based on the current behaviors of stakeholders. For example, managers may assess current levels of employee retention, and then attempt to generate an incremental improvement by exposing a particular segment of employees to CR programs. Goals may also be based on benchmarking, where the performance of market leaders is used as a reference point. For example, a manager may wish to measure improvements in customer loyalty as a result of CR activity and set a goal of reaching the level of a market leader in its industry. Ultimately, what matters most is not how the goal is chosen – which will differ by company and by management style – but that there is a clearly articulated goal of encouraging stakeholders' behavior in some way through CR activity.

The goals of any quantifying exercise are most useful when they are articulated at the individual level. Simply citing correlations between overall CR activity and changes in aggregate performance is not terribly helpful for managers engaged in the complex day-to-day challenges of CR decision-making. Basing decisions on a tenuous link between, say, CR spending and CR performance can be misleading at best and dangerous at worst, because it cannot account for the idiosyncrasies in stakeholder behavior. The most useful way to measure CR value is to track the behaviors of individual people who interact with the company as consumers, employees, investors, or in other capacities.

> Managers need to have clear goals in terms of which behaviors they want to encourage among stakeholders.

The individual level responses to CR are those that can be observed and, generally speaking, are tangible. For example, a consumer who *purchases a product based on his exposure to CR activity* can be considered to reveal a CR response that has tangible value for the company. A person who applies for a job provides another such response.

Of course, these individual behaviors will end up aggregating to improve performance, but measuring them only at the aggregate level inhibits a researcher from knowing which stakeholder segments responded favorably and which did not. Therefore, we advise recording behaviors for individual stakeholders. An example of this sort of indicator of CR value in the consumer realm is purchase. Similarly, programs directed towards employees are sometimes expected to improve employee performance. In this case, managers may wish to track employees' performance according to specific behaviors, indicators, and goals (e.g., courtesy with customers, cooperation with other workers) so that performance can be tied to CR activity.

An important insight in the framework is that CR value can involve *societal* as well as *business value*. Therefore, we recommend tracking stakeholder behaviors towards the selected CR cause whenever possible. These societal behaviors should be considered as an important component in the case for engaging in CR.

How does a researcher or manager go about measuring such responses? Societal value of this kind can be measured through surveys and interviews with stakeholders by asking whether and how the company's CR has encouraged them to increase their donations, volunteering, or positive word-of-mouth for charities that address the same social issues as the company's CR programs. A fine example of these sorts of measures is a study that examined and measured consumer donations to charities sponsored by the company from which they purchase products. In that study, the more consumers felt a sense of Unity with the company, the more they reported donating to these charities.[1]

Ideally, stakeholder behaviors are observed and impartially recorded. Often, however, it is impossible, or at least impractical, to record actual behaviors for every person. In the absence of such data, researchers can measure behavioral *intentions* by using scales administered through surveys.

The examples we provide in Table 9.1 show how stakeholders can be asked of their intent to interact with the company in a number

TABLE 9.1 *Sample items for quantifying how stakeholders respond to CR*

Brand choice	Which of the following brands did you purchase most recently? (provide list)
Brand most frequently bought	Which of the following brands do you purchase most frequently?
Loyalty	I am loyal to this brand.
Advocacy	I would like to try new products introduced under this brand name.
	I talk favorably about this brand to friends and family.
	If the marketer of this brand did something I didn't like, I would be willing to give it another chance.
Reciprocal intention	My community should buy XX [the brand] products to support XX [the name of the CR initiative].
	Buying XX [the brand] products is an excellent way for people in my community to support XX [the name of the CR initiative].
	I am willing to pay a price premium for [the brand] products if it's the only way for [the name of the CR initiative] to continue.
Purchase intent	How likely are you to buy the following brands in the next two months? (very unlikely – very likely)
Employment intent	How likely are you to seek employment with this company within the next two years?
	How likely are you to seek information about jobs at this company in the future?
	In the future, how likely are you to talk-up the company as a good organization to work for? (very unlikely – very likely)
	I would very much like to work for this company.
Investment intent	If you had money to invest, how likely would you be to invest in this company?
Product loyalty	I am loyal to the products that the company makes.
	I like to try every new product the company introduces.
Company promotion	I talk favorably about the company to my friends and family.

TABLE 9.1 (*cont.*)

	I talk favorably about the company's products to my friends and family.
	How many people have you recruited to buy the company's products? (number)
Resilience to negative information	I forgive the company when it makes mistakes.
	I will forgive the company for [specific negative information].
Strong claim on the company	I feel I have a right to tell the company what it should do.
	How frequently have you made demands of the company in the past [time period]? (number)
Product preference	How much would you say you like or dislike [the brand]? (dislike very much – like very much)
	When you buy [the product] to what extent do you buy [the brand]? (never buy – always buy)
	When you buy [the product], to what extent are you "loyal" to [the brand]? (not at all loyal – extremely loyal)
Customer orientation	I make every customer feel like he/she is the only customer.
	Every customer's problem is important to me.
	I give individual attention to each customer.
	I deliver the intended services on time to every customer.
	I always complete tasks precisely for customers.
	I do whatever is necessary to deliver good service to customers.
	I respond very quickly to customer requests.
	I always listen carefully to customers.
Behavior (oral care example)	How often does he/she usually brush his/her teeth? (less than twice a day – twice a day or more)
	How often does he/she usually floss his/her teeth? (less than once a day – once a day or more)
	How often does he/she visit the dentist for routine checkups? (twice a year or less – more than twice a year).

Note: Unless specified otherwise, all items were measured using the strongly disagree – strongly agree scale.

of ways. They include intent to consume the company's products, invest in company stock, apply for jobs at the company, and spread positive word-of-mouth about the company.

Addressing Question 2: How are stakeholders interpreting CR?

> Stakeholders try to make sense of new CR information in light of what they know about the company and in line with what they need themselves.

Managers who wish to optimize their CR engagement need to have reliable means of getting into the mind of the stakeholder, so as to develop a sound understanding of the operation of the psychological engine. As explained in earlier chapters, stakeholders try to make sense of new CR information in light of *what they know* about the company and in synch with *what they need* themselves.

When these two levers – Understanding and Usefulness – are working harmoniously, stakeholders develop a sense of Unity with the company (the third lever), a sense that becomes the primary impetus for CR value. A further look at all three will provide insight into how stakeholders interpret CR and why their perceptions matter to the company and the value of its CR initiatives.

Understanding

In its simplest terms, Understanding is the collection of perceptions that a stakeholder holds about the company's engagement in CR. Understanding develops as stakeholders learn about CR, and as they ask questions such as: What is motivating the company to engage in this CR activity? Is this CR program benefiting society in the way that the company says it is?

Understanding may vary substantially from stakeholder to stakeholder and it may vary greatly in degree, so it is often *best measured at the individual level* using common forms of marketing scales (for example, "To what extent do you agree with the following statement? [Company] initiated their actions out of genuine concern for the environment." 1–7 scale: 1=disagree strongly, 7=agree strongly).

Our framework breaks down each of the 3 U's (Understanding, Usefulness, and Unity) further. It reveals these important aspects of Understanding that managers need to measure and track: (1) awareness, (2) attributions, and (3) efficacy. Each of these can be measured with scales. (See example scales provided in Table 9.2.)

Regarding attributions, both *intrinsic* and *extrinsic* attributions should be measured. As introduced in Chapter 5, extrinsic attributions reflect a belief that the company is acting out of a desire to make money, gain an advantage or otherwise improve its own welfare, while intrinsic attributions reflect the extent to which the stakeholder believes that CR engagement is due to the company's genuine desire to improve societal welfare.

As we reported in Chapter 5, stakeholders tend to balance these two attributions in their interpretations of CR. And *since stakeholders sometimes reward companies precisely for the way in which they combine these two motivations – because they see that approach as innovative – it is best to measure both types so that this interaction can be teased out.*

The third component of Understanding – CR *efficacy* – should be measured at two levels: the program level and the company level. Measuring the efficacy of a particular program is a matter of asking about Understanding with questions that draw out whether and how the programs are "making a difference." The sample items shown in Table 9.2 can be adapted based on the particular societal goals of a program itself, but the theme of providing programs that *make a significant difference to society* should be clear.

TABLE 9.2 *Sample items for measuring parts of the stakeholder psychological engine*

	UNDERSTANDING
Awareness	This brand works for XX [the brand's CR initiative].
Attributions	
Intrinsic attributions	This brand works for [the brand's CR initiative] because it is genuinely concerned about being socially responsible.
Extrinsic attributions	This brand works for [the brand's CR initiative] because it feels competitive pressures to engage in such activities.
Intrinsic attribution	To what extent do you think that the company's genuine desire to help children in need guided its decision to support the cause? (not at all – completely) (oral care example)
Efficacy	
Consumer Realm (oral care example)	[the name of the CR initiative] has improved my child's life.
	[the name of the CR initiative] has enabled my child to take better care of his/her teeth.
Employment Realm	To what extent do you agree with the following:
	The social responsibility initiatives of my employer have a big impact on people's lives.
	My employer's social responsibility initiatives are successful at improving the world.
	The social responsibility initiatives of my employer are highly effective in improving the welfare of people in need.
	USEFULNESS
Self-esteem	To what extent does your overall job:
	Make you feel proud to work at the company.
	Give you a feeling of well-being.
	Make you feel good about yourself.
Work–home balance	Make the transition from home to work easier.
	Make your work and home lives seem almost inseparable.
	Enable you to express your values while at work.

TABLE 9.2 (cont.)

UNITY	
Company attitude	I like this company very much.
Identification	My sense of this brand matches my sense of who I am.
Identification[2]	When someone criticizes the company, it feels like a personal insult.
	I am very interested in what others think about the company.
	When I talk about the company, I usually say *we* rather than *they*.
	The company's successes are my successes.
	When someone praises the company, it feels like a personal compliment.
	If a story in the media criticized the company, I would feel embarrassed.
Identity attractiveness	I like what the company stands for.
Identity similarity	I recognize myself in [the company].
	My sense of who I am matches my sense of the company.
Identity trustworthiness	I don't trust this company.

Note: Unless specified otherwise, all items were measured using the strongly disagree – strongly agree scale.

Measuring the overall efficacy of a company's CR program involves comparing the company to other companies in the same perceived peer group. Some managers mistakenly presume that their only competitors in this sphere are competitors in the same industry. This can be an erroneous assumption when measuring Understanding. Consider the study we did with a Fortune 100 consumer products company. That research revealed that many employees compare their employer's CR efficacy to that of other Fortune 100 companies as well as other consumer goods companies. This expansive view of the competitive set is somewhat unique to the CR realm and must often be considered when quantifying CR efficacy.

Usefulness

Stakeholders can derive many types of benefits, posing a challenge to managers wishing to measure the extent to which stakeholders find CR to be Useful. Because the nature of Usefulness can vary substantially depending on the CR program in question, it is important – before launching a CR program – to use marketing research to establish a set of the benefits that are most important to stakeholders and most likely to be considered Useful to them.

The most likely attributes of Usefulness can be uncovered and slated for tracking by following the process described in Chapter 7, which includes articulation, generation, distillation, and selection. This process can be augmented once the program is launched and the stakeholders gain increasing exposure to its potential benefits. Overall, evaluating the Usefulness of CR programs requires attention to *both functional and identity benefits* so that a holistic sense of how CR improves the individual lives of stakeholders can be obtained.

Functional benefits are those that are largely tangible and are the direct result of features of CR programs. For example, in our study involving the oral care program, parents reported that the program resulted in their children having clean and healthy teeth. In this way, once the key attributes of a program's functional benefits are identified, they can be turned into items like those provided in Table 9.2 so that they can be quantified.

Moreover, functional benefits, in turn, often provide stakeholders with identity benefits. These benefits are much more abstract and relate to thoughts and feelings that people have about their self-image. Identity benefits fulfill two fundamental human needs: *self-esteem* and *self-continuity*. These needs are common to all types of stakeholders, no matter what the nature of their relation with the company may be; however, they often manifest themselves in ways that are *specific to a situation or role*, requiring managers to measure them with a diverse set of contexts in mind.

For example, self-esteem can be very low in the work context even though it is high in the context of one's family life. Therefore, we advise tying questions about identity-related needs to the situation, such as the examples provided in Table 9.2, taken from one of the employee studies. These items examine job self-esteem and work–home balance. That type of balance, as explained in previous chapters, is part of the feeling of self-continuity, which leads to a greater feeling of Unity with the company, and therefore more pro-company behaviors.

Unity

Unity is a summative concept that reflects a stakeholder's overall relationship with the company, indicating whether the stakeholder thinks the company shares his or her values, and whether it is trustworthy enough to warrant a deep stakeholder–company relationship. Typical marketing measures such as customer satisfaction may provide a window into Unity, but they are insufficient at helping us understand the true bonds that can form between individuals and companies, because they do not capture the underlying evaluations that stakeholders make about a company's character or "soul."

We measure Unity in two ways. The first is *identification*, which is the extent to which a stakeholder feels a sense of oneness with, or belongingness to, the company. The second is trust, or the stakeholders' beliefs that the company will act in a benevolent manner going forward.

Researchers Bergami and Bagozzi[3] have empirically tested and validated a two-item scale that is both reliable and extremely easy to implement. It allows respondents to indicate the overlap between themselves and the company in two ways: verbal and pictorial. One item in their two-item scale asks the respondent to indicate the degree to which they agree or disagree with the statement, "The

226 • Putting insight into action

**Measures
Customer Identification with Company**

We sometimes strongly identify with a company. This occurs when we perceive a great amount of overlap between our ideas about who we are as a person and what we stand for (i.e., our self image) and of who this company is and what it stands for (i.e., the company's image).

Imagine that the circle at the left in each row represents your own personal identity and the other circle, at the right, represents the company's identity. Please indicate which case (A, B, C, D, E, F, G, or H) best describes the level of overlap between your and the company's identities. **(Circle Appropriate Letter)**

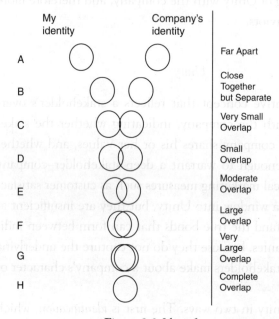

Figure 9.2 Identification measure

values of this company match my own values." The other item is a pictorial scale that uses a series of Venn diagrams involving two circles with varying degrees of overlap (see Figure 9.2); the respondents simply choose *the picture they perceive to best represent the overlap between themselves and the company.*

Calculating the average score on these two items yields a single score that provides a meaningful measure of the stakeholders' perceived match between themselves and the company. Because some individuals are more visual and some more verbal, having the two measures helps account for these differences, thus producing a valid measure.

Not every stakeholder, in every corporate context, however, will feel so close to the company that they perceive an overlap in values. This is why there is a second way we measure Unity: by the degree to which stakeholders "trust" the company. CR programs often communicate that a company is honest and forthcoming, able and willing to deliver on promises. Thus, *trust* is simply a stakeholder's confidence in a company's reliability and integrity.[4]

> It is advisable to measure both identification and trust when quantifying Unity.

There are innumerable measures of trust (or lack thereof) that have been used over the years. (Some examples are provided in Table 9.2.) Trust is integral to any stakeholder–company relationship and is more sensitive to exposure to CR information than identification, because – relatively speaking – identification is more stable. Therefore, it is advisable to measure both identification and trust when quantifying Unity.

STEP 2: Finding linkages between CR value and its drivers

Quantifying stakeholder reactions to CR is clearly important, but managers who stop there will only get a static sense of how CR is "working." To calibrate effectively both current and future CR programs, managers need to develop an understanding of how concepts in the framework relate to one another. In short, they need to do two things:

- First, they need to connect *actions* to *outcomes*, establishing whether their CR *activities* are producing CR *value*.
- Second, they need to know *when* (i.e., in which CR context) these effects are maximally producing this CR value.

Establishing linkages comes down to examining whether a change in one aspect of the framework (i.e., a variable) is related to changes in other variables. Clearly, managers are most interested in variables over which they have at least some control. For example, finding a link between Unity and a stakeholder's intent to apply for employment indicates precisely that managers have to work on Unity if they wish to increase the size of their applicant pool.

Sometimes, this sort of linkage is brought to light based on anecdotal evidence or the managers' experience. More often, though, the complex and highly psychological nature of stakeholder reactions to CR makes anecdotal evidence alone an insufficient basis for effective decision-making. Managers should strive to base decisions on careful analysis that links variables in the framework and reveals the reasons behind stakeholder behaviors.

Methods of establishing linkages

There are two essential steps in validly establishing linkages in our framework:

- The first step entails **sound study design**. This involves collecting data in ways that can shed light on the process. Primary data collected through surveys, laboratory experiments, and field experiments are typically necessary to shed light on the underlying psychological process, although sometimes secondary data collected at checkout counters etc., can also provide rudimentary evidence. As one illustration of study design, as mentioned in other chapters, we used a modified before/after experimental design to evaluate the impact of a million dollar donation by a company to a university. In this instance, we collected data through random surveys of stakeholders before and after the launch of the gift. The findings were clear that stakeholders who became aware of the company's gift had significantly greater intent to apply for jobs, purchase products, and invest in stock of the company than those who were unaware, whether that lack of awareness was due to being surveyed before the announcement, or simply because they had not been reached with the communications campaign. Thus, the experimental study design established that the program succeeded in driving a number of company-favoring behaviors on the part of stakeholders.

- The second essential step in establishing linkages in our framework is the use of **appropriate statistical techniques**. These techniques may be highly advanced or as basic as computing a correlation coefficient, but most techniques are designed to test whether increases (or decreases) in one or more variables result in systematic changes in other variables. For example, in one set of study findings conducted with researcher Shuili Du, increases in Understanding for Stonyfield yogurt consumers were significantly related to corresponding increases in Unity.[5] Both Understanding and Unity were measured using 7-point scales, where 7 represented the most positive Understanding and the highest level of Unity. All other factors being equal (e.g., beliefs about product quality), an increase in Understanding of 1 point on the 1–7 scale was associated with an increase of .3 on our Unity scale. Thus, it became clear how much the company needs to improve Understanding in order to reach a targeted level of Unity. (We provide more detail on such statistical analysis in Chapter 10.)

> In contrast to much market research conducted today that measures psychological variables using a single item, multi-item scales are more effective for assessing any psychological variable.

> Multi-item scales measure a single variable by having respondents answer items that capture a concept using slightly different terminology, and then averaging the multiple responses into a single number. For example, to quantify the extent to which respondents believe a product is socially responsible, the following scale might be used:
>
> Indicate the extent to which you disagree/agree with the following statements:
>
> (1 = strongly disagree and 7 = strongly agree)
>
> - This is a socially responsible product.
> - This product is more beneficial to society's welfare than other products.
> - This product contributes something to society.
>
> Scales such as this are more reliable than single items because they give respondents a chance to rate their thoughts and feelings from a variety of perspectives. We have developed, validated, and deployed dozens of these scales for research projects. Each scale is designed specifically to quantify a distinct concept in our framework.

Focusing on the key drivers of CR value

Our framework emphasizes the importance of stakeholder interpretations for increasing CR value. Many managers, however, view these interpretations merely as a means to an end and don't understand how this extra value is generated – or conversely, how a negative stakeholder perception can work against the company. Finding linkages between stakeholder interpretations of CR activity and CR value is absolutely critical when making the case for engaging in CR activity.

The key drivers of CR value are the levers of the framework: Understanding, Usefulness, and Unity. So linking interpretations to CR value is a matter of finding correlations. That means: first, quantifying these aspects of stakeholder interpretations; then, conducting analyses that can determine the correlation between such perceptions and the forms of CR value they create. Examples of relevant forms of value include customer loyalty, employee intentions to remain employed at the company, or perhaps donations to the issue.

The most straightforward way to record CR value as a function of Unity is to ask survey respondents to rate their purchase intent, or other intended behavior, and then their level of Unity with the company. This is a very common practice due to pragmatic concerns. It does, however, have its limitations, because some respondents may not be able to rate accurately their behavioral intentions, and may be less than forthcoming even if they know their intentions.

That is why, whenever possible, *it is best to record actual behaviors and then match scores for Unity for each stakeholder*. For example, in cases where it is ethical and feasible to do so, managers can find data on consumer purchases or employee work-performance and ask the stakeholders to rate their Unity with the company, stripping the identity of the individual for confidentiality once the data is merged into a single set. This will enable a manager to find – and act upon – the linkage between Unity and targeted behaviors.

Equally important to linking interpretations to CR *value* is linking CR *exposure* to interpretations. The importance of such exposure makes CR communications a critical focus of managers' attention. In short, managers must evaluate whether and how the CR initiative is contributing to Understanding, Usefulness, and Unity. In cases where the program is already running, measuring the impact of program characteristics may be as straightforward as quantifying Understanding, Usefulness, and Unity along with what stakeholders know about the CR activity. Statistical tests can then determine which program descriptions and features are most substantially related to Understanding and Usefulness.

As explained in Chapter 7, to test CR program concepts that have not yet been launched, it may be necessary to design an experiment. For example, the researcher can have stakeholders view one of two or more descriptions of a program, varying the CR issue, CR implementation, or CR resources, or in some cases all three. Then the researcher can compare responses of stakeholders who saw one version to responses of those who viewed another version.

For example, in one of our experiments, respondents were given one of three scenarios to read. In one, the company had a positive record for employee diversity programs; in another, the company's employee diversity record was negative, and in the third, there was no mention of the company's record on employee diversity. Comparing the Unity of prospective customers in each of these conditions, the findings proved that Unity was significantly higher in those respondents who saw the positive CR record.

Factors in producing maximal CR value

CR operates very differently depending on the context in which it is enacted, so managers need to know which context is most fertile for CR engagement. As explained in Chapter 6, there are two levels of contextual factors that managers need to measure, track, and incorporate in their CR decision-making, and then again later (as shown in the section below on calibrating), when they calibrate the effectiveness of CR activities. These two factors are the stakeholder context and the company context.

The stakeholder context is comprised of variables that can differ from stakeholder to stakeholder, while the company context is comprised of factors that are unique to the company or its CR, but which are uniform for all its stakeholders. The best way to understand how context influences the process is to carefully record the effects of CR at every stage of the framework, and then compare how stakeholders view CR, how they *interpret* CR, and how their responses to CR vary under different circumstances.

We have made these comparisons using both qualitative and quantitative data, and using a combination of statistics and careful study design. Some of the results follow.

Stakeholder factors

Stakeholder context factors are often measured through *questionnaires*. For example, in the study regarding a company's diversity program, the stakeholder's level of caring was calculated by listing a number of CR issues and asking the extent to which the respondent supported each issue. (Scale: 1 = do not support at all; 7 = strongly support.)

The list included ten items such as equal opportunity employment practices, special employment support for gays and lesbians, special employment support for disabled people, and special educational opportunities for ethnic minorities. All these ratings were averaged into a single indicator of their caring for the CR issue of diversity. (Table 9.3 shows more examples of stakeholder context items for caring as well as items for closeness.)

In the qualitative case, we spoke to employees in various locations of a Fortune 500 company, asking them about the Usefulness of CR programs. The next step was coding the transcripts from each focus group and comparing responses for employees in various locations. This analysis revealed that *Usefulness varied greatly depending on where the employee worked*. Those at headquarters found CR to be Useful when it helped them become a better employee, by offering them an opportunity to learn new skills, for instance; but those located at an overseas office in a country where the local population was largely hostile to the company found programs most Useful when the program helped them deflect criticism from acquaintances.

TABLE 9.3 *Sample items for quantifying how stakeholder context influences the process*

STAKEHOLDER CONTEXT	
Closeness	
CR Participation	Over the past year, to what extent have you: Donated your own money to social responsibility initiatives of your employer? Volunteered for social responsibility initiatives of your employer? Gone out of your way to tell colleagues, friends, or family about your employer's social responsibility initiatives? (not at all – great extent)
Salience	I think about [the company] often.
Embeddedness	My interactions with the company make me an important player in the organization.
Past purchase	Which of the following brands have you bought in the past two months? (check all that apply)
Caring	
Issue support	I care more than most people about [CR issue]. If I see a news story about [CR issue], I pay close attention to it. [CR issue] is an extremely important issue to me. [Company] addresses societal issues that are important to me. I am personally fond of the issues that [company] supports through its social and environmental responsibility initiatives.

Note: Unless specified otherwise, all items were measured using the strongly disagree – strongly agree scale.

A more quantitative case looked closely at the beneficiaries of the previously discussed oral care program. In that study, those who participated in the CR program had enhanced levels of Understanding and were more likely to purchase the toothpaste brand in the future than non-participants. But going a step further, a set of differences across stakeholder characteristics became clear by comparing the responses of those participants who had lived in the US the shortest amount of time (low acculturation) to those who had lived in the US for the greatest amount of time (high acculturation). Due in part to the more recent generation's desire to fit in to American culture, the low acculturation CR program participants showed enhanced Understanding and greater intent to reward the company through purchase than the highly acculturated group. Thus, although the CR program draws all participants closer to the company, the study revealed that the program proves to be especially effective for those who came to the US recently.

Company factors

In contrast with the stakeholder context factors above, measuring company context factors can be somewhat tricky, because some differences across the company context are objective, while others reside in the mind of the stakeholder. For example, characteristics such as company size can greatly influence how much CR creates value. Size, however, is largely *objective*; almost everyone can agree on whether a company is large or small. But some of the contextual factors we have identified are more *perceptual*.

For instance, Chapter 6 discussed the importance of a company's core business in determining stakeholder Understanding of programs. While for many companies, the industry in which it works is quite obvious, some companies are more difficult to pinpoint. Consider GE, which sells both consumer and business-to-business products, as well as providing an array of services. A stakeholder's reaction to its CR will depend on how knowledgeable he or she is about the company and its competencies. A researcher must tease this information out by asking the stakeholder who becomes aware of the CR activity.

Table 9.4 shows examples of these sorts of perceptual measures used in our studies. More objective measures, however, must be

TABLE 9.4 *Scales for quantifying how company context influences the process*

COMPANY CONTEXT	
CR	
Distinctiveness	(a) The company's program [name] is:
	Not at all unique – very unique
	Typical – Atypical
	Not at all distinctive – Very distinctive
	Ordinary – Unusual
	(b) [CR program] stands apart from other programs that address [CR issue].
Core Business	
Product quality	This product is more advanced than any other product like it.
	This product features advanced components.
	This is a sophisticated product.
	Overall, this brand is of high quality.

Note: Unless otherwise specified, all items were measured using the strongly disagree – strongly agree scale.

incorporated into a study's design. See our discussion and examples in the next section on creating a dashboard.

Determining the influence of context is again a matter of comparing the interpretations and CR value that are found under differing circumstances. For example, one study examined the influence of *CR-core business fit* in interpretations of CR programs. That experiment randomly assigned respondents so that they evaluated either a program that *fit closely* with the products the company sells or *did not fit at all*. The researchers then compared how skeptical respondents were of the motives of the company (an indicator of Understanding) depending on which group they were in – a CR program with good fit or with low fit. The findings were that respondents were less skeptical when CR fit was good than when it was not.

Since fit is somewhat subjective, managers wishing to examine this at their company can measure how much stakeholders perceive a fit, and then compare responses to Understanding related questions for those who perceive a high fit versus those who perceive little fit.

STEP 3: Calibrating CR and stakeholder relationships

Strategic CR management requires a process whereby programs are calibrated regularly for constant improvement. Quantifying and finding linkages are important steps in CR management because they generate knowledge that can be leveraged so that stakeholder relationships are enhanced to the fullest extent possible. But the knowledge generated by these steps must be utilized properly to calibrate CR programs so that they fully improve understanding, satisfy stakeholder needs, and produce maximal CR value.

There are three main applications of this knowledge – with existing CR programs, with future programs, and in other functional areas of the company that could benefit from improving stakeholder relationships. The latter two will spring from assessing the current programs and sharing that information with relevant others.

Applying knowledge to improve CR programs: the CR dashboard

A first step towards calibrating CR programs and stakeholder relationships is aggregating all knowledge about each program on an ongoing basis. Leading companies create dashboard-like systems where managers can find all relevant information in a single source. A CR evaluation dashboard might look like the one shown in Figure 9.3, which provides a high-level view of a company's CR performance at a glance.

Notice that for this program, the key performance indicators of the CR program are tracked for four important stakeholder segments. *These sorts of dashboards can be created for upper-level managers for the entire portfolio of CR programs and also for middle managers in charge of a single CR program.*

Customers

	DESCRIPTION	CURRENT LEVEL	TARGET LEVEL
Understanding	Attributions (genuine concern)		
Usefulness	Self-esteem		
Unity	Identification		
Business Value	Product purchase Positive Word-of-Mouth		
Societal Value	Donations to Cause Volunteering		

Employees

	DESCRIPTION	CURRENT LEVEL	TARGET LEVEL
Understanding	CR efficacy		
Usefulness	Work–home balance		
Unity	Identification with company		
Business Value	Presenteeism Work productivity		
Societal Value	Donations to Cause Volunteering		

Community

	DESCRIPTION	CURRENT LEVEL	TARGET LEVEL
Understanding	Attributions (genuine concern)		
Usefulness	Self-esteem		
Unity	Trust in company		
Business Value	Product purchase Reduced conflict		
Societal Value	Donations to Cause Volunteering		

Investors

	DESCRIPTION	CURRENT LEVEL	TARGET LEVEL
Understanding	CR efficacy		
Usefulness	Self-esteem		
Unity	Trust in management		
Business Value	Investment in stock Positive Word-of-Mouth		
Societal Value	Donations to Cause Volunteering		

Figure 9.3 CR evaluation dashboard

Like the well-known "Balanced Scorecard,"[6] which focuses on sets of business performance measures ("Financial," "Customer," "Internal Business Processes," and "Learning and Growth"), a CR dashboard can be built upon key indicators for each step in our framework. This one has line items for Understanding, Usefulness, Unity, and two forms of CR value (business and societal). The dashboard not only records current performance on these measures, but it also provides a target for the next period.

The dashboard can be used to improve programs – systematically and continually. Learning what is working and what is not can take time. But stakeholders' reactions to CR can evolve over time as well. Very often the fruits of a CR program do not become evident for weeks or even months after their introduction. For this reason, *dashboards can track progress against tangible, agreed upon goals*, so that every CR program is performing up to its fullest.

Gap analyses can be extremely useful when assessing CR performance. When goals are not met, apparent by a gap between targets and actual results, managers can delve into underlying components of Understanding, Usefulness, and Unity for clues as to why the program is underperforming (for more on this see Chapter 10). In many cases, managers can re-calibrate the program based on this information, by improving communication to raise Understanding, or adding features to heighten Usefulness. If enhancing these levers is impractical or overly costly, jettisoning the program may be the best course of action.

Leveraging knowledge to optimize the portfolio of CR initiatives

Quantifying and finding linkages are important steps in CR management because they generate knowledge that can be leveraged so that stakeholder relationships are enhanced to the fullest extent possible.

Leading managers see CR programs as a means to reach broad business and societal goals through stakeholder relationship-building. For this reason, CR *programs should not be viewed as stand-alone endeavors, but rather as a collection or portfolio of initiatives where knowledge is shared so that it may be leveraged by other CR management teams.*

It may seem obvious that this sort of sharing should go on; however, in our experience, it is all too common for programs in marketing, operations, research and development, and corporate affairs to carry on without involving each other. In some large companies, certain CR teams have limited awareness of what other teams are doing outside their functional area, such as marketing, accounting, or operations. For this reason, tools like the CR evaluation dashboard need to be made available to a wide variety of decision-makers. The British retailer Marks & Spencer is an example of a company that involves all departments and its employees in its CR strategy: It measures its performance against 180 social and environmental targets along the entire value chain and communicates the status of accomplishment in real time to all employees at its London headquarters via an electronic ticker.[7]

Knowledge sharing among managers of CR programs is important for two reasons. First, our multi-step framework, from exposure to interpretation to response, is somewhat complex. This complexity makes it unlikely that knowledge of any single CR program – and therefore maximal value of such a program – can be generated by evaluating just that single CR program. Clearly, any CR team can develop more effective CR strategy if they have access to the latest knowledge gleaned from other initiatives. Upper-level managers need to ensure that as many CR managers as possible have access to up-to-date knowledge of how stakeholders react to CR so that future adjustments can be made by considering all the available information.

The second, less obvious, reason that sharing knowledge is important is that many stakeholders are exposed to numerous CR programs simultaneously. Since many stakeholders expect companies' actions to be coherent, lack of coordination between CR programs can lead to confusion, and ultimately suspicion of motives among a stakeholder base.

> Upper-level managers need to ensure that as many CR managers as possible have access to up-to-date knowledge of how stakeholders react to CR so that future adjustments can take into account *all* the available information.

Thus, *CR strategy can be seen as a portfolio of initiatives in which each has a role it plays in providing value to a stakeholder*. Leading companies manage these roles and generate synergies among CR programs by encouraging knowledge sharing.

Summary

Research findings uphold our view that the perceptions and reactions of the individual stakeholder are more significant than a generalized aggregate in determining how to calibrate CR value. Each stakeholder group is different and there are also differences within a group. That is why both qualitative and quantitative research are needed to isolate the factors that lead stakeholders to feel more identified with a company and more trusting of its motives. Then researchers and managers can look for statistical relationships that uncover important links. These links – between various aspects of the psychological levers that influence stakeholder perceptions of the company and its CR efforts – help managers focus on what works and how to make improvements.

Such studies help determine how to improve CR value through a focus on filling stakeholders' needs. When stakeholders understand and perceive the usefulness of a program for themselves, they are more likely to show pro-company behaviors, the program is likely to generate more success, and both social and business benefits will accrue.

Some key points for managers to understand include these:

- Three steps in assessing the value of CR programs are: quantifying responses (for example, using rating scales); finding the links among stakeholder perceptions and CR successes; and calibrating the CR programs to maximize their benefits by using the information generated by such assessment.
- Calibration needs to be an ongoing process because both the variables and relationships among them are subject to change. Managers should keep in mind past efforts, current programs and future initiatives. This broader view will provide insights into the particular circumstances or context (both stakeholder context and company context) that lead to success or a lack of it.
- A company's CR strategy can be seen as a portfolio of initiatives in which each has a role it plays in providing value to a stakeholder.
- A dashboard covering the portfolio of programs the company is engaged in should be made available to all managers so that information is shared widely so as to achieve maximal CR success.

Endnotes

1 D.R. Lichtenstein, M.E. Drumwright, and B.M. Braig, "The Effect of Corporate Social Responsibility on Customer Donations to Corporate-Supported Nonprofits," *Journal of Marketing*, 68(4) (2004), 16–32.

2 F. Mael and B.E. Ashforth, "Alumni and their Alma Mater, a Partial Test of the Reformulated Model of Organizational Identification," *Journal of Organizational Behavior*, 13, 103–23.

3 M. Bergami and R.P. Bagozzi, "Antecedents and Consequences of Organizational Identification and the Nomological Validity of the Bergami-Bagozzi-Scale," working paper, Marketing Department, Jones Graduate School of Management, Rice University (2010).

4 R.M. Morgan and S.D. Hunt, "The Commitment-Trust Theory of Relationship Marketing," *Journal of Marketing*, 58(3) (1994), 20–38.

5 S. Du, CB Bhattacharya, and S. Sen, "Reaping Relational Rewards from Corporate Social Responsibility: The Role of Competitive Positioning," *International Journal of Research in Marketing*, 24(3) (2007), 224–41.
6 R.S. Kaplan and D.P. Norton, "Putting the Balanced Scorecard to Work," *Harvard Business Review*, 71(5) (1993), 134–47.
7 J. Hollender and B. Breen, *The Responsibility Revolution* (San Francisco: Wiley, 2010), 20; and see also http://plana.marksandspencer.com/about, accessed October 29, 2010.

Further reading

Mark J. Epstein, John Elkington, and Herman B. Leonard, *Making Sustainability Work: Best Practices in Managing and Measuring Corporate Social, Environmental and Economic Impacts* (Sheffield: Berrett-Koehler, 2008).

This book provides a comprehensive overview of how to implement and evaluate CR strategies in order to maximize CR value.

Chris Laszlo, *Sustainable Value: How the World's Leading Companies are Doing Well by Doing Good* (Stanford: Stanford Business Books, 2008).

Laszlo uses several case studies to exemplify how companies create CR value and offers a toolkit for managers to implement CR strategies.

Timothy M. Devinney, Pat Auger, and Giana M. Eckhardt, *The Myth of the Ethical Consumer* (Cambridge University Press, 2010).

The authors deconstruct the myth of the ethical consumer by revealing that consumers are more deliberative and sophisticated in their ethical decisions as anticipated by companies.

TEN

Putting the framework to work

A deeper dive

The framework that guides this book synthesizes years of research conducted by us, and also incorporates insights from other leading scholars on CR. The evidence presented so far has provided support for each link in the model. To validate the framework in a comprehensive way, this chapter describes studies conducted in two separate settings: the retail sector and the yogurt industry.

The studies show how the "3 U's" that make up the framework are connected to multiple forms of CR value: outcomes that are of great importance to managers. The full array of levers is then tested as a unified driver of CR value by using a technique known as structural equation modeling. The latter tests have also been designed to isolate the effects of CR activity by controlling for external factors, essentially ruling out alternative explanations. The first study examined reactions of 660 employees in the retail sector. The second study involved the reactions to CR activity of over 1,000 consumers in the yogurt industry.

The framework is designed to guide research on CR activities and inform CR decision-making. In addition to validating the model, we pave the way for practitioners to use the framework by applying our approach in two highly competitive settings. For each of these two studies, we provide an illustration of how the 3 U's might be used by leading companies, focusing on the measures that could be included in a CR "dashboard." Finally, we interpret the findings to provide examples of how these companies can turn the insights of the framework into managerial actions that can improve relationships with stakeholders, and thereby improve corporate performance.

By developing a thorough understanding of the framework's 3 U's, managers can stay ahead of the curve. For example, changes in stakeholder *behavior* may lag behind changes in the 3 U's; as a result, by the time managers detect stakeholder discontent in terms of, say, quitting, it may be too late to address stakeholders' concerns. The framework, on the other hand, helps managers anticipate the factors that stakeholders consider before responding to CR: through purchase, work effort, or investment. In this sense, the levers in the framework can be considered to be *leading indicators of CR value*.

Employee reactions to CR in the retail sector

As we have argued throughout this book, employees represent a critical audience for CR-related information. In the retail sector, employees are particularly vital because many act as the "face" of the company, a conduit through which the company fulfills customer needs. Yet it can be a daunting exercise to leverage CR activity in order to forge strong employee–company relationships. The reason is that employee–company relationships are a complex derivative of everything that employees know about the company. Employees interact with the company more than any other group, and it may be argued that every time they show up for work, or have lunch in the company cafeteria, or hold a meeting with a superior, they are learning something new about the company and what it stands for.

A company's CR record is one of the many pieces of information that employees are exposed to. Most employees want to work for a responsible corporate citizen, and actively look for signals that their employer company fits this bill. This section will illustrate that when designed, implemented, and communicated with the 3 U's in mind, CR activity can drive substantial CR value.

Data collected from a nationwide (US) study will show that even after considering other factors, CR plays a role in fostering strong and committed employee–company relationships, and that based on these bonds, employees are likely to remain employed at the company, work hard, and, become loyal purchasers of the company's products as well.

The data from this study will also show that, in contrast, some CR can actually damage the employee–company relationship, resulting in employees distancing themselves from the company. Thus in each case, the employee relationship can have serious consequences for the company – positive consequences in the former, and negative in the latter. The study findings indicate that the process driving these important outcomes is the stakeholders' interpretation of CR activities: namely, the 3 U's of the framework – Understanding, Usefulness, and Unity.

About the research

The study involved a survey of 660 customer-facing employees at numerous companies in the retail sector. Retailers represented in the study included Walmart, Trader Joe's and Lowe's Home Improvement. Reflecting the wide diffusion of CR in industry today, the majority of our sample (57 percent) was aware of some CR activity at their respective companies. Focusing on the responses of those employees who were aware of at least some CR activity enabled an analysis of how these individuals interpreted and responded to their employers' CR.

The questionnaire, called "Voice of the Employee," was administered through the Internet to a panel of retail employees managed by MarketTools, a leading market research firm. (A list of items used in the study can be found in Exhibit 10.1 at the end of this chapter.) The questionnaire began by delving into aspects of CR value, such as the employee's intent to quit and their work effort at their primary place of employment. Up to this point, the respondent was completely unaware that the survey was intended to investigate their reactions to CR activity. Thus, the Internet platform enabled us to mask temporarily the true intent of the study, which was to examine the linkages between CR activity and CR value.

Once the CR value portion was completed, respondents were asked to indicate whether they were aware of CR activity by their employer. Respondents who were aware of some activity then completed a series of items intended to uncover the 3 U's of the framework. Finally, respondents rated the company on multiple characteristics, described their job and responsibilities, and provided demographic and other respondent characteristic information (e.g., tenure, household income).

Overall, the questionnaire captured elements of companies' CR activities, the 3 U's, CR value, and contextual factors.

Connecting the 3 U's to CR value

How consequential are the 3 U's for retailers? Would improving Understanding, Usefulness, and Unity have any impact on employee behaviors at leading retailers? This section examines the relationships between the 3 U's of the framework and three forms of business value that we explored: employee intent to quit (turnover), employee work effort, and employee purchase loyalty respectively.

Of course, not all of the 3 U's can be expected to drive every aspect of employee behavior. Under some circumstances, Understanding may be the key to forging relationships with stakeholders, while Usefulness takes the proverbial "back seat." In other

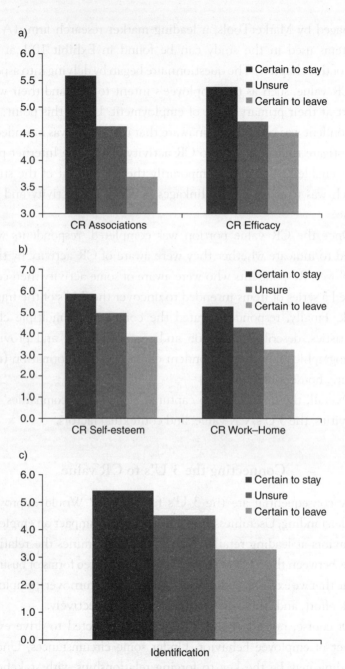

Figure 10.1 Understanding and employee response

cases, Usefulness may be of utmost importance, trumping the effect of Understanding. But consistent across all studies conducted by us is the finding that CR must be successful in moving one or more of the 3 U's if it is to create substantial CR value. Moreover, which of the three is most important will depend on the context.

The data presented in this section, therefore, is not intended to show the definitive links between the 3 U's and CR value (indeed, we do this in the next section: "A Simultaneous Test of All Three Levers"); rather, the following analyses merely provide a glimpse into the relationship between the 3 U's and facets of CR value. In short, presented below are some of the more interesting and powerful effects in this retail context, findings that reveal, once again, the tangible benefits of forging strong employee–company relationships through CR.

Employee turnover

Employee turnover has plagued retailers for years. In some companies, it can feel as if the hiring process is nothing more than a revolving door, with new employees quitting almost as quickly as they arrive. To understand the link between CR and employee turnover, the employee study asked respondents to indicate the probability that they would leave their current employer within the next year. This was asked on an 11-point scale, with 0 indicating no chance, and 10 indicating a 100 percent chance; thus, a lower number indicates a more favorable response for the company.

Consider Figure 10.1 (panel a), which shows the relationship between employees' intent to quit and two measures of Understanding: CR associations and CR efficacy. For each indicator of the 3 U's: the column furthest left represents the Understanding of respondents who responded that there was no chance of quitting within the next year (i.e., certain to stay); the second column represents those who indicated between a 10 percent and 90 percent chance of quitting in the next year and are therefore somewhat uncertain (i.e., unsure); and finally, the column furthest right represents those who said there is a 100 percent chance of quitting within the year (certain to leave).

Employees' commitment to stay employed at the company corresponds with clear downward steps (those certain to stay have the greatest CR associations, those unsure are lower, and those certain to leave are lowest), suggesting that this lever may play a role in their decision-making. As explained by the framework, CR associations help employees develop a sense of the company's benevolence and trustworthiness, which improves the employee–company relationship.

The same is true for CR efficacy, where it appears that employees' commitment to remain at the company is in part a function of how much the company's CR programs benefit society. Highly effective CR activities have a great impact on society, and are, not surprisingly, preferred by employees. Employees want to know not only that their respective companies are involved in CR, but also that these programs are not wasteful – that each dollar or hour or product donated makes as great a difference as possible (see Figure 10.1 panel a).

The same pattern can be found for the Usefulness of CR activities. Once again, one witnesses an almost linear relationship between both CR and self-esteem and between CR and work–home integration (see Figure 10.1 panel b).

These two forms of Usefulness correspond to fundamental socio-psychological needs: the need for a sense of self-worth and the need to have a coherent self, where spheres of one's life do not contradict one another. These data suggest that highly Useful CR activities can give employees a reason to remain employed at the company. In fact, CR activity may provide even more reason to stay for employees who have no other means of integrating their work and home lives.

> Chapter 6 stressed that the effects of the 3 U's often depend heavily on the context. We therefore examined whether the effect of CR work–home integration on an employee's intent to quit was different depending on whether the employee has flexibility in determining his or her work schedule. Comparing employees with little control over their work schedule to those with a lot of flexibility revealed that CR work–home integration reduces intentions to quit more for those without a flexible schedule than those with great flexibility, suggesting that it is an especially effective strategy when other means (i.e., flex-time) are not available.

Unity is the third lever in the framework, and the one that reflects the overall psychological bond between a stakeholder and a company. By communicating a set of socially desirable values held by the company, CR can strengthen this employee–company bond considerably. In some cases, these bonds may become so robust that employees begin to incorporate their sense of the company into their sense of self. A strong identification like this, a sense of oneness or sameness with the company, will embolden employees to deepen their relationship with the company, committing themselves fully to its goals – which are, after all, considered their own as well.

A manifestation of such CR-driven attachment to the company can be seen in employees who commit themselves to remain employed at their company over the long haul. Panel c of Figure 10.1 shows that there is also a tight relationship between Unity and CR value. Consistent with the other two panels of the dashboard, identification – a central indicator of Unity – aligns with employee commitment to remain with their employer. Reading left to right once again, one sees substantial declines in identification across the three groups.

Work effort

Most managers would agree that filling a job position means more than just adding a warm body to the retail floor. Managers want their employees to be engaged in the job and to work hard to serve customer needs. Such engagement can boost productivity and improve customer satisfaction considerably. In this study, employees indicated their work effort by scoring two aspects of their own work performance.

Obviously, this is somewhat subjective as it is a self-rating; however, it does provide a window into an employee's mental state on the job, especially their desire to work hard for the company. Each employee respondent rated his or her performance along two dimensions compared to their peers at the company: the quantity of work performed and the quality of work performed. These scores were averaged to create an overall work effort score. Scores were, not surprisingly, quite high (on average 6.05 on a 7-point scale), but insight can be gleaned by examining differences against the 3 U's.

Because a component of Understanding is the employee's CR associations, to assess the impact of Understanding on work effort, employees rated the company on how responsible the company was perceived to be. Then the employees were divided into two groups: by those whose assessment of the company was either above or below the median of all employees in the sample. This enabled a comparison of work effort for these two groups.

The average score for those with the most favorable CR associations (6.21) was significantly higher than those with relatively poorer CR associations (5.80). This is an indication that employees are more motivated to work hard for companies that they believe are responsible corporate citizens. A similar analysis of the relationship with CR efficacy finds the same result. Employees who scored the company as having high CR efficacy reported a significantly greater work effort (6.19) compared to those whose Understanding of the company's CR efficacy was poorer (6.00).

Taken together, these results indicate that on the whole, Understanding is associated with a boost in work effort. It is worth noting that because employee interpretations are the basis of these effects, they are often complex and heavily dependent on the contextual factors, such as whether or not the employees participate in the company's CR activities.

> The study examined the level of *participation* in the company's CR (e.g., donated money, volunteered time), another contextual factor likely to influence the effects of the 3 U's. Respondents were grouped based on whether they were above or below the median score for self-reported participation. The most negative reaction to CR came from those with high participation who *also* viewed the company's CR as ineffectual.
>
> To appreciate this effect, imagine an employee who has given time, money, and effort to supporting the company's CR programs only to find out that these efforts have done little to improve the environment or people's lives. These employees are likely to feel disappointed, perhaps even somewhat betrayed by the company. They may transfer some of these feelings to the workplace, wondering whether their efforts on the job are worth the trouble.

Purchase loyalty

A third way in which employees can create value for the company is through their own purchase loyalty when it comes to the company's brands. Having employees that are loyal customers provides the obvious benefit of contributing an additional revenue stream. But loyal customers also make great brand ambassadors. Employees who enjoy shopping where they work are likely to convey their personal enthusiasm to customers and prospects. Since they are familiar with

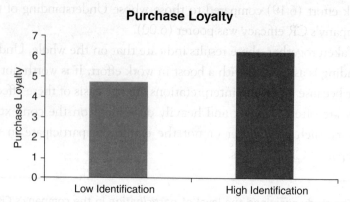

Figure 10.2 Identification and purchase loyalty

the product line of the retailer from a consumer perspective, they are also highly prepared to help match customers with the product that will most fulfill the customers' needs.

When employees believe that their employer company is responsible, they are likely to feel a sense of Unity with it. Scores on identification with the company (i.e., Unity) were standardized such that the mean score was 0 (positive scores are above the mean and negative scores below it). Such identification scores are significantly higher for employees that have very positive CR associations compared to scores for employees that do not see the company as very responsible (.55 and .35, respectively).

This sense of Unity is subsequently associated with employee-driven value through purchase. In the present study of customer-facing employees, respondents who identified with the company reported significantly greater purchase loyalty than employees who did not perceive an overlap between their values and those of the company (Figure 10.2). Employees who identify strongly with the company see themselves as true members of the company, committed to its goals, and motivated to help it succeed in any way possible. Thus, if nurtured properly, the bonds of an employee–company relationship can spill over to purchase of its products and possibly even other company-benefiting behaviors (e.g., stock purchase).

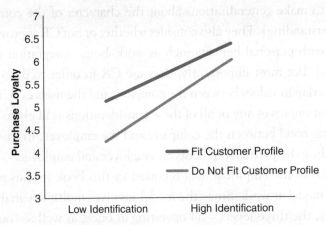

Figure 10.3 The influence of customer similarity

Interestingly, the effects of identification on loyalty appear to be robust for all employees. The psychological bonds of identification encourage employees to become loyal customers, even when employees do not fit the classic customer profile. This conclusion is based on the demographic profile of employees who took the survey. A series of questions asked the extent to which they fit the demographic profile of customers in terms of age, gender, income, and education. We then analyzed the effect of identification on purchase loyalty, finding a significant and positive effect for *both* groups. In fact, employees who do not fit the classic customer profile, yet feel a sense of Unity with the company, have nearly identical loyalty to those who fit the profile very closely (Figure 10.3). This suggests that CR, if executed so that it engenders Unity, can convert even the most unlikely employees into loyal customers, another way in which the employee–company relationship manifests itself.

A simultaneous test of all three levers

The portrait that these analyses paint is of employees who are more than just passive bystanders of a company's CR activities. When employees learn about these activities, they evaluate them and use them to make generalizations about the character of the company (Understanding). They also consider whether or not CR is providing them with personal benefits such as work–home integration (Usefulness). But most importantly, they use CR in order to determine the overlap in values between the company and themselves (Unity). CR that improves any or all of these considerations is likely to forge a lasting bond between the company and the employee, in this case extending the partnership between employer and employee.

Much of the empirical data reported in this book reveals pieces of the model at work. Since the model involves multiple variables – namely, the three levers – all operating at once, as well as "outside factors" that may also contribute to purchase behavior, readers may ask whether this framework holds up as a whole, with CR producing value for the company when these outside factors are considered. To test the full framework in a comprehensive way, the data was analyzed using a statistical technique known as structural equation modeling. The technique is widely used by scholars interested in estimating relationships that involve interplay between multiple variables that occur over multiple steps. In the present research, the technique was applied to test the validity of the levers highlighted throughout this book.

The variables used to test the framework among these customer-facing employees are depicted in Figure 10.4. As in the book's framework, employees will behave in ways that are favorable to the company to the extent that they (1) develop a favorable Understanding of CR activities, (2) find the company's CR to be Useful, and (3) develop a sense of Unity with the company.

To test this line of reasoning, we used two measures for Understanding (CR associations and CR efficacy), two measures for Usefulness (CR self-esteem and CR work–home integration), and one measure for Unity (identification). Unity, or the overall strength of the employee–company relationship, is expected to have an impact on three intended behaviors: the employee's intent to leave the

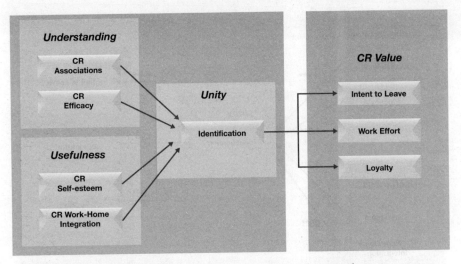

Figure 10.4 A simultaneous test of the framework

company within a year, the employee's work effort, and the employee's purchase loyalty towards the company's products and services. Additionally, non-CR aspects of the job were included as control variables, so that the analysis captures the impact of the levers *beyond* satisfaction with pay, support from the supervisor, and the tenure of the employee in years.

Our analysis reveals that Understanding and Usefulness work together to influence Unity with the company, and that based on this employee–company relationship, employees can be expected to behave in ways that benefit the company. The impact factor for each variable in the model is shown in Figure 10.5; every predicted path is statistically significant ($p < .05$) as indicated by the asterisks.

The impact factor should be interpreted as the expected change in the dependent variable for each unit change in the independent (i.e., predictor) variable. For example, for every unit increase in CR associations (Understanding), we can expect an increase in identification (Unity) of .11 points. Similarly, the impact of CR efficacy, CR self-esteem, and CR work–home integration on Unity are .05, .12, and .08 respectively.

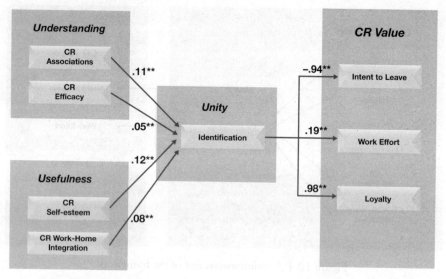

Figure 10.5 Impact factors for each of the links in the framework

Notes: Key fit indicators indicate that the framework adequately fits the data – GFI = .98, CFI = .99, NFI = .98, SRMR = .04, RMSEA = .07 (.05–.09), $\chi^2(15) = 50.48$, p < .05. Control variables (included, but not pictured) are degree of supervisor support, and satisfaction with pay. **p < .05.

Perhaps more pressing for many managers is the contribution of Unity to CR value. Every unit increase in Unity (a point on our value overlap index) is associated with a .94 reduction in an employee's intent to leave the company in the next year; nearly a one-to-one relationship. Similarly telling, the impact of Unity on work effort and purchase loyalty is .19 and .98 respectively. *Note that these effects are above and beyond the effects of the employee's satisfaction with pay, the level of support received from his or her supervisor, and the number of years that the employee has worked at the company.* The positive outcome of this test indicates that the logic behind the framework is sound and robust across numerous employee behaviors.

In the next section, we delve deeper into stakeholder reactions to CR by providing an illustrative example in the retail sector. More specifically, the framework is applied to examine the reactions of Walmart employees to its CR programs and initiatives.

> The 3 U's drove CR value for employees even after accounting for other factors such as satisfaction with pay.

Illustrating the approach with Walmart

Who among us is not familiar with the extraordinary success of Walmart? The world's largest retailer by revenues also employs more people than any other company in the private sector. Walmart has more than 2.1 million employees (1.4 million in the US), most of whom interact with customers every day. Like other retail chains, Walmart has devoted substantial resources to developing a motivated staff of customer facing employees. And like most retail chains, its internal marketing efforts constitute an ongoing struggle, with many bright spots but also numerous setbacks.

For example, in 2000, Walmart launched an aggressive program, which overhauled their employee orientation process, providing training during those critical days when employees learn about the company and the job, forming a first – and lasting – impression. The aim was to reduce employee turnover by 50 percent and motivate workers so that they were fully engaged on the job.[1]

This and other programs improved Walmart's situation, but the company still had an annual turnover rate of about 44 percent in 2004 – a figure that is somewhat elevated, but not inconsistent with the retail sector at large (about 35 percent, according to the Department of Labor).[2] More troubling, 70 percent of new hires leave Walmart within the first year of employment.[3] To put this in perspective, each 10 percent in employee turnover at Walmart translates to roughly 140,000 jobs that must be filled in the US; thus, Walmart must replace hundreds of thousands of employees each year. With the total price tag for replacing a single hourly retail sector employee (non-union) estimated at $3,372, Walmart's total quitting-related costs may exceed a billion dollars.[4]

But employee turnover isn't the only employee-related issue facing retailers like Walmart. Employee motivation is a key ingredient in driving customer satisfaction and sales. Customer-facing employees who are motivated to provide superior service to customers can help the bottom-line by working hard to encourage customers to return again and again. Moreover, motivated employees may use service encounters as opportunities to communicate positive aspects of the company personality; for example, caring, honesty, and integrity. Customers then use this information to determine whether they wish to engage the company or move their purchase to another one that better suits their values.

Walmart knows that its "associates" are central to its mission, and it is constantly seeking methods to encourage employees to become better and more satisfied. The corporation is in the process of creating clear career paths for employees, and it has been overhauling its health and other employee benefits.

The company also frequently stresses the importance of good customer service. "Everything we are trying to do, it is focused around the customer" said Eduardo Castro-Wright, president and chief executive of Walmart's US division. Company spokeswoman Sarah Clark admits that at times Walmart has "not [been] as sharp as it could have been," but claims that a renewed focus means that "we're always wanting to be relevant to the customer."[5]

Overall, work effort, especially work towards satisfying customer needs, is an outcome that managers are eager to track due to its link to business performance. Tom Mars, executive vice president and chief administrative officer of Walmart US, told *The New York Times*, "If we want to make [jobs at Walmart] great jobs, we really have to do something different to distinguish those jobs and our company from everyone else in retail."[6]

One way that Walmart has tried to distinguish itself is through its corporate responsibility activities. The company's CR activity is wide ranging, touching almost every facet of its operations, and addressing numerous CR domains: the environment, employee work conditions, and ethical supply chain practices. For example, Walmart's environmental efforts are vast, ranging from reducing waste to increasing the efficiency of its vast fleet of trucks to encouraging customers to purchase environmentally responsible products, such as compact fluorescent light bulbs (CFLs). The size of its charitable donations through its foundation is jaw-dropping. At the time of the employee study reported in this book, Walmart estimated its giving at more than $300 million, with giving by its customers and employees exceeding $100 million.

For example, Walmart had partnered with the Salvation Army, resulting in collections outside Walmart stores of more than $30 million – amazingly, one in every four "Red Kettle" dollars was collected at a Walmart site – and the Walmart Foundation gave an additional $1.25 million to the charity. The company had given $34 million dollars to the Children's Miracle Network (including customer donations), in order to help children's hospitals in North America. Walmart donated millions in cash and food to America's Second Harvest (now called Feeding America), including a grant to help the hunger organization improve its warehousing capabilities and increase the size of its fleet of trucks.

Walmart's performance on the 3 U's

Walmart hopes that these endeavors will improve societal wellbeing, but to be sustainable over the long term, they also need to show some business benefits, such as improved relationships with employees, reduced employee turnover, heightened customer service, and increased sales. Of course, as argued throughout this book, the link between CR activity and these various forms of CR value is anything but guaranteed. Managers need to track the 3 U's of the framework if they are to effectively co-create, communicate, and calibrate their CR efforts in ways that drive CR value.

A first step is to create a dashboard that tracks stakeholder perceptions of CR activity. Such a dashboard can paint a vivid picture of how stakeholders are interpreting CR activity. Companies need to pay particular attention to the framework's three levers as a primary means of assessing the value that CR can generate. These serve as a guide for which configurations of CR are most likely to result in positive responses – and, conversely, which will lead stakeholders to turn away from the company.

We now revisit the retail employee study above with an accent on the specific case of Walmart. As a first step we examine Walmart's CR performance in terms of the 3 U's in the framework. These should not be examined in a vacuum, however. Stakeholders interpret CR activity based in part on their expectations of the company in comparison to competitors. Therefore, managers would do well to track the 3 U's against competitors, focusing on where they exceed or fall below stakeholder expectations.

In Walmart's case, it can be difficult to narrow the field, because the company competes across so many markets. To provide an overview, Walmart's CR performance is compared to both Target and to the retail sector at large. It is worth noting that the incidence of Walmart and Target employees in our sample is somewhat low; *the analysis is presented here as an illustration of our approach, not as a conclusive assessment of employee perceptions at companies in the retail sector.*

More than three-quarters (77 percent) of Walmart employees in the sample were aware of its CR activity, comparable to Target's awareness of around 80 percent. Table 10.1 drills deeper, showing the percentage of these aware employees who knew about activities targeted at nine domains. (These are employee perceptions; in actuality, Walmart reports that it addresses all of these domains.) Walmart performs well in its environmental endeavors; 89 percent

TABLE 10.1 *Awareness of CR activity in numerous domains*

	Walmart	Target	All other Retailers
Environment (e.g., reducing carbon emissions or waste)	89%	47%	42%
Community (education of children in need, food for the hungry)	82%	94%	69%
Health and Eradication of Disease (e.g., cancer, AIDS)	56%	59%	36%
Diversity in the Workplace	75%	76%	51%
Employee Well-being (e.g., workplace safety)	80%	82%	64%
Fair Labor (e.g., eradication of sweatshops)	60%	53%	36%
Product Safety	69%	65%	48%
Humane Treatment of Animals	27%	29%	14%
Governance (e.g., reporting honestly to investors)	49%	41%	21%
Other	4%	0%	3%

of Walmart employees indicated that they knew about its environmental programs versus only 47 percent for Target employees and 42 percent for employees at other retailers. However, Walmart appears to have communicated its community programs less effectively than Target among its employees (awareness of 82 percent and 94 percent, respectively). Although both Walmart and Target are ahead of other retailers on the whole (69 percent), in numerous other domains, Walmart is essentially at parity with Target.

Unfortunately, and more importantly, this awareness does not seem to be generating a sense that Walmart is a socially responsible company (Figure 10.6 panel a). Walmart scores are somewhat lower than both Target and the retail sector in CR associations, or the extent to which employees find the company to be a responsible corporation (5.03 compared to 5.21 for Target and 5.25 for other retailers). However, Walmart gets higher marks for the efficacy of its CR programs, nearing parity with Target and outstripping the retail sector at large. Overall, Understanding for Walmart's CR activity is a mixed bag. The company has driven high awareness of many of its

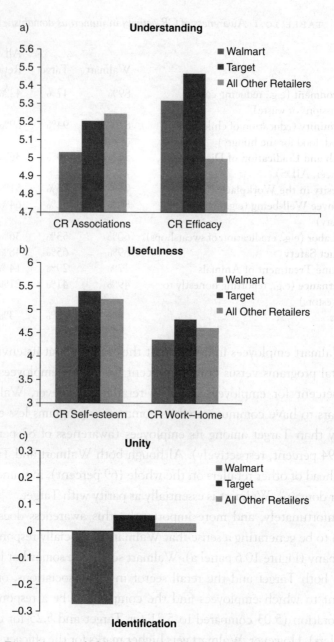

Figure 10.6 A dashboard of stakeholder reactions to CR activity

programs, but has not yet convinced its employees that it is a socially responsible company, and could still improve on perceptions that its CR is effective in changing people's lives.

In terms of Usefulness, Walmart's absolute scores on 7-point scales for CR self-esteem (5.06) and CR work–home integration (4.36) are respectable. However, when compared to Target (5.39 and 4.80, respectively) and to the industry (5.22 and 4.61), the picture is a bit more discouraging (panel b of Figure 10.6). Walmart appears to lag behind both Target and the industry. Thus, Target's employees are deriving more psychosocial benefits from Target's CR than Walmart's employees are deriving from Walmart's CR.

Unity is arguably the most critical lever, because it represents an overall assessment of a stakeholder's bond with the company. Measured by identification – a mean-centered index, where scores are above or below an average score of 0 – Walmart lags behind one of its key competitors and the retail sector in general. On panel c of Figure 10.6, the average level of identification with Walmart is −.27, while employees at Target (.06) and other retailers perceive a greater overlap between their values and those of their employer (.03).

Implications for Walmart

What is a company like Walmart to do with this information? To review, an assessment of Walmart's position relative to industry peers is mixed. Despite fine employee awareness of many of its programs – for the environment, the community, fair labor, and corporate governance – Walmart has not been as successful at using CR to "connect" with its employees. Its good deeds have not been enough to develop a bond of Unity with employees.

The framework suggests that Walmart needs to forge this bond if it is to reduce staff turnover, especially among the highly vulnerable new hires. Such bonds would also drive employee work effort and leverage its base of over two million potential customers around the world (i.e., their employees). The research findings suggest that Walmart could substantially reduce intent to leave, while increasing work effort and purchase loyalty by fostering a sense of Unity with employees. More specifically, by leveraging CR in order to improve Unity, Walmart may well see corresponding gains in employee retention, work effort, and purchase loyalty.

The first change that Walmart needs to implement is to make its CR activity more compelling and relevant to employees. Its employees know that Walmart is engaged in CR all over the world, but these efforts appear to be perceived as distant to them. Walmart needs to find ways to design CR programs that provide direct psychological benefits to employees, either in terms of self-esteem, or work–home integration. By enhancing the self-esteem that employees derive from CR activities, the data suggests that Walmart could realize a significant gain in Unity.

On the other hand, if Walmart does not generate self-esteem and work–home integration benefits for employees, some employees are likely to view CR at Walmart as ivory tower initiatives that have little to offer them personally. These initiatives are unlikely to foster the strong sense of Unity necessary to drive retention, work effort, and purchase loyalty.

The 3 U's dashboard also suggests that a potential point of differentiation, versus the industry at large, is for Walmart to leverage its ability to implement highly effective and impactful CR programs. The framework indicates that real improvements in CR efficacy would give employees a sense that the company truly wants to make a difference in the world. But if Walmart wishes to see improvements in CR associations and ultimately Unity, it may wish to shift some communication emphasis from the size of its programs to the concrete ways that Walmart's CR is changing people's lives for the better.

Due to its sheer size, Walmart is uniquely positioned to concentrate on a few CR programs that are highly effective in changing people's lives on a grand scale. This may involve pruning some of its many initiatives to include those that are most impactful for employees and other important constituents.

We are encouraged by changes Walmart has made over the past year. Since this data was collected, the company has issued reports suggesting that management is now using CR to give tangible and psychological benefits to its employee base. For example, in its 2010 corporate responsibility update, Walmart reports that it has "awarded more than $6.5 million in grants to programs that help train and deploy a skilled workforce." The company is reassessing its efforts to encourage employee participation in CR activity and states that it is in the process of revamping these efforts. In the past year, the Walmart Foundation has also given $1.2 million to the National Council of la Raza (NCLR) in order to enhance job prospects for Latinos, a segment of Americans with a historically high unemployment rate. These new programs may yield greater benefits for employees compared to the programs of years past, which in turn is likely to create substantial CR value for Walmart. But there is still much work to be done in co-creating, communicating, and calibrating Walmart's hugely diverse portfolio of CR programs.

Consumer reactions to CR in the yogurt industry

In Chapter 3, results of a study in the yogurt industry were shown, revealing that Stonyfield yields greater benefits from CR activity because it is a "CR brand." But can more mainstream companies, such as Dannon and Yoplait, gain from engaging in CR? This section revisits that study. The findings suggest that mainstream yogurt brands such as Dannon and Yoplait can reap rewards, but only to the extent that they leverage the 3 U's in the framework.

About the research

The study surveyed 3,384 yogurt consumers across the US. The consumers were part of an opt-in panel managed by MarketTools, a leading market research company. As in the employee study described in the previous section, respondents began the study by providing data on their behavioral intentions (i.e., the three forms of CR value) for four major yogurt brands (Dannon, Yoplait, Stonyfield, Colombo, and the option of naming any other brand they purchase). They were first asked to give the probability that they would purchase a number of yogurt brands (including Dannon and Yoplait); this measure might alternatively be thought of as the "share" of their intended purchases because the sum of these various probabilities equaled 100 percent. Respondents then indicated their willingness to pay a premium and their likelihood of being resilient to negative information on 7-point scales. (See Exhibit 10.2 at the end of this chapter for items used.)

At this point, respondents were asked about CR activities for the yogurt brands in the study. Six domains were explored, which matched the highest-profile CR activities undertaken by yogurt companies at the time: eradication of hunger, fight against breast cancer, conservation of national treasures, protection of the environment, humane treatment of animals, and use of organic ingredients. Respondents indicated whether each brand was actively involved in each of the CR domains. The questionnaire then turned to the 3 U's in the framework, before finally asking respondents to rate their preferences for CR activity (e.g., overall demand for CR, personal support for issues such as the environment and breast cancer), to state their perception that the yogurt brand was of high quality, and to provide some demographic information (e.g., age).

Connecting the 3 U's to CR value

Understanding, Usefulness, and Unity may ultimately lead to many forms of consumer behaviors. In the present study, three critical outcomes in the yogurt industry are examined: (1) purchase intent, (2) willingness to pay a premium, and (3) resilience to negative information. Taken together, these forms of CR value give a fairly comprehensive view of the health of a brand. Purchase intent is an indicator of future market share gains or losses; willingness to pay a premium gives a sense of the brand's potential for high margin sales; and resilience to negative information can serve as a gauge of the long-term viability of the brand, given the very real possibility that the brand is faced with a recall or other setback. Each of these outcomes is now taken in turn, and related to the 3 U's.

As stated in the section on retail sector employees, these three levers cannot be expected to influence consumer behavior in the same way under every circumstance. The data presented in this section offers some illustrative, intriguing examples of how CR activity creates CR value via the central pathway comprised of the 3 U's.

Purchase intent

Perhaps the form of CR value that managers prize above all else is purchase. Purchase is the most straightforward way to tell if marketing is doing its job, and many managers are rewarded primarily for reaching market share goals. We find a strong effect of identification on purchase intent. Respondents in our study were asked to give the probability that their next yogurt purchase would be Dannon, Yoplait, or a host of other brands. Their responses closely mirrored the degree to which they sense Unity with the brand. When Unity was low with a brand, the intent to purchase was rated 25 on the 100-point scale. But when Unity was high, intent to purchase soared to 44. *The closer the psychological connection with a brand, the more likely consumers are to purchase it.*

Willingness to pay premium

According to the framework, another important contributor to CR value is the Usefulness of the CR activities. In this nationwide study of yogurt consumers, we measured the self-esteem that respondents get when they purchase the brand. The questions we sought to answer were: Does this dimension of Usefulness add value to the brand at purchase? And might this become reflected in the consumer's willingness to pay a premium?

> Respondents rated the product quality of each brand in the study, a key company characteristic that influences how CR "works." The effect of Usefulness on willingness to pay a premium differed for brands with high versus low product quality. Usefulness was associated with higher levels of willingness to pay for high quality brands versus low quality brands.

We recorded respondents' willingness to pay a premium, as expressed in our survey, and examined the effect of Usefulness on this important outcome. We used self-esteem as the central measure of Usefulness for this part of the analysis. As expected, the effect of Usefulness is positive, with consumers willing to pay a premium for brands that give them Usefulness (i.e., self-esteem). Those that got little self-esteem from the brand rated their willingness to pay a premium for the brand as a 2.4 on our 5-point scale. But those with high self-esteem had significantly higher willingness to pay a premium for the brand (3.5). Brands that are already of high quality may stand to benefit even more. Overall, this analysis suggests that consumers receive added value from CR activities that provide them with self-esteem, and that this added value is reflected in the price they are willing to pay at the register.

Resilience to negative information

Businesses today face the reality that negative information about the company may surface at any moment. This may involve product safety issues, publicity campaigns by NGOs, and other threats. For example, in 2008 Stonyfield voluntarily recalled batches of its yogurt after it found some fragments of glass in containers. Fortunately, Stonyfield has developed such a strong and loyal following of consumers that long-term sales were not harmed. Stonyfield's customers were quite resilient to this negative information in part because the company is perceived as caring about others; consumers likely reasoned that it must have simply been an accident that was outside its control.

The strongest brands are also those that are able to overcome these obstacles and continue to sustain relationships with customers. And forward-looking managers find ways of fortifying the brand for moments when news about the brand turns negative. The following data bears out the logic that consumers' Understanding of CR can make a brand resilient.

Consumers were separated into four groups based on two factors: (1) the extent to which the consumer believed that the brand engaged in CR out of genuine concern, and (2) the extent to which he or she believed it was motivated by profits. Consumers with greater attributions of a company's genuine concern reported greater resiliency to negative information, suggesting that these consumers were willing to "give the brand a break" if it was thought that its "heart" was in the right place. Those with low attributions of genuine concern (Understanding) gave brands an average rating of 3.1 on the 5-point scale for resilience to negative information, while those with high attributions of genuine concern gave an average rating that was significantly higher (3.7). Interestingly, this is unaffected by consumers' perceptions that the brand is motivated by profits; the aforementioned bump in resilience is roughly the same whether the consumer believes that the company is motivated by profits or not (Figure 10.7). Thus, consumers are perfectly willing to accept profit motives; in fact, they appear to matter very little, as long as the company is also acting out of genuine concern.

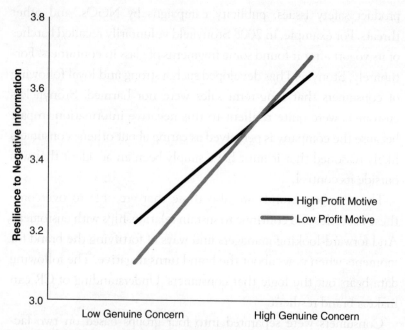

Figure 10.7 Understanding and resilience to negative information

A simultaneous test of all three levers

Consumers, like their employee counterparts, can engage in considerable thought and interpretation when they learn about a company's CR activities. The framework in this book predicts that consumers will reward companies to the degree that (1) Understanding is favorable, (2) CR is deemed by the consumer to be personally Useful, and (3) CR contributes to a sense of Unity with the company. This framework was tested with the same structural equation modeling technique used in the employee study. The results are consistent with the employee study, illustrating the robust nature of the framework.

The variables used to test the framework among these consumers are depicted in Figure 10.8. Two measures of Understanding were used: (1) the extent to which these activities are effective in making a difference in society (CR efficacy), and (2) how much the

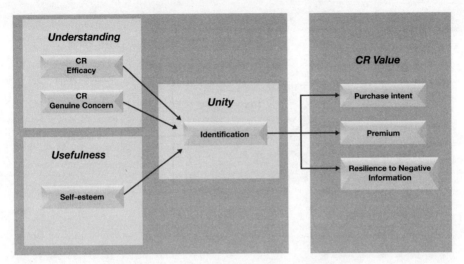

Figure 10.8 A simultaneous test of the framework

consumer believes that the company is motivated by an authentic sense of altruism (genuine concern). Usefulness was represented by the extent to which the brand provides the consumer with a sense of self-worth (i.e., self-esteem). Unity was captured by identification with the company. Unity is expected to drive CR value, which in this study was measured as purchase intent, willingness to pay a premium, and resilience to negative information.

Additionally, to control for a number of extraneous factors, respondents were asked to indicate whether they have purchased the brand previously, the extent to which the brand "tastes good," the extent to which the brand is high quality, and the sex of the respondent. A full set of scales can be found in Exhibit 10.2 at the end of this chapter.

Once again, multiple components of Understanding and Usefulness are shown to work together to influence Unity with the company. Furthermore, based on this customer–company relationship, employees plan to purchase the product, pay a premium, and remain resilient. Figure 10.9 shows the impact factors for each of the paths,

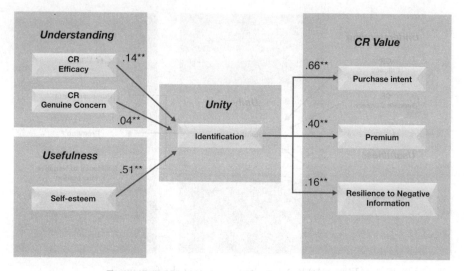

Figure 10.9 Impact factors for the predicted paths

Notes: Key fit indicators indicate that the framework adequately fits the data – GFI = .97, CFI = .96, NFI = .96, SRMR = .04, RMSEA = .09 **p < .01 Control variables (included, but not pictured) are tastes good, high quality, sex, and prior purchase of the brand.

all of which are statistically significant (p < .05) as indicated by the asterisks.

Regarding the 3 U's, increases in CR efficacy and attributions of genuine concern each contribute to identification (impact factors of .14 and .04 respectively). Self-esteem (.51) enhances identification as well. Finally, identification has a positive effect on all three forms of CR value; that is, every unit increase in identification is associated with an increase in purchase intent by .66, willingness to pay a premium increases by .40, and resilience to negative information strengthens by .16.

All of these effects are incremental to the effects of respondent sex, perceived quality ratings, taste, and prior purchase. In other words, these control variables are also significant predictors of the CR value variables, but the 3 U's provide additional explanatory power, supporting the logic behind the framework once again.

> The 3 U's generated CR value among yogurt consumers above and beyond the effects of taste and prior purchase of the brand.

Illustrating the Approach with Dannon and Yoplait

People tend to associate yogurt with a relaxing break, perhaps as a refreshing escape from a hectic day. But behind the scenes of these carefree consumer experiences is an epic battle between two juggernauts of the grocery world: Dannon and Yoplait. Dannon (owned by Group Danone) and Yoplait (owned by General Mills) are firmly entrenched as the two market leaders. Collectively, they now account for around two-thirds of all yogurt sales. For more than twenty years, Dannon and Yoplait have battled for supremacy in the nation's grocery stores. Dannon was once the market leader; but after steadily gaining market share for years, Yoplait now reigns supreme.

The battle continues to play out in the choices people make at shelves of supermarkets across the country and around the world. These are the moments when consumers decide which brand to purchase, how much to pay, and in cases where they perceive corporate malfeasance, whether to give the yogurt brand another chance.

CR in the yogurt industry

Dannon and Yoplait are already using CR as an element in their marketing mix, tactics designed to distinguish the brand from competitors. A contributing factor to Yoplait's success is the high-profile promotion of its CR activities. Yoplait has been a long-time supporter of Breast Cancer research, most notably, through its Save Lids to Save Lives campaign (Figure 10.10). During these drives, Yoplait produces containers with pink lids. For every lid mailed in to Yoplait, the company donates 10 cents (up to $1.6 million) to Susan G. Komen for the Cure. After twelve years of running the program,

276 • Putting insight into action

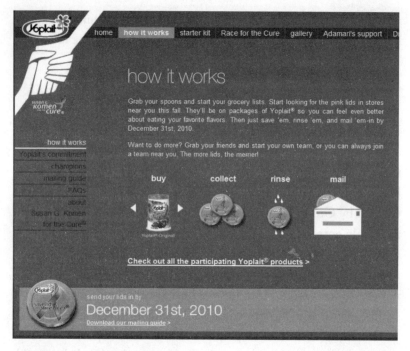

Figure 10.10 Yoplait's "Save Lids to Save Lives" Program: How It Works

Yoplait has donated more than $25 million through this signature program, and there are no signs it plans to slow down. The brand already encourages people to form groups of friends and co-workers so that Yoplait can reach this year's goal.

Dannon, for its part, is also involved in CR activity. It supports nutritional education to reduce obesity and encourage healthy lifestyles, especially among children. For example, its Dannon Institute (Figure 10.11) maintains a portal-style website that serves as an informational resource for researchers and health and education professionals; it includes directories of nutritional organizations, a database of nutritional guidelines, and a listing of research support opportunities. Dannon also has an ongoing relationship with Feeding America (formerly known as America's Second Harvest), with which it works to fight hunger in America.

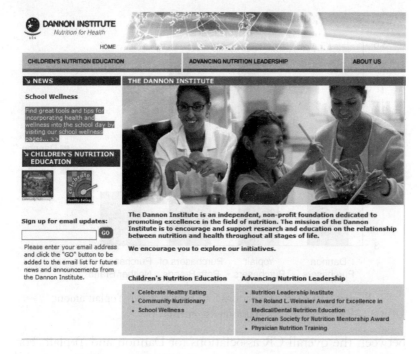

Figure 10.11 The Dannon Institute: About Us

Both brands are involved in CR activity. Both brands promote these activities among their stakeholders, including consumers. But is this activity having any impact on the 3 U's in the framework? When and how is it creating value for these brands? As an illustration of the approach proffered in this book, we now analyze the data for Dannon and Yoplait specifically, as a brand manager might view them.

Dannon and Yoplait's performance on the 3 U's

Understanding

Concerning the first lever, Understanding, consumers in the study gave their impressions of the CR activities at both Dannon and Yoplait. Perhaps surprisingly, there was virtually no difference

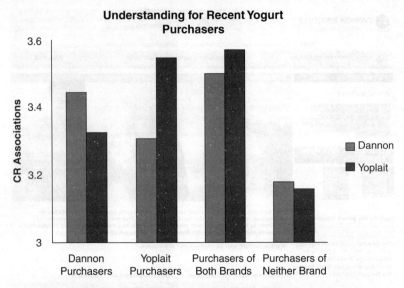

Figure 10.12 CR associations for Dannon versus Yoplait among customer segments

between the overall CR associations for Dannon and Yoplait. For the total sample, the average response to the item "this is a socially responsible brand" yielded an average response of 3.32 for both Dannon and Yoplait. But upon closer examination, we see that Yoplait has created strong associations as a responsible company with certain segments of consumers.

For example, Dannon customers (those who have recently purchased the Dannon brand) view the brand as more responsible than Yoplait, perhaps due to communications and packaging messages. This is true for Yoplait customers as well, who have a much stronger sense that Yoplait is responsible compared to Dannon. This suggests that in each case, consumers are receiving information about each brand's CR activities, a form of learning that becomes reinforced each time they buy. Although it is impossible to be sure from this study alone, Yoplait appears to have the upper hand in priming these associations (see Figure 10.12). This figure suggests that Yoplait customers view the Yoplait brand as more responsible than Dannon customers view the Dannon brand.

Of course, in such a competitive market, many gains in market share must come at the expense of other brands, so it is particularly important to look at customers who are "on the fence" between the two market leaders. With these customers (the third column from left in the figure), both brands are perceived as responsible, but Yoplait maintains a relative advantage among the two brands.

This result is an early indication of the psychological process that customers go through as they compare brands in highly competitive situations. Customers forced to make a choice will often revisit their impressions of the CR activities of the brands in question in order to help differentiate between the two manufacturers. The data in this study reveals that if a consumer has recently bought both Dannon and Yoplait, that consumer's CR associations are likely to favor Yoplait.

To find out what is driving these associations, one must examine more specific CR domains that consumers associate with a brand. Recall that respondents in our study were asked to indicate the extent to which each brand was active in each of the six domains. Figure 10.13 shows that for hunger, national treasures, animals, the environment, and organics, Dannon and Yoplait are essentially at parity. Of these issues, there is a small spike for both companies recognizing their environmental initiatives. The obvious difference in consumers' Understanding of these competitors' CR activities is in the breast cancer domain. Clearly, Yoplait's twelve-year program "Save Lids to Save Lives" has helped it take ownership of the breast cancer issue, providing it with a strong point of differentiation.

Usefulness

The second lever in the framework is Usefulness, and this study sought to document the influence of Usefulness on yogurt consumers as well. To capture Usefulness, we examined the degree to which the brand gave consumers self-esteem, the sense of self-worth that can come from purchasing brands that do good in the world. Since these

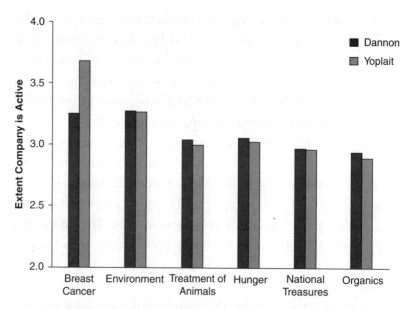

Figure 10.13 Perceived CR activity across six domains: Dannon versus Yoplait

brands give a portion of proceeds to charity, consumers can feel that they are actively – albeit indirectly – contributing to helping someone in need, which adds to the sense of pride.

On an overall basis, Dannon and Yoplait are on par in terms of self-esteem. (Average scores on the 1–5 scale are 3.08 and 3.01, respectively.) The main differences become apparent once self-esteem is related to CR activity. For example, there is a substantial difference in self-esteem from buying Yoplait for those who perceive Yoplait to work hard to fight breast cancer versus those who do not (3.27 compared to 2.88 respectively on a 1–5 scale).

Unity

Perhaps the most critical indicator of the success – or failure – of CR in creating value is the stakeholder's sense of Unity with the company. Unity is a holistic representation of the individual's relationship with the company. We focus specifically on one component of this relationship because of its broad set of implications for CR value: identification. As we have mentioned elsewhere, identification is easily thought of as the perceived overlap between the values of the individual and the values of the company. This sense of overlap, or oneness with the company, enables stakeholders to express aspects of their self-concept each time they interact with the company, giving them a coherent sense of self, and potentially affirming to themselves and others what they stand for.

Yogurt purchasers behave in such a way as well; and we find that CR communicates the values of the company as well as any other actions we know. Most consumers see themselves as honest, caring people, and a company that engages in CR can straightforwardly signal that it shares these important social values. It can thus encourage consumers to feel closer to the company.

> Respondents were asked how important it is that companies engage in CR activity, something we call CR demand. Respondents were categorized into two groups, those who care deeply about CR (high CR demand) and those who are relatively lukewarm to the idea (low CR demand).
>
> For both Dannon and Yoplait, the relationship between CR associations and identification is significantly stronger for consumers with high CR demand than for consumers with low CR demand. This suggests that CR is especially potent for consumers who hold responsibility as a core personal value.

Dannon and Yoplait both have levels of identification just under 3 on the 5-point scale (2.93 and 2.85 respectively). These indicators, hovering at the mid-point of the scale, seem to suggest that the average consumer is neither particularly drawn to nor repelled by Yoplait or Dannon. These consumers identify to some extent, but are a long way from the ideal, where they see many of their personal values reflected in what the company does. However, CR, because it can reveal the character or soul of a company, is capable of engendering a sense of Unity with the company. And this effect is especially strong for consumers who believe that companies have a responsibility to society.

Implications for Yoplait and Dannon

Yoplait's steady market share gains over the last twelve years coincide with its CR activity. The data presented here suggests that the connection between their strong sales performance and continued CR performance is more than mere coincidence. Yoplait has successfully differentiated itself from its main rival, Dannon, by claiming the breast cancer initiative as its signature issue.

Recall that the Understanding of Yoplait and Dannon was comparable except for a large spike for Yoplait when consumers were asked the extent to which each brand addresses breast cancer (Figure 10.13). By "owning" breast cancer as a cause, Yoplait has successfully differentiated itself and signaled to its consumers (particularly those who care about breast cancer) that it shares values with them (Unity).

Yoplait customers also view Yoplait as a more responsible brand than Dannon customers view Dannon. Perhaps more importantly, those people who buy both brands view Yoplait as more responsible than Dannon. The result has been a continuous creation of CR value where CR serves as a complement to Yoplait's high quality products.

Does this mean that the future is bleak for Dannon? Not at all. While there is probably little opportunity to claim the mantle of breast cancer from Yoplait, Dannon has an opportunity to take ownership of other CR domains. For example, with the environment commanding ever-increasing attention in the media and among consumers, there may be an opportunity to promote the work that they are already doing in this area. Our research suggests that it would be especially wise to hone in on environmental efforts that are closely related to their operations, such as factory improvements, or recycling measures that involve consumers. As an issue, the environment may actually provide flexibility to Dannon in targeting the quickly expanding male segment of the market. Yoplait is well positioned in the female market but it is not clear how compelling breast cancer will be as an issue to prospective male customers.

The research findings suggest that if Dannon were to improve the self-esteem that customers and prospective customers get from the brand, they are likely to see a deepening of the customer–company relationship (Unity). Such an increase would then drive purchase intent, willingness to pay a premium, and resilience to negative information. In a commoditized industry like the yogurt business, these sorts of changes can mean the difference between gaining or losing ground on a competitor.

Summary

The 3 U's of the framework provide managers with intermediate goals that research shows are intrinsically linked to stakeholder responses to CR. Thus they serve as a critical foundation for CR management, becoming *leading indicators* of CR value.

This chapter examined reactions to CR in two contexts, the retail sector and the yogurt industry. Each of the analyses not only finds broad-based support for the framework, but also rules out other factors by including numerous control variables in the model.

The chapter also took a closer look at some leading brands within these contexts, providing actual data to illustrate the recommended approach. In sum, these are some main findings of the research:

- The framework – more specifically, the 3 U's – explains stakeholder responses to CR activity even when other factors are considered. Thus, when managed carefully, CR can generate incremental value for both business and society.

- Taken together, the two studies reveal that while particular circumstances may differ greatly from one context to another, the essential psychological process underlying the responses to CR activity is surprisingly consistent. Stakeholders tend to weigh similar factors, and they react based on their personal interpretation of the 3 U's – Understanding, Usefulness, and Unity.
- Managers need to remain cognizant that the effects of the 3 U's are often influenced by contextual factors such as closeness of stakeholders to the organization and characteristics of the company enacting the CR activity.
- By linking CR activities to the 3 U's, a portrait of stakeholder reactions can be painted – a portrait that can be leveraged so that CR strategy is kept on track and areas of potential growth can be further evaluated and calibrated.

Endnotes

1 http://findarticles.com/p/articles/mi_m3092/is_5_39/ai_60122332/, accessed March 22, 2011.
2 www.pbs.org/wgbh/pages/frontline/shows/walmart/transform/protest.html; www.super-solutions.com/pdfs/EmployeeTurnoverExpensive2004.pdf, accessed March 22, 2011.
3 www.pbs.org/itvs/storewars/stores3.html, accessed March 22, 2011.
4 http://gsmweb.udallas.edu/faculty/bfrank/CCRRC/CCRRCStudy1.14.pdf, accessed March 22, 2011.
5 J. Waters, "Wal-Mart wants focus on customers: Two days of talks to outline vision, bathroom cleanings," MarketWatch: Wall Street Journal Digital Network (2006), available at www.marketwatch.com/story/wal-mart-wants-media-to-focus-on-customer, accessed March 22, 2011.
6 www.inc.com/news/articles/2010/06/wal-mart-worker-retention.html, accessed March 22, 2011.

Further reading

N. Craig, CB Bhattacharya, David Vogel, and David I. Levine, *Global Challenges in Responsible Business* (Cambridge University Press, 2010).

This book addresses the implications for business of CR in the context of globalization, social, and environmental problems. It focuses on the major themes embedding CR, CR and marketing, and CR in developing countries.

Mark Maurer, *Corporate Stakeholder Responsiveness* (Bern: Haupt, 2007).

This book proposes a corporate stakeholder responsiveness model that helps companies to improve their learning processes and illustrates its findings with case studies of Swiss phone companies.

Auden Schendler, *Getting Green Done: Hard Truths from the Front Lines of the Sustainability Revolution* (Philadelphia, PA: Public Affairs, 2009).

Schendler, Executive Director of Sustainability at the Aspen Skiing Company, shares his company's journey towards sustainability and provides an array of case studies from other companies as well.

Exhibits

> ### Exhibit 10.1 Retail customer facing employee questionnaire items
>
> ### UNDERSTANDING
>
> **CR awareness** (Yes – No)
> Now, we'd like to know about social responsibility initiatives at the company you work for. These include things like charitable giving, conservation of the environment, and teaming up with non-profit organizations (e.g., United Way, Habitat for Humanity, etc.). Are you aware of any social responsibility initiatives that are sponsored by your employer?
>
> **CR activity** (select all that apply)
> To the best of your knowledge, which of the following issues do the social responsibility initiatives of your employer address? Check all that apply.
>
> - Environment (e.g., reducing waste or emissions)
> - Community (e.g., education of children in need, food for the hungry)
> - Health and eradication of disease (e.g., breast cancer, AIDS, malaria)
> - Diversity in the workplace
> - Employee well-being (e.g., workplace safety)
> - Fair labor practices (e.g., eradication of sweatshops)
> - Product safety
> - Humane treatment of animals
> - Governance (e.g., reporting honestly to investors)
> - Other (specify)
>
> **CR associations** (1–7 scale, disagree strongly – agree strongly)
> - The company is an excellent corporate citizen.
> - The company is socially responsible.
> - The company always tries to do "the right thing."

The company cares deeply about all its stakeholders (i.e., community, customers, investors, suppliers, etc.).
The company supports initiatives that improve society at large.

CR efficacy (1–7 scale, disagree strongly – agree strongly)
The social responsibility initiatives of my employer have a big impact on people's lives.
My employer's social responsibility initiatives are successful at improving the world.
The social responsibility initiatives of my employer are highly effective in improving the welfare of people in need.

USEFULNESS

CR self-esteem and CR work–home integration (1–7 scale, Not at All – To a Great Extent)
Setting aside all the other aspects of your job... To what extent do your company's social responsibility initiatives?
Make you feel proud to work at the company.
Give you a feeling of well-being.
Make you feel good about yourself.
Make the transition from home to work easier.
Make your work and home lives seem almost inseparable.
Enable you to express your values while at work.

UNITY

Identification
The values of the company overlap with my own values. (1–7 scale, disagree strongly – agree strongly)
Imagine that one of the circles at the left in each row represents your own self-definition or identity and the other circle represents the identity of the company. Please indicate which case (A, B, C, D, E, F, G, or H) best describes the level of overlap between your own and the company's identity (choose one).

A: Far apart
B: Close together but separate

C: Very small overlap
D: Small overlap
E: Moderate overlap
F: Large overlap
G: Very large overlap
H: Complete overlap

CR VALUE

Intent to quit (0% chance – 100% chance)
How likely are you to quit your job within the next year?

Work effort (1–7 scale, Among the worst in the company – Among the best in the company)
How do you rate yourself compared to other employees at the company?

   Overall quality of work performed.
   Overall quantity of work performed.

Purchase loyalty (1–7 scale, disagree strongly – agree strongly)
I think of myself as a loyal customer of the company.

OTHER CR RELATED

CR demand (1–7 scale, disagree strongly – agree strongly)
For your primary employer, indicate the degree to which you disagree/agree with the following.

   I believe that this company has a responsibility to make the world a better place.
   I care greatly whether or not this company acts as a good corporate citizen.
   It is very important to me for this company to be socially responsible.
   I want this company to expand its social responsibility initiatives.
   I want this company's social responsibility initiatives to be successful.

I always look for opportunities to familiarize myself with this company's social responsibility initiatives.
I would be extremely disappointed if this company eliminated its social responsibility initiatives.

CR participation (1–7 scale, Not at All – To a Great Extent)
Over the past year, to what extent have you:
Donated your own money to social responsibility initiatives of your employer?
Volunteered for social responsibility initiatives of your employer?
Gone out of your way to tell colleagues, friends, or family about your employer's social responsibility initiatives?

CONTROL VARIABLES

Customer contact (0–10 scale, None at All – All of My Time)
In the course of a typical day, what proportion of time do you spend in contact with customers?

Pay satisfaction (1–7 scale, extremely unsatisfied – extremely satisfied)
How satisfied are you with your paycheck?

Supervisory role (1–7 scale, Not at All – My Primary Responsibility)
To what extent is supervising other employees part of your job description?

Hours worked per week
How many hours per week do you typically work at your primary employer? (1–15, 16–25, 26–35, 36–45, 46–55, 56–65, 66 or more hours)

Work flexibility (1–7 scale, disagree strongly – agree strongly)
The company enables me to determine my own work schedule.
My supervisor allows me to juggle my work schedule if I need to.
I have a lot of say when it comes to my work schedule.

Commission-based compensation (1–7 scale, Not at All – My Primary Responsibility)
To what extent are you rewarded in your job (e.g., your paycheck, promotions, awards) based on:

The quantity that customers purchase?
The amount that customers spend?

Supervisor support (1–7 scale, Does not describe him/her at all – Completely describes him/her)
How closely do the following statements describe your immediate supervisor?

Listens to your problems.
Shares ideas or advice with you.
Is supportive to you.

Fit with customer profile (1–7 scale, Not Close at All – Very Close)
To the best of your knowledge:

How close in age are typical customers to your age?
How close is the household income of typical customers to your household income?
How close is the level of education of typical customers to yours?
The gender of customers is... (1–7 scale, 1 = Predominantly Male, 4 = Equally balanced between Male/Female, 7 = Predominantly Female)

Demographics

Sex
Age
Household income
Education attained
Years employed by company

Exhibit 10.2 Yogurt consumer questionnaire items

UNDERSTANDING

CR associations (1–5 scale, not at all – very much)
This is a socially responsible brand.

CR activity (1–5 scale, disagree strongly – agree strongly)

[Brand] works for the eradication of hunger.
[Brand] is active in the fight against breast cancer.
[Brand] helps in the conservation of national treasures (e.g., rare copies of the Declaration of Independence).
[Brand] is committed to the humane treatment of animals.
[Brand] is environmentally responsible (i.e., uses recyclable packaging, conserves energy, minimizes solid waste).
[Brand] uses only organic ingredients.

CR efficacy (1–5 scale, disagree strongly – agree strongly)
This brand has made a real difference through its socially responsible actions.

CR attributions (1–5 scale, disagree strongly – agree strongly)

[Brand] works for the eradication of hunger. This is because...
[Brand] is environmentally responsible. This is because...
[Brand] uses organic ingredients in its products. This is because...
[Brand] treats animals in a humane fashion. This is because...
[Brand] is active in the fight against breast cancer. This is because...
[Brand] helps preserve national treasures. This is because...

a. They are genuinely concerned about being socially responsible.
b. They want to make a profit.

USEFULNESS

Brand self-esteem (1–5 scale, disagree strongly – agree strongly)
Buying this brand over other brands makes me feel good about myself.

UNITY

Identification (1–5 scale, disagree strongly – agree strongly)
My sense of this brand matches my sense of who I am.

CR VALUE

Purchase intent (0%–100%)
The next time you buy yogurt, what is the probability that you will buy each of these brands? Please provide a percentage for each brand, and have the percentages add up to 100%.

Willingness to pay premium (1–5 scale, disagree strongly – agree strongly)
I am willing to pay a premium for this brand.

Resilience to negative information (1–5 scale, disagree strongly – agree strongly)
If the maker of this brand did something I didn't like, I would be willing to give it another chance.

OTHER CR RELATED

CR demand (1–5 scale, disagree strongly – agree strongly)
In general I like brands that are socially responsible.

CONTROL VARIABLES

Prior purchase (select one)
Which of the following yogurt brands did you buy most recently?
  Dannon, Yoplait, Stonyfield, Colombo, other, please specify.

Product quality (1–5 scale, disagree strongly – agree strongly)
Overall, this brand is of high quality.

Tastes good (1–5 scale, disagree strongly – agree strongly)
This brand tastes good.

Demographics
  Gender
  Age
  Highest level of education attained
  Annual household income before taxes

ELEVEN

Conclusion

The long and winding road revisited

What then of Chevron and Shell? In our opening chapter, we discussed the struggles of these two massive and influential global oil companies to engage in meaningful, useful, and impactful CR. While each was trying to do right by its desire simultaneously to help itself and the world around it, both companies found themselves buffeted by the uncertain storms of increasingly influential and competing stakeholder demands and actions. These stakeholder reactions derailed company efforts, literally in the case of Shell, at being socially responsible. In other words, the actions taken by these companies in Barendrecht and the Yadana Valley resonated far beyond – their success in creating value for the company, as well as for the world at large, turned out to be contingent on the thoughts, feelings, and actions of important stakeholders.

In this book, we have made the case for why all companies, large and small, local and global, *must ground their CR strategies in a sound and thorough understanding of their impact on two key stakeholder groups: consumers and employees.* In making our case, we have drawn on academic research in this domain to proffer an individual stakeholder perspective on CR, providing a sense for when, why, and how stakeholders respond to a company's initiatives. In particular, we have presented a stakeholder psychology model of CR, which underscores the need for three psychological levers – Understanding, Usefulness, and Unity – to work in unison in order for CR to create maximal stakeholder value. The power behind these levers is, in turn, impacted by several stakeholder- and company-specific features, which amplify or dampen the extent to which they create CR value for both the stakeholder and the company.

Applying our model to the Chevron and Shell scenarios makes apparent the failure of these companies to take into full account the importance of these psychological levers in setting off the *reactions* of their stakeholders to their CR *actions*. For instance, our model suggests that Shell would have been much more likely to achieve its CR goals had it taken into consideration the needs of the residents of Barendrecht and what it would have taken for the residents to benefit personally from Shell's actions. Putting insight into action, this book draws on our stakeholder psychology model to also suggest ways, in which a company might want to co-create, communicate, and calibrate its CR initiatives with the goal of maximizing business and social value.

That said, the field of CR is vast and our book only addresses a small piece of the puzzle. In the remainder of this final chapter, we look ahead to outline a few key areas that we believe merit further investigation and that hold rich promise for companies wishing to fully leverage CR's potential.

Understanding the reactions of other stakeholder realms

Given that most of our empirical research to date has focused on consumers and employees, this book primarily dealt with these two stakeholder groups. But even though studies have shown that these are the two predominant stakeholder groups, and although our general framework and approach should hold for many of the other stakeholders, it would be helpful to gain a deeper understanding of some of these other groups. To make the case for such investigation, we outline here what we have learned to date about how the investment, procurement, and government communities help create business value for the company.

Investment

Just as CR can create company value in the consumption and employment realms, so can it also create company value by increasing the intent of individuals to invest in the company. We find evidence in our work that, again, given the right conditions, individuals are prone to invest in companies that engage in CR initiatives. Investors today have an unprecedented selection of investment alternatives. With so many companies to choose from, it is not surprising that many individual investors, institutional investors, fund managers, and analysts are looking to incorporate non-economic criteria into their investment decisions. Investors subscribing to a philosophy of socially responsible investing (SRI) can place as much weight on social and environmental criteria as they do on financial returns.

SRI is no longer just a fringe phenomenon; rather, it appears to be having an impact on the financial markets as a whole and the trend towards SRI grows ever stronger. According to Ceres, a network of investors and NGOs, SRI is growing at a much faster pace than other professionally managed assets (18 percent compared to less than 3 percent between 2005 and 2007).[1] Friends Provident has a staff of 14 full-time SRI researchers who manage a total of £2.1 billion in ethically screened funds. Friends Provident's chief executive, Keith Satchell, says: "These funds specifically look at companies' social and environmental performance; and lack of disclosure, or poor reporting, is often a key factor in making the decision about whether we are willing to invest."[2]

Recall once more our study of stakeholder responses to a large corporate donation to a child development center. The results clearly showed that stakeholders who were aware of the gift had significantly greater intentions to purchase stock in the company than either of the two control groups that consisted of unaware respondents. Once again, further analysis showed that the primary driver of this effect was the enhanced sense of Unity that developed as a result of the CR activity.

Beyond the purchase of stock, shareholders are now generally more active and discerning with their proxy votes and are filing more shareholder resolutions than ever before; a growing proportion of these are related to responsibility issues, especially in the oil, gas, food, and waste sectors. For example, one resolution filed at Cabot Oil & Gas gained 35.9 percent support and at ExxonMobil, where a low vote total would not be unexpected due to dispersed ownership, a social and environmental resolution won 26.3 percent of shareholder support. A vote on potentially toxic Bisphenol A (BPA) at Coca-Cola gained 21.9 percent support.[3]

To the extent that investors find a company's CR activity to be Useful, we believe they will be willing to sacrifice time and effort on the company's behalf to file these resolutions. Such shareholder resolutions are typically constructive and improve both business and societal outcomes. For example, the Interfaith Center on Corporate Responsibility (ICCR) had planned to introduce a shareholder resolution at the company's annual general meeting forcing environmental compliance. However, when Ford announced details of an initiative that would cut new vehicle emissions by 30 percent before 2020, ICCR agreed to shelve the resolution.[4]

Overall, there is a need to establish more rigorously the various ways in which investors respond to a company's CR initiatives and, more generally, to establish how well our individual stakeholder psychology model holds up in the investor realm.

Procurement

In many industries, quality suppliers are a scarce yet mission-critical resource. Suppliers provide resources that can arm companies with a sustainable competitive advantage. These stakeholders supply materials, goods, and services, and otherwise enable the company to provide value to its end-customers.

When buyers compete for the attention of these suppliers, CR activity can provide an edge in tipping the scales in favor of one buyer over another. CR does not automatically increase the likelihood that suppliers will seek out a company and remain committed suppliers. Rather, in keeping with our framework we believe that CR builds a sense of Unity and reassures suppliers that a company is good to work with. Suppliers are likely to make efforts to partner closely with the buyer to the extent that suppliers feel that they can trust a buyer. The buyer's CR record can enhance that trust.

Consider Green Mountain Coffee Roasters, which is widely heralded for both its CR activity and its first-rate supplier relationships. Green Mountain knows that its CR activity indirectly attracts high quality suppliers because it communicates the values of the company in a way that fosters trust among the coffee-growing community. "There is always a risk that you'll have fewer suppliers in a market with growing demand," says Michael Dupee, vice president of corporate responsibility at Green Mountain Coffee Roasters. "By being active in your outreach you are sending a signal to high quality specialty coffee suppliers that we are good people to work with. Actions speak louder than words, and [CR] can strengthen relationships by showing how far you are willing to go in the relationship."[5]

CR can also lead suppliers to seek stronger relationships with their client companies through greater information sharing. Information sharing in supplier–buyer relationships can reduce conflict, improve efficiency and in some cases lead to significant innovations. The high quality relationships that CR creates can act as an incentive, which increases the likelihood that suppliers will share ideas and knowledge.

Consider once again Green Mountain's experience with one of its suppliers, which enabled them to introduce a groundbreaking advance before competitors. As Michael Dupee puts it, "[CR] sometimes enables us to engage in a commercial relationship at a higher level than we would otherwise. [A supplier] might bring us an idea before they bring them to other people." This happened when International Paper approached Green Mountain about introducing a paper cup that used a bio-liner polymer made from corn sugar. It would be the first commercially available compostable cup for hot liquid made entirely with renewable resources. (Most cups are made with a petroleum-based liner.) "International Paper knew who we were and the things we care about and *they came to us*. So here we are with a great product and a great story that reinforces the brand for both companies."

Again, although this is a good start, there remains a clear need to research more companies such as Green Mountain as well as the supplier community at large to validate our model.

Government

Government can have an undeniably strong impact on the regulatory environment in which companies operate. As we have shown with other instances of how CR enhances a stakeholder's relationship with the company and leads to pro-company behaviors, we conjecture that, similarly, it can lead to favorable actions from the government in the regulatory arena. While the details of a CR-regulation link remain largely unexplored, there is anecdotal evidence that a company's CR actions can create value through stakeholder activism and behaviors that, over time, influence government regulation. Such activism may be positive, in which government officials lobby others to support the company and promote its interests, or negative, where the government puts pressure on the company to change its behaviors. As one researcher has put it: "A firm's CR decisions can engender regulatory and political – as well as competitive – effects that companies need to understand and respond to."[6]

Other benefits of CR in the government realm are that it helps to maintain flexibility in negotiations with host governments in foreign markets, and helps to prevent government actors from erecting legal constraints on the business.[7] In other words, the success of CR activity can be measured in terms of the degree to which it motivates government officials to regulate in ways that help the company's business performance. Since many government officials depend on the electorate, these outcomes should be seen as the outgrowth of the relationship between the company and the citizenry at large, not just the legislators and regulators.

Similar to the investment and procurement realms, more research is needed to establish whether, why, how, and when government officials are affected by a firm's CR initiatives.

The cross-stakeholder effect

In this book, we studied how each individual stakeholder group – say, consumers and employees – responded to a firm's CR initiatives. For instance, we learned that employee engagement in CR leads to increased employee retention and positive word-of-mouth. But what if employee engagement in CR prompts them to be more customer-focused, which in turn increases customer satisfaction and loyalty? Or, do accounts of happier suppliers of a company prompt regulators to look on it more kindly? In other words, do the effects of CR cross over stakeholder groups and thereby compound their effects? Answers to these questions are important as they would shed invaluable light on the potential of CR to create shared value.

To date, we have conducted one study where we observed whether and how employee engagement in CR made them more customer-focused. Specifically, the study sought to understand whether and how CR drives a special case of workplace performance, the customer orientation of frontline employees. Customer orientation is the degree to which frontline employees "practice the marketing concept by trying to help their customers make purchase decisions that will satisfy customer needs."[8] Customer-oriented employees seek ways to benefit customers over the long term, rather than sacrificing the welfare of the customer in the interest of making an immediate sale.

To investigate the link between CR and customer orientation we surveyed more than 900 full-time employees in the retail and hospitality industries. (The panel was provided by a leading marketing research provider and the survey was administered as a programmed questionnaire over the Internet.) The central finding of this study is that engagement in CR initiatives *can* make employees more customer oriented. More specifically, the relationship between CR and customer orientation is driven by two intermediate steps: (1) the Usefulness of the programs to employees, and (2) the sense of Unity that employees sense *between themselves and customers*.

The first finding, that Usefulness drives customer orientation, is consistent with our framework. Highly effective CR programs underscore the relational aspect of frontline employees' job-roles as service providers[9] and help people develop a sense of work–home balance (a component of Usefulness). Likewise, participation in CR initiatives, whether through donations, volunteering, or other means, provides employees with self-esteem and work–home balance because through participation, employees are enabled to co-create initiatives so that they maximally fulfill their personal needs.

The sense of *Unity with customers* is more counterintuitive. We find that employees feel psychologically closer to customers when they believe that customers support the same CR programs that they do. Having common CR goals signals an overlap in values between employees and customers. This "kinship" with customers ends up being a catalyst for great customer service, because employees not only want to serve those with whom they share values, but also feel more capable of doing so, because they can more easily put themselves "in the customer's shoes," gaining insight into their needs.

Overall, through this research we learn that CR can enhance customer relationships not only through consumers' direct exposure to the activity itself, but also through indirect effects via employee behaviors. Thus, the sense of customer and employee Unity with one another in relation to CR represents an additional factor by which companies can multiply the value of their CR among two of their primary stakeholder audiences, employees and consumers. Going forward, we need to conduct more studies in other stakeholder realms to learn more about these cross-stakeholder effects.

Longer term perspective and emphasis on social value

We emphasized time and again in the book that creating business value through the indirect route of stakeholder reactions is highly contingent on creating social value first. However, the emphasis was always on indices and metrics that companies care about: purchase, loyalty, word-of-mouth, etc., and for the most part the measures we obtained were at a point in time. We believe that going forward, we need to (1) broaden the portfolio of measures and include more measures related not only to social and environmental performance of the firm but also to other outcomes relevant to stakeholders such as "quality of life," and (2) take a longer term as well as longitudinal measurement perspective. These two issues are inextricably related; we elaborate the need for each below.

In early 2008, the French President, Nicolas Sarkozy, created The Commission on the Measurement of Economic Performance and Social Progress (which included economists such as Joseph Stiglitz and Amartya Sen) to identify the limits of GDP as an indicator of economic performance and social progress and to identify more relevant indicators of social progress. In their interim report, the Commission suggested that the time is ripe for our measurement system to *shift emphasis from measuring economic production to measuring people's well-being.*[10]

In other words, we (as a collective) are slowly but surely recognizing that economic indicators are imperfect proxies for social progress. Beyond measuring brand loyalty and word-of-mouth then, companies can also broadly measure subjective well-being for relevant stakeholder groups – e.g., happiness and/or pride at being a consumer, employee, or investor – and try to relate these outcomes to CR. Given that these measures are applicable to virtually all stakeholder groups, adopting such measures may even ultimately help blur the distinction between business and social outcomes and help us view everything from a societal welfare perspective.

It is equally important to measure diligently the impact of CR initiatives, especially in the social arena. For example, in the example of the oral health program, the prevalence of "lost school days" was touted as a major motivation for investing in children's dental hygiene. The reaction to the program would likely be more positive had the executing company actually estimated roughly the school days that were "saved" (rather than lost) because of the program.

Similarly, the "school readiness" program of PNC Bank and many other programs related to childhood education in underprivileged communities would benefit from trying to assess school performance, drop-out rates, and other longer term measures of social progress traditionally used by researchers in social marketing and social work. Note that these are just examples; depending on the program, the metrics could relate to malnutrition, mortality, disease, environmental footprint, and other relevant issues, again culminating in quality of life indicators such as satisfaction, pride, happiness, and security about the future. Importantly, increased emphasis on social and environmental measures could also spur greater collaboration between researchers who have thus far maintained largely parallel lives.

As may be evident from the discussion above, one of the key impediments for businesses to be engaged in such measurement schemes is the long-term nature of the beast. In an environment where institutions are largely rewarded for short-term performance, it is hard to sustain energy and enthusiasm in the long haul. However, as businesses are recognized more for their achievements in the social sphere rather than solely for their financial performance, such a longer-term perspective may gain greater currency.

Even from a strictly business standpoint, a longer time horizon and ongoing measurement are useful. For example, tracking studies of the 3 U's could reveal what parts of a strategy need strengthening. Furthermore, given that akin to brand communication, CR communication will occur according to a "plan," it may help to ask questions such as: (1) What does the "decay curve" for CR awareness look like? (2) How long do positive attitudes and behaviors stemming from a CR initiative typically last? Answers to these questions can only be obtained through ongoing, longitudinal measurement and can help optimize the CR communication strategy.

Bringing the multi-minded stakeholder to life

In this book, we introduced the notion that all of us play multiple roles in our lives – consumer, employee, investor, family member, community participant, regulator, etc. – to make the point that social responsibility initiatives touch us all. However, there is a bigger issue to be explored – perhaps in a future book. One of the key impediments to the long-term success of sustainability strategies is our tendency to view each role through a separate lens, e.g., all else equal, as consumers, we want to pay the lowest possible price; as employees, we want to earn the most amount of money; and as investors, we want to earn maximum possible returns. No wonder then that companies are under tremendous pressure to think short-term – cut prices, produce dividends... the works.

But if all of us (as multi-minded stakeholders) could somehow dissolve the partitions in our minds to practice "responsible stakeholder-ism" across all realms and roles, all parties alike would be able to focus more wholeheartedly on the single goal that affects everyone on our planet: a sustainable future.

Endnotes

1 Ceres: The 21st Century Corporation: The Ceres Roadmap for Sustainability, available through www.ceres.org/ceresroadmap, accessed March 22, 2011.
2 www.independent.co.uk/news/business/analysis-and-features/do-blue-chips-green-reports-show-their-true-colours-466969.html, accessed April 9, 2009.
3 www.justmeans.com/Sustainable-Shareholder-Resolutions-Gain-Record-Levels-of-Support-in-2010/21874.html, accessed March 22, 2011.
4 www.mallenbaker.net/csr/CSRfiles/page.php?Story_ID=2055, accessed July 1, 2008.
5 Telephone conversation, November 12, 2008.
6 D.A. Detomasi, "The Political Roots of Corporate Social Responsibility," *Journal of Business Ethics*, 82 (2008), 807–19, 807.
7 J. Peloza (2005), "CSR as Reputation Insurance," University of California, Berkeley Working Paper (2005), #24, available at: http://repositories.cdlib.org/crb/wps/24, accessed April 9, 2009.
8 R. Saxe and W.A. Barton, "The SOCO Scale: A Measure of the Customer Orientation of Salespeople," *Journal of Marketing Research*, 19(3) (1982), 343–51.
9 A.M. Grant (2007), "Relational Job Design and the Motivation to Make a Prosocial Difference," *Academy of Management Review*, 32(2) (2007), 393–417; D.M. Sluss and B.E. Ashforth, "Relational Identity and Identification: Defining Ourselves Through Work Relationships," *Academy of Management Review*, 32(1) (2007), 9–32.
10 www.stiglitz-sen-fitoussi.fr/documents/rapport_anglais.pdf, accessed August 23, 2010.

APPENDIX

Our research program

Our research program

This book brings together a series of studies that we have conducted over a period of about ten years. Our research program has examined stakeholder responses to CR in numerous stakeholder realms, across a wide range of settings, and utilizing a variety of research methods. The breadth of our research agenda enables us to triangulate our findings, examining the issue from multiple standpoints. This substantially increases the validity and generalizability of our framework. Below we describe a number of the studies that are profiled frequently in the chapters above; additional information about the studies is available from the authors.

General CR Insights Study[1]

Multiple methods were used to assess consumer responses to CR. About 100 respondents took part in a series of focus groups and interviews conducted with the general population of the US. The studies covered all major aspects of the framework. The central objective of the studies was to understand how CR inputs lead to Understanding, Usefulness, and Unity, and how these initial internal outcomes (i.e., outcomes that occur in the mind of the consumer) lead in turn to business value and social value. Findings established these linkages and identified a number of context factors that influence the linkages.

Technology Company Study[2]

Multiple experiments were run with consumers to determine the effect of a company's CR record on purchase intent. Subjects were recruited from student pools at multiple universities in the Northeast. A total of 622 people participated in the experiments. In both studies, subjects began by reading a short statement about a well-known company selling calculators, printers, or computers (the company name was disguised). The statement included a description of the company's CR activities. Some participants were given a statement describing a positive CR record (e.g., an employee diversity program, a program to eliminate sweatshops in the company's factories) while others were given information about a negative CR record (e.g., eliminating an employee diversity program, having sweatshops in the company's factories); a third group of subjects served as a control and received no CR information. In addition to CR record, respondents were also informed through the description that the company's product quality was either high or low. Identification and evaluations (Unity), attributions (Understanding), and purchase intent (business value) were measured after exposure to the descriptions. Subjects also reported their support of the CR issue (a context factor). We analyzed the effects of CR record, product quality, and issue support on Unity and business value using a statistical technique called three-stage least squares regression, finding that the effects were significant and that the three factors interacted significantly.

Yogurt Study[3]

In this field survey, consumer opinions about three leading yogurt brands were sought in order to understand the multiplying influence of CR positioning on Unity and business value. The survey was delivered over the Internet to a nationally representative panel of consumers supplied by a leading market research firm. Our questionnaire asked respondents questions about Understanding, Unity, and business value as well as their preferred brand of yogurt. Each of the yogurt consumers included in our final sample (a total of 1,062) was a frequent purchaser of one of three brands: Stonyfield, Dannon, or Yoplait, and aware of the brands' CR initiatives. Responses for frequent purchasers of Stonyfield, a brand strongly associated with its social responsibility practices, were compared to responses from frequent buyers of Dannon and Yoplait, which both run CR initiatives but not as the central feature of what the brands stand for. Results revealed that awareness and attributions (Understanding), identification (Unity), and loyalty and brand advocacy (business value) were all more favorable for the CR brand than either of the control brands (i.e., non-CR positioned).

Employee Study[4]

The study was designed to examine the impact of CR in the workplace. Eight focus groups were carried out in various locations of a consumer products multinational including the company's world headquarters, a manufacturing plant, a regional sales office, and one non-US location. Groups of 5–8 people were structured to represent a broad cross section of the company's employee base. Topics included in the two hour discussions were their conceptualization of CR, perceptions of the company's CR efforts (Understanding), needs fulfilled by CR (Usefulness), identification with the company (Unity), work effort and retention (business value), and volunteering outside of work (social value). The results established a clear set of relationships between CR, Understanding, Usefulness, Unity, and value. The research was augmented – and further supported – with additional in-depth interviews and a follow-up survey conducted by the company of more than 10,000 members of its global workforce.

Frontline Employee Study[5]

A field survey of over 900 employees in the retail and hospitality industries was carried out to understand the effect of CR on workplace behaviors of frontline employees. The sample was taken from a nationwide panel of employees provided by a leading market research company. All respondents had regular and direct contact with customers as part of their job. The instrument began with business value such as customer orientation behaviors, and went on to assess their awareness, perceptions of the efficacy of their employers' programs (Understanding), work–home balance, pride in the company (Usefulness), and identification with the company (Unity). The 557 survey participants who were aware that their employer engaged in CR activities were analyzed using a number of statistical techniques including multiple regression and structural equation modeling with manifest variables. Results supported our contention that Understanding and Usefulness work together to improve Unity and, ultimately, business value.

Firm Market Value Study[6]

This study examined the market value of companies as a function of CR activity. The study aggregated secondary data from a set of 113 Fortune 500 companies which spanned a number of industries, including auto, household appliances, personal computers, cigarettes, athletic shoes, airlines, hotels, utilities, department stores, discount stores, and supermarkets. Measures were taken from multiple third-party sources including COMPUSTAT, Fortune America's Most Admired Companies (FAMA), the American Customer Satisfaction Index, Competitive Media Reporting, and the Center for Research in Security Prices. The variables included in the study focused on CR record, evaluations (Unity) and stock price returns, and Tobin's Q, a measure of a firm's intangible value (business value). Product quality and innovativeness capacity (context factors; both measured using FAMA ratings) were also analyzed to see how they influenced the CR-Unity link and the CR-business value link. Analysis using a statistical technique called structural equation modeling showed that CR drives business value by first leading to Unity; analysis of the context factors showed that the effect of CR is much stronger for high product quality and high innovativeness companies than for peers that are low on either dimension.

Consumer Oral Care Program Study[7]

A two-phase, multi-method approach was used to assess the responses of families to a CR program in which they participated. The research looked at the business and social value of the oral care program run by a global consumer products company. The program is named after the toothpaste brand of the company and targets disadvantaged youths mainly through the company's alliance with the Boys and Girls Clubs of America. The research examined responses of Hispanic families since this was one of the key target segments of the program. The first phase involved focus groups with parents whose children participated in the program. The focus groups, which were conducted in Spanish, began with general discussions of oral and dental hygiene, perceptions of the program (Understanding), benefits of the program (Usefulness), their relationship with the consumer products company and the toothpaste brand (Unity), intentions to purchase the brand (business value), and the changes in oral and dental hygiene habits of themselves and especially their children (social value). Phase two was a quantitative survey which examined Understanding, Usefulness, Unity, value, and the degree of acculturation of respondents. The responses of program participants were compared to a control group comprised of Hispanics in the general population with a similar demographic profile to program participants (household income, education, employment status, marital status). Results supported our assertion that Understanding and Usefulness contribute to Unity, which drives business and social value, but that these are dependent upon context factors such as acculturation of stakeholders.

Childhood Development Center Study[8]

A quasi-experiment was conducted in the field to examine responses to the announcement of a $1 million gift by a global corporation to a child development center at a major state university. The gift was announced with a week-long communications campaign involving emails, newspaper articles, announcements at the homecoming football game, and other means. A total of 948 undergraduate students at the university were invited to participate in a web-based survey. The study was conducted using a variation on a pre-post design with some respondents invited before the announcement, and others invited two weeks after the announcement had been made. Unity, Understanding, and business value in the consumption, employment, and investment realms were recorded for all respondents, and post-announcement respondents were asked whether or not they were aware before taking the survey that the company had given a $1 million gift to the university. Ninety-eight respondents were aware of the donation; we compared their responses to two control groups: (1) those who answered before the announcement and were therefore unaware, and (2) those who responded after the announcement, but were not aware of the donation. On numerous measures, we found no difference between the control groups, but significant differences between the aware group and *both* control groups. As a result we were able to establish that the gift yielded business value and that Unity was the driving force behind these behaviors.

Endnotes to Appendix

1. CB Bhattacharya and S. Sen, "Doing Better at Doing Good: When, Why, and How Consumers Respond to Corporate Social Initiatives," *California Management Review*, 47(1) (2004), 9–24.
2. S. Sen and CB Bhattacharya, "Does Doing Good Always Lead to Doing Better? Consumer Reactions to Corporate Social Responsibility," *Journal of Marketing Research*, 38(2) (2001), 225–43.
3. S. Du, CB Bhattacharya, and S. Sen, "Reaping Relational Rewards from Corporate Social Responsibility: The Role of Competitive Positioning," *International Journal of Research in Marketing*, 24(3) (2007), 224–41.
4. CB Bhattacharya, S. Sen, and D. Korschun, "Using Corporate Social Responsibility To Win the War for Talent," *MIT Sloan Management Review*, 49(2) (2008), 37–44.
5. D. Korschun, When and How Corporate Social Responsibility Makes a Company's Frontline Employees Customer Oriented, Doctoral Dissertation, Boston University, Boston, MA.
6. X. Luo and CB Bhattacharya, "Corporate Social Responsibility, Customer Satisfaction, and Market Value," *Journal of Marketing*, 70(4) (2006), 1–18.
7. S. Du, S. Sen, and CB Bhattacharya, "Exploring the Social and Business Returns of a Corporate Oral Health Initiative Aimed at Disadvantaged Hispanic Families," *Journal of Consumer Research*, 35(3) (2008), 483–94.
8. S. Sen, CB Bhattacharya, and D. Korschun, "The Role of Corporate Social Responsibility in Strengthening Multiple Stakeholder Relationships: A Field Experiment," *Journal of the Academy of Marketing Science*, 34(2) (2006), 158–66.

Index

Index of names

Arnould, Eric J., 174, 175

Bagozzi, Richard P., 225
Becker-Olsen, Karen, 137
Bergami, Massimo, 225
Bhattacharya, CB, 15, 140, 142
Blazing, J., 203
Bloom, P.N., 203
Brugmann, Jeb, 168

Cadbury, George, 27–28
Castro-Wright, Eduardo, 260
Clark, Sarah, 260
Copeland, Jim, 29
Cotte, June, 55
Curtis, Paul, 79

Dawkins, Jenny, 90, 204
Du, Shuili, 196, 229
Dupee, Michael, 298, 299
Durgee, Jeffrey, 163

Elfenbein, Hillary Anger, 31
Ellen, Pam Scholder, 94
Epstein, Marc, 45

Forehand, M.R., 198
Friestad, M., 192

Greening, Daniel, 57
Grier, S., 198

Hamilton, Lisa, 121
Henderson, Judy, 29

Irmak, Caglar, 156

Jayachandran, Satish, 156

Kahn, B.E., 191, 193
Kemp, Danny, 4
Klein, Jill Gabriele, 97
Kramer, Mark R., 8

Laberge, Myriam, 158, 177
Langers, Bob, 91
Lichtenstein, Donald R., 61
Luo, Xueming, 15, 140, 142

Margolis, Joshua D., 31
Markus, Frits, 16
Mars, Tom, 260
Menon, S., 191, 193
Mohr, L.A., 193, 194
Muniz, Albert M., 174, 175

Naing, Htoo, 5

Owen, Robert, 27

Porter, Michael E., 8
Prahalad, C.K., 157, 168, 177
Pringle, Hamish, 29

Ramaswamy, Venkat, 157, 177
Rosen, Stefanie, 156
Ruete, Matthias, 17

Salt, Sir Titus, 27
Sarkozy, Nicolas, 302
Satchell, Keith, 296
Schau, Hope Jensen, 174, 175
Sen, Amartya, 302
Silten, Bobbi, 59
Sorrell, Sir Martin, 45
Stiglitz, Joseph, 302
Svendsen, Ann, 158, 177
Syzkman, L.R., 203

Thompson, Marjorie, 29
Trudel, Remi, 55
Turban, Daniel, 57

van der Veer, Jeroen, 17
van Heugten, Marianne, 16
Vogel, David, 28

Walsh, James P., 31
Watanabe, Katsuaki, 29
Webb, D.J., 193, 194
Whooley, Niamh, 113
Widener, Sally, 45
Wright, P., 192

Yoon, Y., 203

Index of subjects

3M, 42

Accenture, 8
AccountAbility, 167
advertising, 189, 202
AIDS International, 184
Air France, 207
American Customer Satisfaction Index, 15
American Diabetes Association, 201
America's Second Harvest, 261, 276
annual reporting, 75
Apple, 93, 109
Aramark, 160
  Aramark Building Community, 161, 170
Article 13, 163
associations
  corporate ability associations, 110
  CR associations, 110
  and employees' commitment, 250
  and identification, 281
AT&T, 167
attributions, 92–96, 115, 190, 198
  and consensus, 96
  and consumer responses to CR initiatives, 96, 200
  and CR efficacy, 96
  extrinsic, 93, 94, 200
  intrinsic, 93, 94–95, 193, 200
  and trust, 114
Avon, 200

Back to Sleep campaign, 195
Balanced Scorecard, 239
Barendrecht, Netherlands, 15–17, 294
BASF, 79
Ben & Jerry, 200, 205
benefits of CR activity, 31, 62, 101
  empirical evidence for identity-related benefits, 102–07
  functional benefits, 100–07, 163, 165, 179
  identity-related benefits, 102–07, 163, 164, 165
  psychosocial benefits, 179

Bentley Center for Marketing
    Technology, 92
Body Shop, 54, 200
Boys and Girls Club of America, 37
BP, 93
branding, 78, 143–44, 174, 176
Budweiser, 201
Business Ethics, 139
Business for Social Responsibility, 44
business value, 36, 45–46, 47, 49–60,
    63, 140, 247, 302
  effects of CR on, 140
  and product quality, 143

calibration of CR strategies, 213, 214
  assessment of the effectiveness of CR
    programs, 215–20
  assessment of stakeholders'
    interpretations of CR, 220–27
  factors in maximizing CR value,
  focusing on the key drivers of CR
    value, 230–32
  measurement of individual behavior,
    217, 231
  measurement of stakeholder
    relationships, 214–19, 227, 233,
    237
  method of establishing linkages,
    228–30
  ongoing nature of, 242
  qualitative and quantitative
    research, 241
  questionnaires, 233
  statistical techniques, 229
  structural equation modeling, 244,
    272
  study design, 228
  Understanding, 220
Carrefour, 198
causal thinking, 92
cause advocacy, 60–61
CDA Collaborative Learning Projects,
    5

Center for Corporate Citizenship, 160
Ceres, 296
Chevron, 1–6, 11, 294
  Myanmar Community Development
    Program, 2–3
  Yadana Valley Project, 2–3, 294
child development center, corporate
    donation to, 89, 111, 296
Children's Miracle Network, 261
Clorox
  Green Works products, 79
  Reverse Graffiti Project, 79, 80
Coca-Cola, 74
Commission on the Measurement of
    Economic Performance and Social
    Progress, 302
community of virtue, 174, 175, 179
companies
  annual reporting, 75
  CR-positioning of, 144, 145
  CR reporting, 77
  culture of service, 146
  customer-centric, 147
  engagement of employees with, 57
  expectations of, 28, 114, 142
  need for sensitivity to context,
    121
  quality or product/service dimension
    of, 144
  regulation of, 299
  social dimension of, 143
  social legitimacy, 154
  third-party evaluations of, 81, 196
  views of CR, 29–32
  websites, 79
company characteristics, 144–47
  organizational culture, 146–47, 148
  reputation, 145–46, 148, 159
  size and demographics, 146
company context, 135–47, 232
  company characteristics, 144–47
  core business, 140–44
  CR-positioning, 144, 145

company context (*cont.*)
  factors in, 135
  measurement of factors in, 235–37
  and type of CR activity, 136–40
Cone Communications, 10–11, 49
consumers, 10; *see also* customers
  demand for CR, 29
  as embedded stakeholders, 123
  as enactors of CR initiatives, 173
  engagement with CR, 156, 174
  intent to purchase products, 33, 49, 216
  involvement in creation of CR initiatives, 157
  loyalty, 54–55, 144
  perceptions of value co-creation, 157
  process of comparing brands, 279
  reactions to information about companies, 7
  self-esteem, 279
  surveys of, 10
consumption
  measurable aspects of, 50–56
  purchasing, 50–54
  willingness to pay, 55–56
  word-of-mouth, 56, 205, 209
context
  company context, 122, 232
  examples of, 134
  factors in, 122, 232–37
  influence of, 119–50
  significance of, 119–20
  stakeholder context, 122–35
core business, 144, 145
  and CR issues, 200
  factors in, 140
  marketing strategy, 143–44
  product quality, 140–43
corporate responsibility, 3, 7, 30
  benefits of, 44
  characteristics sought by stakeholders, 70–76
  communication channels for, 76–82
  companies' view of, 29–32
  and a company's long-term strategy, 30
  demand for, 28, 29, 281
  diffusion and prominence of, 28
  history of, 27–28
  implementation, 72, 73–74
  reporting on, 77, 98, 187, 202, 209
  research on, 295, 306–12
  resources for, 75–76
  stakeholder reactions to, 48, 85–118, 218–19
  strategic approach to, 8, 29
  in the yogurt industry, 275–77
Corporate Social Opportunity, 30
CR activities, 88
  assessment of, 139, 170
  awareness of, 87–92, 263
  benefits for the company, 31
  benefits for management, 62
  co-creation of, 125
  community engagement in, 174
  and customer orientation of employees, 301
  distinctiveness of, 136
  examples of, 183–85
  executive buy-in, 160
  as an expression of a company's character, 113, 225, 282
  features of, 168
  and financial performance, 11
  and fit with the company, 136–37, 148, 199–201
  formulation and implementation of, 158
  functional benefits, 116
  goals of, 61, 121, 159, 179
  government responses to, 299–300
  history of, 153–57

and identification, 110
and improvement of lives of
    stakeholders, 14
investors' responses to, 296–300
as a means to reduce the cost of
    capital, 159
motivations behind, 43, 92, 198
optimization of a portfolio of,
    239–41
participation in, 128
pilot testing of, 170
and procurement decisions, 297–99
and reputation, 145
and self-continuity, 105
and social capital, 175
societal value, 195
stakeholders' interpretation of, 35,
    138–40
tailored to stakeholders' needs, 39
uniting employees in multiple
    locations, 106
CR communication, 77, 137–38, 172,
    209, 231, 304
  about social issues, 192
  acknowledgement of failures, 197
  and awareness of CR activities, 90
  breadth of, 77–78
  channels for, 76–82, 188, 201–06,
    209
  commitment to the issue, 192–94
  consumer reactions to, 191
  content of the message, 191–201
  control over content, 203, 206,
    208
  creation of, 199
  credibility of, 188, 198, 201, 203,
    205, 206, 208
  to customers, 9
  and education, 206–08
  effectiveness of, 187, 194–97
  to employees, 9
  examples of effective use of, 78–79
  factors in commitment, 193
  of the fit between a company's CR
    issues and its identity, 199
  goals of, 191
  "guerilla" communications, 80
  and identity-related needs of
    stakeholders, 107
  innovations in, 79–81
  internal, 204
  and issue-oriented TV programs, 80
  of motives for CR activities,
    197–99
  and optimizing the 3 U's, 188–91
  potential negatives of, 81–82
  quality of, 138
  quality of attention to, 91, 115
  risks in, 189, 190
  target of, 189
  top-down or bottom-up approach,
    139
  and trust, 139
  and viral media, 79
CR dashboard, 237–39, 242, 244, 262,
    264
CR demand, 28, 29, 281
CR formulation process, 158
  articulation, 159–61
  creating partnerships, 168–69
  culture of participation, 161
  dialog with stakeholders, 158,
    161–63, 164
  distillation, 166–67, 179
  experimentation, 169–71
  follow-up questions, 170
  formation of a development team,
    168
  generation, 161–66, 179
  laddering, 163–66
  market research with stakeholders,
    163
  quasi-experiments, 169
  selection of initiatives, 167–71, 179

CR implementation, 73–74, 171–78, 179
    enactors versus enablers, 172–74, 179
    examples of, 72
    factors in success of, 171–72
    formal versus informal, 176–78
    horizontal versus vertical, 174–76, 179
    laddering, 179
    monitoring, evaluation, and reward systems, 177
    top-down, 155, 172
    types of, 73
CR issues, 29, 70–71
    categories of, 71
    commitment to, 192–94
    company's involvement with, 167, 191
    prioritizing of, 71
CR performance; see also calibration of CR strategies
    interpretation of, 197
    measurement of, 196
    third-party certification, 196
CR programs, 17; see also CR activities
    applying knowledge to improve, 237–39
    coordination between, 241
    and employee–company relationships, 246
    goals for evaluation of, 216
    influence of context, 119–50
    key performance indicators, 237
    link between spending and results, 98
    meeting their intended effects, 215–20
    'one size fits all', 121–22
    partnerships with non-profit organizations, 38
    as a portfolio of initiatives, 241, 242
    processes for evaluation of, 214, 242
    providing a win-win-win solution, 37, 96
    and stakeholders' needs, 18
CR strategy
    and closeness, 186, 190
    co-creation of, 153–81
    communication of, 186–212
    involvement of stakeholders in creation of, 157–59
CR value, 1–22, 25
    business value, 36, 45–46, 47, 49–60, 63, 140, 247, 302
    co-creation of, 148, 172
    consumption and business value, 49–56
    creation of, 13, 25, 31, 45
    direct route to, 31, 39, 42, 43, 62, 148, 155
    employment and business value, 52, 56–60
    formal versus informal, 179
    framework for achieving, 34–36
    generation of, 213
    indicators of, 283
    indirect route to, 31
    individuality of, 42
    and management decision-making, 45
    measurement of, 47
    and the psychological drivers of stakeholder behavior, 227–37
    quantification of stakeholder perceptions, 214–27
    societal value, 36, 46, 60–62, 63, 195, 199, 217, 302–04
    and stakeholder behavior, 215
    stakeholder route to, 31–32, 39, 62, 148
    and the 3 U's, 247–55
    types of, 45–46
    and Unity, 231

customers, 255; *see also* consumers
   and CR management, 9
   loyalty, 216
   target of CR communications, 9

Dannon, 14, 54, 144, 275–83
   CR activities, 276
   CR associations, 278
   implications of the evaluation of its CR activities, 282–83
   self-esteem, 283
   and the 3 U's, 277–83
   Understanding, 277–79, 282
   Unity, 280–82
   Usefulness, 279–80
Dannon Institute, 276, 277
dashboard for calibrating CR strategies, 237–39, 242, 244, 262, 264
Deloitte, 29
Den Tek Oral Care, 201
Diageo, 73, 201
Diet Coke, 202
Disney, 'Give a Day, Get a Disney Day' program, 173, 174
donations to charity, measurement of, 217
Dow Jones Sustainability Index, 204

Earthkeepers, 175–76, 205–06
EarthRights International, 4
efficacy of CR programs, 96–99, 125, 172, 194–97, 221–23, 250, 252
   empirical evidence on, 97
   and negative perceptions, 97
   and positive attributions, 96
employees
   advocacy for the company, 204
   attributions and efficacy of CR programs, 97
   awareness of CR activities, 89, 126–27, 247

benefits of CR activity, 101, 102, 165, 301
and company size and demographics, 147
and CR management, 9
customer-service focus, 34, 300
defense of companies' reputation, 103
demand for CR, 29
and development of CR initiatives, 155–56
as embedded stakeholders, 123
empowerment of, 156
as enactors of CR initiatives, 172
engagement with CR, 57, 105, 156, 300
evaluation of CR activities, 255
guidance and resources for CR activities, 172
identification, 254
location of work and engagement with CR, 106–07, 126–27, 233
opportunities to gain skills from CR activities, 101
organizational self-esteem, 103
participation in CR activities, 128, 253
performance of, 217
reactions to CR in the retail sector, 245–46
reactions to information about companies, 7
recognition and reward, 173
recruitment and retention of, 57–60, 159, 176, 216, 249–51
relationships with companies, 245, 254
self-esteem, 102, 301
sense of Unity with employers, 59
skills gained through participation in CR programs, 165
support for CR activities, 172–73

employees (*cont.*)
    target of CR communications, 9
    trust and CR activities, 114
    work–life balance, 106, 107, 251, 265, 266
    work performance, 57–59
Emporio Armani, 73, 136
equity, 29
Extreme Makeover Home Edition, 80

Feeding America, 261, 276
financial performance, and CR investment, 11
Fleishman-Hilliard, 91
Fortune magazine, 204
framework for achieving CR value, 34–36, 230–32, 244–84
    and context, 36
    benefits for management, 37–38, 39
    impact factors for, 258, 274
    the 3 U's, 35, 85–87
Friends Provident, 296

GAP, 59
gap analyses, 239
GE, ecomagination brand, 14, 78, 95, 235
General Mills, donations to charity, 14, 75
Girl Guides and Girl Scouts, 120
Global Compact, 8, 9, 155
Global Reporting Initiative, 29, 42
Godrej, 154
Google, 58
government responses to CR activities, 299–300
Green Mountain Coffee Roasters, 59, 298–99
Greenpeace, 204
greenwashing, 6, 187

Home Depot, 73, 74
    and Habitat for Humanity, 137

IBM, volunteering, 75
identification, 50, 108–12, 116, 251
    and loyalty, 255
    measurement of, 225, 226
    and purchase loyalty, 254
identity, core defining characteristics of, 111
information overload, 91, 115, 208
information, sharing of, 298
integrated marketing communications, 77, 82
interdependence of stakeholders and companies, 158
Interfaith Center on Corporate Responsibility, 297
International Paper, 31, 32, 299
investors, 296–300
    demand for CR, 29
    heterogeneity of, 33
    responses to CR, 296–300
Ipsos-MORI survey, 90
Ipsos-Reid survey, 90

Johnson & Johnson, 192
JustMeans, 82

Kellogg, 82
KLD Research Analytics, 71
knowledge, sharing of, 160, 240

loyalty, and identification, 255

market for virtue, 27–29, 39
market research, 163, 221, 229–30
marketing strategy, and CR activities, 77, 82, 143–44
MarketTools, 267
Marks & Spencer, 240
matching gift programs, 156
materiality matrix, 163, 167
McDonald's, 80, 91
McKinsey survey, 9, 44, 159
Microsoft, 73, 109

MTV, 80
multipliers, 119, 147
  caring, 129
  closeness, 124–29
Myanmar, 1, 2–3, 4–6

National Council of la Raza, 267
National Institute of Child Health and Human Development, 195
Neighborhood Centers Inc., 170–71
Nestlé, 46–48, 204
  CR initiatives, 71
  framework for creating shared value, 47
  outcomes of CR initiatives, 47
  participation in CR conferences, 206
  stakeholder-related drivers of societal value, 47
networking, 101
Newman's Own, 62
nongovernmental organizations, 154, 168

Océ UK Ltd., 207
Ogilvy & Mather, 80
oral health program, 37–38, 51–54, 62, 88, 95, 97, 127, 186–87, 310–11
  benefits of, 100, 182, 303
  consumption realm outcomes of, 53
  effects of closeness, 127
  efficacy of, 97
  functional benefits, 100–01, 224
  influence of acculturation of participants, 133–35, 235
  measurement of functional benefits, 224
  measurement of Understanding, 234–35
  motivations behind, 95
organizational self-esteem, 103

Pampers, "One Pack = One Vaccine" program, 195
Patagonia, 187
PepsiCo, Pepsi-Refresh project, 161
PNC Bank, Grow Up Great program, 162, 165, 166, 198, 303
Procter & Gamble, 14
procurement, 297–99
product quality, 140–43, 148
  and business value, 143
  and purchase intentions, 141
Product(RED), 73, 136
psychological drivers of stakeholder behavior, 13, 14, 19, 85–118, 147, 284, 294, 295
  attributional beliefs and, 92
  closeness and, 124
  and CR value, 227–37
  empirical test of, 255–59
  impact factors for, 257
  measurement of, 222
  and specific CR initiatives, 162
  Understanding, 87–99; see also separate entry
  Unity, 107–14; see also separate entry
  Usefulness, 99–107; see also separate entry
purchase intentions, and product quality, 141
purchase loyalty, 253–55
  and identification, 254

questionnaires, 233, 246

Reebok, 160
reputation, 145–46, 148, 159
  and identity-related benefits of CR activities, 103
research methods, 14
  descriptive studies, 15
  experiments, 15
  field surveys, 15

research methods (*cont.*)
　focus groups, 14
　interviews, 14
research program, 306–12
　child development center study, 311
　consumer oral care program study, 310–11
　employee study, 308
　firm market value study, 309–10
　frontline employee study, 309
　general CR insights study, 306
　technology company study, 307
　yogurt consumers, study of, 307–08
resources for CR activities, 75–76, 138
　and awareness of CR activities, 75
　measurement of, 76
　size of commitment, 75
　types of, 75
retail sector, research on employees in, 246–47, 309
　employee turnover, 249–51
　purchase loyalty, 253–55
　questionnaire, 246, 286–90
　work effort, 252–53
Revlon, 137
Ritter Sport, 194

Salvation Army, 261
Scandic, 158
Sears, 80
self-confidence, 100, 164
self-continuity, 102, 105, 116, 165
self-esteem, 100, 102, 116, 164, 165
shared value, 8, 19, 46–49, 63
shareholder resolutions, 297, 299
Shell, 15–17, 173, 294, 295
　carbon capture and storage, 16, 294
　CR reporting, 187
　stakeholder opposition to, 17
social acceptance, 100
social capital, 175–76

social justice, 29
social marketing initiatives, 173
social media, 204, 205, 209
social progress, 303
socially responsible investing, 296
societal value, 36, 46, 60–62, 63, 195, 199, 217, 302–04
　behavior changes, 61–62
　cause advocacy, 60–61
　measurement of, 60, 217
stakeholder activism, 299
stakeholder context, 122–35, 232
　caring, 129–32, 148
　characteristics of stakeholders, 132–35
　closeness to the company and to CR activities, 123–29, 147, 157
　empirical studies on caring, 131–32
　empirical studies on closeness, 125–29
　measurement of factors in, 233–35
　participation in CR activities, 129
　and product quality, 141
stakeholder route to CR value, 31–32, 39, 44–45, 62, 148
stakeholders
　advocacy behavior, 127, 204, 208
　assessment of their interpretations of CR, 217–23
　attributions, 92–96
　awareness of CR activities, 111, 138, 190, 207
　benefits of CR activities, 48, 99
　and co-creation of CR programs, 19
　complexity of responses to CR, 12
　concern for corporate responsibility, 10–11
　confidence in the reliability and integrity of a company, 112

and CR communications, 69–84, 189
and CR implementation, 74
the cross-stakeholder effect, 300–02
cultural factors, 133–35
demographic factors, 132–33
donations to charity, 60
education of, 206–08
and the effectiveness of CR initiatives, 194
embedded, 123, 125, 174
employees, 179
empowerment of, 171
engagement with CR, 12, 18, 154
evaluation of CR activities, 69, 95, 164
heterogeneity of, 30, 33, 122, 129, 304–05
identification of specific segments of, 167
importance of, 7–10
individuality of, 27–34, 36, 40
interpretation and evaluation of CR activities, 13, 98, 114, 123, 215, 231, 246
knowledge of a company's marketing strategy, 143
knowledge of a company's social impact, 196, 228
measurement of behavioral intentions, 217–23
needs of, 99
negative reactions to CR activities, 125
perceptions of companies, 34
psychological drivers of stakeholder behavior, 67, 178, 191
purchasing, 127
quantification of perceptions, 214–27
reactions to information about companies, 7, 11–12, 14, 188, 199, 208–09
relationships with companies, 13, 19, 34, 37, 45, 49
response to CR, 36, 42–64, 93–96, 110, 228
self-esteem, 103
sense that their values overlap with the company's, 109
skepticism among, 190, 192, 198, 203, 236
stakeholders other than employees and customers, 295–96
surveys of, 11, 215
volunteering, 60
word-of-mouth, 60
Starbucks, 160
stewardship, 8
Stonyfield Farm, 56, 62, 144, 202, 205, 229, 271
  customer loyalty, 144
  integration of CR with the core business, 144
structural equation modeling, 244, 272
  variables, 256–57, 272–73
Sudden Infant Death Syndrome, 195
Susan G. Komen for the Cure, 73, 78, 275
sustainability, 7

Target, 193, 265–67
team-building, 101
Telefónica, 154
the 3 U's; *see also* Understanding, Unity, Usefulness
  communication to optimize, 188–91
  and context, 251, 284
  and CR value, 247–55
  empirical test of, 255–59
  as indicators of CR value, 283
Timberland, 175–76, 205–06

TNT, 197
Total, 4–6
Toyota, 29
trust, 50, 112–14, 116, 139, 225, 227, 298
   and attributions, 114
   empirical evidence for the link between CR and trust, 113–14
   measurement of, 227
   and Unity, 126
   and Usefulness, 114

Undercover Boss, 81
Understanding, 35, 87–99
   attributions, 92–96, 221
   awareness, 87–91, 92
   closeness and, 124, 125, 129
   and commitment to CR programs, 194
   and company size and demographics, 146
   and the core business of the company, 235
   CR associations, 249, 252
   and CR communications, 207
   CR efficacy, 249
   and CR implementation, 177
   definition, 86
   efficacy, 96–99, 221–23
   and employees' responses to CR activities, 248
   and functional benefits, 133
   and identity-related benefits, 135
   measurement of, 217–22, 223, 229
   and reputation, 145
   and resilience to negative information, 271, 272
   and stakeholder acculturation, and Usefulness, 247
   and work effort, 253
United Nations Children's Fund, 195
Unity, 35, 58, 107–14, 257
   assessment of, 108
   and awareness of CR activities, 112
   caring and, 131
   closeness and, 125
   and company size and demographics, 146
   context and, 119
   and CR communications, 199
   and CR value, 251, 258
   and customer orientation of employees, 301
   definition, 86
   effect on purchase intent, 119
   and employees' commitment, 251
   and identification, 108–12, 254
   investors and, 297
   measurement of, 223, 225–27, 229, 231
   and purchase loyalty, 258
   and reputation, 145
   and societal value, 60
   and stakeholder acculturation, 133
   and stakeholders' intentions, 228
   and trust, 112–14, 126
   and Understanding and Usefulness, 108, 273
   and work effort, 258
UPS, 120–21
Usefulness, 35, 99–107, 269
   caring and, 130
   closeness and, 125, 127, 129
   and CR activities, 104
   and CR communications, 207
   and CR implementation, 177
   and customer orientation of employees, 301
   definition, 86
   functional benefits of CR activity, 100–07, 224

identity-related benefits of CR
    activity, 102–07, 224–25
measurement of, 222, 224–25, 233
and reputation, 145
and self-esteem, 250
and trust, 114
and Understanding, 247, 257
and willingness to pay, 270
and work–life balance, 128

values, overlap between stakeholders'
    and company's, 108–09, 156, 281
Verizon, 160
virtue
    community of, 174, 175, 179
    market for, 27–29, 39
volunteering, 60, 61, 75

Wainwright Bank, 200
Walmart, 14, 202, 259–67
    and America's Second Harvest, 261
    charitable donations, 75, 261
    and the Children's Miracle Network, 261
    communication of its CR activities, 263
    CR activities, 62
    CR performance, 262
    customer satisfaction, 260
    efficacy of CR programs, 263, 266
    employee awareness of CR activities, 262, 263
    employee participation in CR activities, 267
    employee turnover, 259
    environmental efforts, 261, 262
    implications of the evaluation of its CR activities, 265
    orientation and training, 259
    relevance of CR activities to employees, 266, 267
    and the Salvation Army, 261
    self-esteem, 265, 266
    and the 3 U's, 261–65
        Understanding, 263
        Unity, 265
        Usefulness, 265
    work effort, 260, 265
    work–home balance, 265, 266
Walmart Foundation, 261, 267
websites, corporate, 79, 189, 198, 202, 209
Wharton School, 155
win-win programs, 96
work–home balance, 106, 107, 251
    caring and, 130
    closeness and, 128
    Usefulness and, 128, 250, 301
World Association of Girl Guides and Girl Scouts, 120
World Economic Forum, 43
World Wildlife Fund, 192
WPP Group, 45

Yadana Valley Project, 2–3, 294
yogurt consumers, study of, 54, 56, 144, 267–75, 307–08
    and company size and demographics, 146
    and the efficacy of CR programs, 274
    purchase intent, 268, 269
    questionnaires, 291
    resilience to negative information, 268, 270–71
    self-esteem, 270, 274
    and the 3 U's, 268–69, 272–75
        Understanding, 271
        Unity, 144
    willingness to pay, 268, 269
Yoplait, 54, 144, 275–83
    breast cancer research, 275, 282
    CR activities, 275–76
    CR associations, 278

Yoplait (*cont.*)
  CR initiatives, 73, 74
  implications of the evaluation of its CR activities, 282–83
  market share, 282
  "Save Lids to Save Lives" campaign, 78, 275, 276, 279
  and the 3 U's, 277–83
  Understanding, 277–79, 282
  Unity, 280–82
  Usefulness, 279–80

Zoominfo, 169